THE ISRAEL TEST

By George Gilder

THE
ISRAEL
TEST

GEORGE GILDER

RICHARD VIGILANTE BOOKS

PUBLISHED BY RICHARD VIGILANTE BOOKS

Copyright © 2009 by George Gilder

All Rights Reserved

www.richardvigilantebooks.com

RVB with the portrayal of a Labrador retriever in profile is a trademark
of Richard Vigilante Books

Book design by Charles Bork

Library of Congress Control Number: 2009929489

Applicable BISAC Codes:

HIS019000   HISTORY / Middle East / Israel

ISBN 9780980076356

PRINTED IN THE UNITED STATES OF AMERICA

10 9 8 7 6 5 4 3 2 1

First Edition

For Midge Decter

CONTENTS

PART ONE

Zerizus

CHAPTER ONE

The Central Issue

The central issue in international politics, dividing the world into two fractious armies, is the tiny state of Israel.

The prime issue is not a global war of civilizations between the West and Islam or a split between Arabs and Jews. These conflicts are real and salient, but they obscure the deeper moral and ideological war. The real issue is between the rule of law and the rule of leveler egalitarianism, between creative excellence and covetous "fairness," between admiration of achievement versus envy and resentment of it.

Israel defines a line of demarcation. On one side, marshaled at the United Nations and in universities around the globe, are those who see capitalism as a zero-sum game in which success comes at the expense of the poor and the environment: every gain for one party comes at the cost of another. On the other side are those who see the genius and the good fortune of some as a source of wealth and opportunity for all.

The test can be summarized by a few questions: What is your attitude toward people who excel you in the creation of wealth or in other accomplishment? Do you aspire to their excellence, or do you seethe at it? Do you admire and celebrate exceptional achievement, or do you impugn it and seek to tear it down? Caroline Glick, the dauntless deputy managing editor of the *Jerusalem Post*, sums it up: "Some people admire success; some people envy it. The enviers hate Israel."

The Israel test is a moral challenge. The world has learned to see moral challenges as issues of charity and compassion toward victims, especially the poor, whose poverty is seen as proof of their victimization. Israel is not poor. And it is a victim only of resentment toward superior achievement and capability.

In countries where Jews are free to invent and create, they pile up conspicuous wealth and arouse envy and suspicion. In this age of information, when the achievements of mind have widely outpaced the power of masses and material force, Jews have forged much of the science and wealth of the era. Their pioneering contributions to quantum theory enabled the digital age. Their breakthroughs in nuclear science and computer science propelled the West to victory in World War II and the cold war. Their bioengineering inventions have enhanced the health and their microchip designs are fueling the growth of nations everywhere. Their genius has leavened the culture and economy of the world.

Israel today concentrates the genius of the Jews. Obscured by the usual media coverage of the "war-torn" Middle East, Israel's rarely celebrated feats of commercial, scientific, and technological creativity climax the Jews' twentieth-century saga of triumph over tragedy. Today tiny Israel, with its population of 7.23 million, five and one-half million Jewish, stands behind only the United States in technological contributions. In per-capita innovation, Israel dwarfs all nations. The forces of civilization in the world continue to feed upon the quintessential wealth of mind epitomized by Israel.

Today in the Middle East, Israeli wealth looms palpably and portentously over the mosques and middens of Palestinian poverty. But dwarfing Israel's own wealth is Israel's contribution to the world economy, stemming from Israeli creativity and entrepreneurial innovation. Israel's technical and scientific gifts to global progress loom with similar majesty over all others' contributions outside the United States.

Though Jews in Palestine had been the most powerful force for prosperity in the region since long before the founding of Israel in 1948, more remarkable still is the explosion of innovation attained through the unleashing of Israeli capitalism and technology over the last two decades. During the 1990s and early 2000s Israel sloughed off its manacles of confiscatory taxes, oppressive regulations, government ownership, and Socialist nostalgia and established itself in the global economy first as a major independent player and then as a technological leader.

Contemplating this Israeli breakthrough, the minds of parochial intellects around the globe, from Jerusalem to Los Angeles, are clouded with envy and suspicion. Everywhere, from the smarmy diplomats of the United Nations to the cerebral leftists at the Harvard Faculty Club, critics of Israel assert that Israelis are responsible for Palestinian Arab poverty. They imply that Israelis' success imposes upon them heavy obligations to Palestinian Arabs. Violence against Israel is seen as blowback from previous crimes of the Israelis. With little or no extenuation for the difficulties of a targeted defense against guerrilla attacks and suicide bombers, the world condemns the Israelis' efforts to preserve their country against the evil that would destroy it. Denying to Israel the moral fruits and affirmations that Jews have so richly earned by their paramount contributions to our civilization, the critics of Israel lash out at the foundations of civilization itself—at the golden rule of capitalism, that the good fortune of others is also one's own.

In simplest terms, amid the festering indigence of Palestine, the state of Israel presents a test. Efflorescent in the desert, militarily powerful, industrially preeminent, culturally cornucopian, technologically paramount, it lately has become a spearhead of the global economy and vanguard of human achievement. Believing that this position was somehow captured, rather than created, many in the West still manifest a primitive zero-sum vision of economics and life.

Assuming that wealth is distributed from above, chiefly by government, rather than generated by invention and ingenuity, Israel's critics see the world as a finite sum of resources. They regard economic life as a possibly violent struggle of each against all for one's "fair share." Believing that Israel, like the United States, has seized too much of the world's resources, they advocate vast programs of international retribution and redistribution. They imagine that the plight of the Palestinians reflects not their own Marxist angst, anti-Semitic obsessions, and recidivist violence but the actions of Israel. In their view, Israel's wealth stems not from Jewish creativity and genius but from cadging aid from the United States or seizing valuable land and other resources from Arabs.

In the blinkered vision of economists and politicians in international organizations and elite universities, this tiny bustling country, confined in a space smaller than New Jersey, is a continuation of the history of Western colonialism and imperialism. It is as if an embattled span of a few miracle miles in the desert echoes in some way a map of the world bathed in British pink or Soviet gray. In an elaborately mounted argument, full of pedantic references to Algeria and other colonial wars, a former Israeli army officer, now Indiana University professor, Rafael Reuveny declares that Israel is "The Last Colonialist." From the midst of the fruited plains of America, he actually finds it possible to write of Israel's now "vast lands."

The irony is that Israel is an imperial influence. Its hegemony stems not from its desperate efforts to contrive a defensible country amid compulsively predatory neighbors but from the global sway of its ideas and technologies.

To mistake the globally enriching gifts of mind for the brutal exercise of force is the central lie of Marxist economics. Although Marx sometimes affirmed the role of the bourgeoisie in creating wealth, he believed that the entrepreneurial contribution was transitory. The crude Marxian deceit was to declare that all value ultimately derives from labor and materials. Denying the necessary role of creative mind as embodied in capital and technology, Marx ended up vindicating the zero-sum vision of anti-Semitic envy, in which bankers, capitalists, arbitrageurs, shopkeepers, entrepreneurs, and traders are deemed to be parasitical shysters and dispensable middlemen.

As one of the world's most profitable economies built on one of the world's most barren territories, Israel challenges all the materialist superstitions of zero-sum economics, based on the "distribution" of natural resources and the exploitation of land and labor.

This crippling error of zero-sum economics manifests itself around the globe. It is still the chief cause of poverty. It can destroy any national economy. Perhaps some of you readers share it. You believe that capitalist achievement comes at the expense of others or of the environment. You believe that "behind every great fortune is a great crime." You advocate the redistribution of wealth. You think we all benefit when the government "spreads the wealth around." You imagine that free international trade is a mixed blessing, with many victims. You want to give much of Israel's wealth to its neighbors. You think that Israel's neighbors—and the world—would benefit more from redistribution than from Israel's continuing prosperity and freedom. You believe that Israel is somehow too large rather than too small. You believe, fantastically, that poverty is caused not by envy and rapine but by enterprise and property—that poverty is a major side effect of wealth.

Just being facetious. I would not imagine that any of my sophisticated readers could entertain such notions.

But let us continue along this line. Anti-capitalists, like anti-Semites throughout history, have always been obsessed with the "gaps" everywhere discernible between different groups: gaps of income, power, achievement, and status. Against the background of Palestinian poverty, anti-capitalists and anti-Semites alike see Israel as primarily a creator not of wealth but of gaps. With a gross domestic product of around $200.7 billion (2008), per-capita income of some $28,200, and close to a trillion dollars of market capitalization for its companies, Israel these days is rich, they say. But look at the gap between its luxuries and Palestinian privation. Look at the gap between Jews in Israel and Arabs in Israel—sure evidence of "discrimination" and "exploitation." Look at the gaps in the United States. Tax rates are clearly too low. The rich top 10 percent, who pay more than 70 percent of the income taxes in the United States, are obviously undertaxed according to the gapologists' model. Jews lead all other American groups in per-capita income, signifying another gap, presumably rectifiable by the United Nations.

Shaping the clichés of the gapologists is a profound misunderstanding. What makes capitalism succeed is not chiefly its structure of incentives but its use of knowledge and experience. As a knowledge system, capitalism assigns to the entrepreneurs who have already proven their prowess as investors—who have moved down the learning curve in the investment process—the right to shape the future pattern of investments. The lessons of one generation of successful investments inform the next generation. The lessons of failure are learned rather than submerged in subsidies and gilded with claims of higher virtue and purpose. Information is accumulated rather than lost. Under capitalism, knowledge grows apace with wealth. The executors of entrepreneurial knowledge extend it to new ventures and investments and become the economic leaders of the age.

Nothing is more destructive to opportunities for the poor than diverting resources from entrepreneurs who know how to use them profitably and giving them to government to spend politically. Greasing and disguising this destructive process in the United States is the guidance of handi-capitalists in nominally "private" institutions—from Wall Street money-shufflers to corn-state ethanol farmers—that are dependent on public handouts and guarantees. If governments were superior investors, the Soviet bloc would have been an economic triumph rather than an economic and environmental catastrophe. China would have thrived under Mao rather than under the current regime that claims, "To get rich is glorious." Whether in the United States or in Israel, at Harvard or at the United Nations, an obsessive concern with gaps between rich and poor is the signature of a deep and persistent Marxism that is intrinsically hostile to the wealth-producing work of Jews in the world. At the heart of the UN's case against Israel is the UN's focus on gaps.

Misunderstanding the nature of capitalism, the critics turn to challenge Israeli democracy. They charge that Israel's Jewish identity creates serious problems for its democratic values. Like former president Jimmy Carter in his book *Palestine: Peace Not*

Apartheid, former Israeli foreign minister Shlomo Ben-Ami in an article in *Foreign Affairs*, the flamboyant Frenchman Bernard-Henri Lévy in articles and a book, *Left in Dark Times*, and Thomas Friedman in a series of books and in his *New York Times* columns, many people raise the chimera of a Jewish "apartheid" regime that will mar the purity of Israel as a homeland for Jews. But creating no such problem of apartheid worth mentioning by such gentlemen are the vast *Judenrein* realms of Arabia accomplished by evicting up to some 800 thousand Jews from their midst immediately following Israel's War of Independence in 1948, capturing some $2.5 billion of their property. Rivaling every Nazi dream of ethnic purity are these domains ruled by Arab *sharia* law, autarky, anti-Semitism, and socialism. Equating democracy not with the rule of law but with the claims of racist self-determination, these writers implicitly propose that 5.5 million Jews are morally obliged to entrust their fate to some 100 million Arabs pledged to their destruction.

This bizarre conclusion is the perfectly logical result of the fondest dream of the twentieth-century Left, to reconcile democracy and socialism, to imagine democracy without economic freedom or a system of law and property rights that transcend the vicissitudes of elections. Without such well-established rights, which in the most successful democracies are always established before democracy itself, elections themselves are undermined and come to be decided in the streets. Democracy without capitalism has no content, since no power-centers outside the state can form and sustain themselves. As a form of politics, dealing with relative power, democracy by itself is a zero-sum game, in which the winnings of one group come at the cost of others. There are only a limited number of seats in a legislature or executive positions in a government. By contrast, capitalism is a positive-sum game, based on an upward spiral of gains, with no essential limits to the creation of wealth. Under capitalism the achievements of one group provide markets and opportunities for others. Without an expanding capitalist economy, democracy becomes dominated by its zero-sum elements—by mobs and demagogues.

Throughout history, in any nation with a significant Jewish presence such mobs and demagogues have turned against the Jews. Today they have turned against Israel. And Jimmy Carter, Thomas Friedman, and all the rest who advocate the claims of Arab "democracy" over Israeli accomplishment unintentionally side with the mobs and demagogues.

If democracy is the rule of the people, then the first right of every democratic citizen is self-rule—the authority to govern his own affairs peaceably on the basis of predictable rules of law conducive to a happy and productive life. The equation of democracy with ethnic self-determination replaces this orderly and profoundly human life with a savage division of spoils among members of the victorious tribe.

Thus many people regard Tibet or Burma or Kosovo as "nations" comparable to Israel. Non-capitalist self-determination, though, is entirely self-defeating. Sleek new automobiles across the United States—Volvos and Priuses galore—bear bumper stickers declaring, "War is Not the Answer" or urging a "Free Tibet." Without capitalism and free trade, however, self-determination is a pretext for constant civil wars, as each shard of nationality is sharpened into a sword implanted in its own specified holy soil, presumably defended by the United States or the United Nations.

The critical test of democracy is its ability to free human energies and intellect on the frontiers of human accomplishment.

More than any other country in the world, Israel manifestly passes this test. It is the test of *zerizus*, Hebrew for "alacrity," or, as Rabbi Zelig Pliskin describes it on the *Jewish World Review* Web page, "the blessed willpower and aspiration that leads to exceptional achievement." Passing this test, Israel is precious. All the carps and criticisms of Israel reflect a blind proceduralism and empty egalitarianism. The test of virtue is not mere procedure; it is content and accomplishment. If a system cannot pass this test—democratic or not, concerned with electoral politics or not—it is just another form of barbarism.

José Ortega y Gasset in his masterpiece *The Revolt of the Masses* described the essential barbarian mentality as a failure or refusal to recognize our dependency on the exceptional men and women who created the civilization in which we live and on which we subsist. Like monkeys in the jungle reaching for low-hanging fruit without any clue of its source or science, the barbarian politicians leading the ranks of modern anti-Semitism promiscuously pick the fruits of modern capitalism and the pockets of capitalists without a clue as to the provenance of their own largely parasitical lives and luxuries.

More sharply and categorically than any other conflict, the Israel-Palestine dispute raises these issues of capitalism and democracy, civilization and barbarism. By merely foreswearing violence and taking advantage of their unique position contiguous with the world's most creative people, the Palestinians could be rich and happy. Civilized people with the good fortune to live near brilliant entrepreneurs or thinkers go to work for them and attempt to learn their skills and master their fields of knowledge. Then they may start similar ventures on their own. It is the only way to succeed. In the past, Palestinian Arabs have often excelled as entrepreneurs, and some do around the world today. But nowhere are the Palestinians less likely to prosper than under the current Palestinian regimes. Palestinian leaders tell their people to disdain the peaceful and collaborative demands of democratic capitalism. Palestinians are taught to say they find it "humiliating" to work for Jews. Instead the Palestinians "elect" democratic jihadists. So do the Iranians and the Syrians.

In the West, anti–Semitic parties are mostly exponents of the "democratization" of everything, including businesses and corporations. They uphold a regime of "social justice" against a free regime of equality under the law. The effect of this disorder is to allow envious majorities to harass and dispossess the successful, who are disproportionately Jews. Israel's enemies are mostly self-styled "democrats." This is inevitable, since Jews and Israelis inexorably put the lie to the cherished ideal of cultural, national, and intellectual equality of outcomes anywhere.

The Israel test forces confrontation with the central moral and practical issues of capitalism. Israel has become one of the world's leading capitalist powers. The issues it raises loom in every capitalist country where Jews excel. These issues are not chiefly of religion or democracy or territorial legalities but of the inevitable inequalities of capitalist outcomes. Are entrepreneurs, in Israel and around the world, chiefly givers and benefactors, or are they predators and exploiters? Should policy focus on fostering economic growth for all or on closing gaps between rich and poor, on enabling an economic spearhead of excellence and creativity, or on dispossessing the successful to subsidize the wretched of the earth? Clutching their Fanon and their Koran, their Howard Zinn and their Noam Chomsky, the ersatz voices of the "wretched of the earth" punctuate their claims by flaunting fists of hate, clenched minds of murder. Do true democrats owe anything at all to such people?

To many observers—in the army of the Left—it is obvious

that Israeli wealth causes Palestinian misery. How could it be otherwise? Jews have long been paragons of capitalist wealth. Capitalist wealth, as Pierre-Joseph Proudhon put it in regard to "property," is "theft." Karl Marx was said to have shaped his opposition to property rights and his Jewish self-hatred by reading the even more virulently anti-Semitic Proudhon. In an 1883 diary entry, Proudhon declared, "The Jew is the enemy of mankind. One must send this race back to Asia or be exterminated." This fits well with Osama bin Laden's view that warping the entire U.S. economy and its global impact has been the effect of Jewish usury.

History, however, favors the view that poverty springs chiefly from envy and hatred of excellence—from class-war Marxism, anti-Semitism, and kleptocratic madness. It stems from the belief that wealth inheres in things and material resources that can be seized and redistributed, rather than in human minds and creations that thrive only in peace and freedom. In particular, the immiseration of the Middle East stems chiefly from the covetous and crippling idea among Arabs that Israel's wealth is not only the source of their humiliation but also the cause of their poverty.

Most of the world, even many citizens of Israel itself, wants to muddle these issues. The favored answer to all trade-offs among different values is: "All of the above." Democracy, equality, multiculturalism, *sharia* law, gay marriage, anti-globalization, capitalism, and freedom—the children of the coddled West want it all in a cornucopian cocktail party of inebriated contradictions, from green austerity to entitled affluence. They mix ritualistic political support for Israel with celebration of Palestinian voters who elect and applaud anti-Semite terrorists. They match a devout belief in abortion with fears of demographic disaster in Israel and with continual bows of political reverence toward an ever-diminishing complement of children. They combine opposition to nuclear weapons and U.S. defense spending with speculative demands for American intervention in places the United States has no conceivable national interest, from South Ossetia to Tibet. They oppose nuclear proliferation while urging U.S. nuclear disarmament that hugely enhances the incentives for *secret* nuclear programs. Without peremptory U.S. nuclear superiority, a small complement of nukes can confer global dominance and make it impossible for the United States to defend Israel or anyone else.

The Israel test forces a remorseless realism. It disallows all the bumper-sticker contradictions of pacifistic bellicosity. Either the world, principally the United States, supports Israel, or Israel, one way or another, will be destroyed. There are no other realistic choices. And if Israel is destroyed, capitalist Europe will likely die as well, and America, as the epitome of productive and creative capitalism spurred by Jews, will be in jeopardy.

This is the most portentous form of the Israel test. Inescapably, it poses the questions of life and wealth that lie behind nearly all the holocausts and massacres of recent world history, from the genocidal attacks on European Jews and the pogroms of Russian Kulaks and Jews to Maoist China's murderous "cultural revolution," from the eviction of white settlers and Indian entrepreneurs from Africa to the massacres of overseas Chinese businessmen in Indonesia. The pattern recurs even in the rout and rapine of "privileged" shopkeeper Kikuyus and "rich" Rift Valley distance runners after the 2007 Kenyan elections.

"Everywhere," as I wrote in *Wealth & Poverty* nearly thirty years ago, "the horrors and the bodies pile up, in the world's perennial struggle to rid itself of the menace of riches"—[of the shopkeepers, the bankers, the merchants, the *middlemen*, the traders, the landowning farmers, the entrepreneurs]—"at the same time that the toll also mounts in victims of unnecessary famine and poverty." Everywhere nations claim a resolve to *develop*; but everywhere their first goal is to expropriate, banish, or kill the existing developers. At the United Nations, these contradictions reach a polyglot climax, with alternating zeal against the blight of want and against the Americans and Zionists, creators of wealth.

"There is something, evidently, in the human mind, even when carefully honed at Oxford or the Sorbonne, that hesitates to believe in capitalism: in the enriching asymmetries and inequalities of all creative achievement, in the inexhaustible mines of the division of labor, in the multiplying miracles of entrepreneurial economics, in the compounding gains from global trade and protected rights to property. It is far easier to see the masters of these works as evil—demonic bookkeepers sustained by the blood of children or usurious parasites on the regional economy or conspiratorial bankers and robber barons—and to hunt them as witches or leeches, favored by occult powers and Faustian links."

With wealth seen as stolen from the exploited poor, the poor in turn win a license to dispossess and kill their oppressors and to disrupt capitalist economies. This is the foul message of Frantz Fanon, Hamas, al-Qaida, Hezbollah, and the academic coteries of Chomsky, Zinn, and a thousand Marxist myrmidons across the campuses of the world. But no capitalist system can sustain prosperity amid constant violence. The idea that suicide bombing is a tolerable policy that can be extenuated by alleged grievances is preposterous. It is the violence that makes necessary the police measures that render economic progress impossible, particularly for the groups associated with the attacks. By justifying violent attacks on a civilized democracy—and then condemning the necessary retaliatory defense—leftists would allow no solution but tyranny. Since across the world economy today this scenario is most starkly enacted in the Middle East—in the Palestinian territories—all these synaptic suicide bombers of the brain focus instinctively on the Israel test. They know well which side they are on.

Which side are you on?

CHAPTER TWO

The Blindness of the Experts

Most of the world's experts—advocates and critics of Israel alike—are blind to the Israel test. G. K. Chesterton got it right. "The Fabian argument of the expert, that the man who is trained should be the man who is trusted, would be absolutely unanswerable if it were really true that a man who studied a thing and practiced it every day went on seeing more and more of its significance. But he does not. He goes on seeing less and less of its significance."

From the virtuoso tracts of Alan Dershowitz to the demented screeds of Noam Chomsky or Naomi Klein, from the casuistic pirouettes of Michael Lerner and *Tikkun* magazine to the pro-Israel celebrations of the Religious Right, from Jeffrey Goldberg in the *Atlantic* to Bernard-Henri Lévy in scores of books and articles, the literature of Israeli condemnation and support—however coherent on its own terms—seems mostly irrelevant to the real test and trial of Israel.

Beyond the wholehearted endorsements of the Religious Right, which are unlikely to convince unbelievers, the general position of the experts is that Israel is deeply flawed but commands a colorable case for continued existence. Coloring the case entails much knowledge of the intricacies of international law and the history of UN resolutions. Israel's historical record is said to be full of excessive violence, but it is extenuated by the violence inflicted on the Jews in the Holocaust. Israel may not be good, but it has rights that should be respected, provided that it improves its behavior.

By clinging to liberal policy and democratic processes, Israel, in this view, may justify its claim to continued American aid. Under these conditions, says even the third worldly president Barack Obama, the United States should continue to affirm and guarantee the country's defense. Because of Israel's legal rights and democratic processes, the United States should ignore its dire unpopularity with nearly all U.S. allies, international organizations, and trading partners that condemn its allegedly lawless and aggressive foreign policy.

At their best, these defenders of Israel pile up impressive mountains of evidence that Israel is "not guilty" of charges only a madman, delusional academic, or UN human rights expert could have believed in the first place. Alan Dershowitz, the distinguished American professor of jurisprudence at Harvard University, has contributed two popular books, *The Case for Israel* and *The Case Against Israel's Enemies*, that offer over thirty chapters of evidence against the standard propaganda. He is about the best and most tenacious defender Israel has, outside of the incandescent pages of *Commentary, and he has* millions more readers than that remarkable publication.

Dershowitz cogently contests the proposition that Israel is a racist bastion of apartheid, a genocidal expansionist power, and a crypto-Nazi perpetrator of "massacres." He ably refutes the verdict of the relevant UN committee that Israel is "the world's primary violator of human rights"—and even, it seems, "meta-human rights," whatever they are and whatever kind of meta-violations they endure.

Dershowitz devastates the likes of the president of the UN General Assembly, Miguel d'Escoto Brockmann of Nicaragua, who in 2008 declared that Israel's policies are "so similar to the apartheid of an earlier era that the world must unite against them, demanding an end to the massive abuse of human rights and isolating the offending nation as it once isolated South Africa with boycott, divestment, and sanctions." Dershowitz also eviscerates the UN Commission on Human Rights, which has awarded 27 percent of its condemnatory resolutions to Israel, far ahead of any rival. He cogently dispatches the World Court's 2004 ruling that Israel's splendidly effective system of protection against suicide bombers, a security fence, violates international law. Emerging slowly but surely in the annals of global jurisprudence, so it seems, is a "human right" to commit suicide with a bomb on a bus.

Dershowitz even takes the trouble to answer the charges of the ineffable Iranian president Mahmoud Ahmadinejad as if the ruler were moved by legal niceties and resourceful argument. Not for nothing is Dershowitz one of the world's leading defense attorneys. But the very act of responding to the claims of diabolical maniacs puts this great advocate of Israel in an oddly defensive posture, as if a country that requires so resourceful, agile, punctilious, and high-priced a defense—like Dershowitz's most notable former client, Claus von Bulow—must have something to hide, a skeleton in its Knesset, a metastasized horror in its history.

The central error of Israel's defenders is to accept the framing of the debate by its enemies. The idea is that peace depends on some marginal but perpetually elusive improvement in Israel's behavior. Prefacing the usual defense are concessions that Israel is "far from perfect" and "has made mistakes" in "overreacting to terrorism and other threats." As Larry Summers put it, "There is much . . . in Israel's foreign and defense policy that can and should be vigorously challenged." Such statements from Israel's nominal defenders slip readily from meaningless negatives: "Israel is not perfect"—to crippling concessions: "Israel overreacts to terror." Locked in a debate over Israel's alleged vices, they miss the salient truth running through the long history of anti-Semitism: Israel is hated above all for its virtues.

No failure to comply with the dictates of World Court rulings defending the free movement of suicide bombers, no falling short of the standards devised by UN human rights committees dominated by demented tyrants can even begin to explain, let alone *excuse,* the celebrated beheadings, kidnappings, plans for genocidal torture, and frothy prophecies of extinction that reverberate daily through the streets and mosques of the Middle East with the regularity of the muezzin call to prayers and pogroms.

Long preceding the formation of Israel, Arab anathemas swelled to a chorus as statehood loomed. Azzam Pasha, the secretary general of the Arab League, in 1948 called for the extinction of Palestinian Jews in a radio speech, declaring, "This will be a war of extermination and a momentous massacre." In 1948, the founder of the Muslim Brotherhood in Egypt, Hassan al-Banna, told the *New York Times* correspondent in Cairo, Dana Adams Schmidt: "If the Jewish state becomes a fact, [the Arabs] will drive the Jews who live in their midst into the sea."

In *Dialogues and Secrets with Kings,* published after the 1967 war, the very first official Palestinian Liberation Organization (PLO) leader, Ahmad Shuqeiri, also upheld the sea-water solution: "I frequently called on the Arabs to liquidate the state of Israel and to throw the Jews into the sea. I said this because I was—and still am—convinced that there is no solution other than the elimination of the state of Israel."

From the PLO's 1964 announcement, long before Israel's capture of the West Bank or Gaza, of the PLO's resolve to extinguish the state of Israel by "armed struggle" to the daily calls by the venerable president of Egypt Gamal Abdel Nasser for "Israel's destruction" in the 1967 war; from the prime minister of Syria, Haffez Assad, invoking "a battle of annihilation," now to two recent presidents of Iran pledging to "wipe Israel off the map"; from the endless proclamations by Palestinian terrorist politicians seeking "liberation from the Jordan River to the sea" to the various men of Allah declaring that Israelis are "filthy bacteria" that must be "butchered and killed . . . wherever you meet them"; from the sponsorship and celebration of suicide bombers by various imams and exalted rulers to polls of the Palestinian people affirming the same murderous worldview; these statements are no frenzied war cries uttered only during actual combat and regretted in peacetime. Representing the essence of the Palestinian movement, rabid anti-Semitism continues a commitment that began with Palestinian complicity in the Holocaust.

Everyone knows that the word "Nazi" is used promiscuously in today's world. But the word does have a real meaning. It means a National Socialist Movement dedicated to murderous anti-Semitism. Socialism everywhere expresses envy of excellence by treating the works and wealth of the successful as the wages of sin. Nazism simply sees the sin as a Jewish conspiracy.

By this measure, the PLO has always been essentially a Nazi organization. The first move toward pushing the Israelis into the sea came during World War II from the Grand Mufti of Jerusalem, Haj Amin al-Husseini. "Germany," as the Mufti put it, "is the only country in the world that has not merely fought the Jews at home but has declared war on the entirety of world Jewry; in this war against world Jewry the Arabs feel profoundly connected to Germany."

Fresh from aiding the massacre of Jews in Romania and Bosnia and recruiting Bosnian Muslims into the Nazi forces, the Mufti was a fanatical participant in the European Holocaust. His most passionate goal was to extend it to the Middle East. After visiting Auschwitz with Himmler, this founder-hero of the Palestinian movement urged the Nazis to accelerate and intensify the killings and then join him in extending the carnage to Palestine by massacring the half-million Jews living there. In this pursuit, he conspired with the Nazis under Walther Rauff, engineer of Auschwitz, to create a special force in Greece ready to make the attack. Only General Montgomery's defeat of Rommel at El Alamein prevented the Mufti and his friends from pursuing their plan. Still unsated in his killing frenzies in late 1944, Husseini launched an attack of parachutists on the Tel Aviv water supply with ten containers of toxin. Failing in the attempt, he devoted the rest of his life to the cause of destroying Israel.

Cited as a war criminal, Husseini gained asylum with the similarly rabid Holocaust celebrants among the Muslim Brotherhood in Egypt. For his barbarities, the Mufti remains a revered historical figure in the Palestinian territories. Beginning in the 1930s, his Nazi animus originated long before any of the supposed Israeli offenses that are now cited to justify Palestinian violence and hatred against the Jews in Israel.

When Husseini died in 1974, his anti-Semitic cause was taken up by his distant relative Yasser Arafat, the PLO leader and eventual Nobel "Peace" laureate. Arafat characteristically bought Hitler's *Mein Kampf* in bulk and distributed it to his followers in Arab translation under the title *My Jihad*, as Israeli soldiers discovered on capturing his abandoned camp in southern Lebanon in 1982. Arafat was a master of the duplicitous art of recanting in splenetic Arabic to his followers any public professions of peace he may have espoused in international meetings.

Arafat's successor as head of the Palestinian Authority, Mahmoud Abbas, is supposedly a "moderate." This seems to be the term for anti-Semites who are ambivalent about whether to celebrate the Holocaust or to deny that it occurred. Devoted to the destruction of Israel, Abbas was a Holocaust denier from the time of his doctoral thesis—in his own words, a study of "the Zionist fantasy, the fantastic lie that 6 million Jews were killed." Contesting with Abbas for power and winning Palestinian elections in 2006 was Hamas, an organization whose founding charter proclaims its devotion to the killing of Jews.

Perhaps the most menacing leader of Palestinian "liberation" is Hamas' ally Hezbollah, whose leader, Hassan Nasrallah, declared in 2002 that if all the Jews gather in Israel, "they'll make our job easier, and will keep us from having to go hunt them down all over the world."

When experts in the United States urge the creation of a Palestinian state, they are effectively endorsing a Nazi national movement with roots in Europe. Pointless and fantastical are claims to favor a Palestinian national movement that renounces the murder of Jews. Murdering Jews is the essence of the only Palestinian national movement we have ever known.

The creation of a peaceful and productive Palestinian state would require support from neither Harvard nor Hezbollah, nor any force outside Palestine itself. The Palestinian Arabs could be a nation tomorrow and a state the day after, if their leaders could let go of the notion that the Jews must die before Palestine can live.

In no way do the usual defenders of Israel so clearly concede the National Socialist framing of the debate as on the question of "settlements": the fate of the several hundred thousand Jews living on West Bank territory that some Israeli government might concede to a Palestinian state. Dershowitz and scores of other defenders of Israel, including Bernard-Henri Lévy and Jeffrey Goldberg, join the chorus of critics regarding as a "serious" or even a "catastrophic error" settlements that plant productive people on mostly undeveloped areas of Judea and Samaria that once chiefly sprouted missiles and mortars overlooking Jerusalem and Tel Aviv. Once again, nominal defenders of Israel give up the key point without even seeing it. For the dispute over the settlements is an argument over whether Jews may reasonably expect to be permitted to live among Arabs anywhere.

After the Arabs refused all offers of land for peace in the wake of the 1967 war, the Israelis were necessarily responsible for the West Bank and Gaza. Israel's government under Levi Eshkol initially barred settlements on the grounds that the land would one day be relinquished to Jordan under a peace agreement. When the Jordanians joined the rest of the Arab states in adamantly refusing any negotiations, Israel inherited the land. Under Israeli management, economic growth in the West Bank and Gaza surged for some twenty years at a rate as high as 30 percent in 1979, averaging 25 percent per year, and the number of Arabs grew from roughly 1 million to almost 3 million in some 261 new towns, while the number of Jews in the territories rose merely to 250 thousand, settled on land not exceeding 2 percent of the area of the West Bank. As the Israelis spurred development, Arabs thronged in to participate in it. Between the 1967 war and the first intifada in 1987, Arab settlers moving in from Jordan and other Arab countries to the West Bank and Gaza came to outnumber Israeli settlers by a factor of ten.

Since Israel's creation, while it was accommodating massive immigration from Arab nations dedicated to its destruction, essentially every Arab state expelled its own Jews, many resident for generations. Evicted were more than 800,000 people. Confiscated was some $2.5 billion in land and wealth.

Every proposal for a Palestinian state, even from Israel's usual supporters, takes this crime for granted and proposes that Israel preemptively repeat it by itself uprooting the Jewish settlers from the West Bank. Though Israel accepts both Christians and Muslims as citizens, both Israel's enemies and its defenders assume that any future Palestinian state will exclude any remaining Jews from the homes and neighborhoods, communities, shops, and schools they have built. Too bizarre to be contemplated, apparently, is the possibility that the Jews, if they chose, could be allowed to live in a Palestinian state, or be safe if they did.

At home in the United States, if some locally dominant ethnic group violently protested against Jews being allowed to live on property amounting to 2 percent of "the neighborhood," all these supposed defenders of Israel would know exactly whom they were dealing with and how to respond. But in the case of the Palestinians, we are to take as natural and right their claims to be squeamish about living anywhere near Jews. Since Arabs in the area have consistently gravitated to neighborhoods where they can enjoy the prosperity and order that the Jews create, their leaders must rely on the Israelis to remove the offending settlements.

But without the presence of the Jews, there is no evidence that the Palestinians would particularly want these territories for a nation. When they were held under Jordanian and Egyptian auspices between 1948 and 1967, after all, there was no significant move to create a Palestinian state, but there was a continuing migration toward the peace and prosperity that the Jews were creating. Hostility toward Jews stems not from any alleged legal violations or untoward violence but from their exceptional virtues. This is the essence of anti-Semitism.

Winston Churchill proclaimed the essential dynamic in a speech in Parliament in 1939 responding to efforts to withdraw

British support for a Jewish state. Describing "the magnificent work which the Jewish colonists have done," he said: "They have made the desert bloom . . . started a score of thriving industries . . . founded a great city on the barren shore . . . harnessed the Jordan and spread its electricity throughout the land . . . So far from being persecuted, the Arabs have crowded into the country and multiplied till their population has increased more than even all world Jewry could lift up the Jewish population. Now we are asked to decree that all this is to stop and all this is to come to an end. We are now asked to submit—and this is what rankles most with me—to an agitation which is fed with foreign money and ceaselessly inflamed by Nazi and by Fascist propaganda."

That says it all, for the ages. Eighty years later nothing much has changed.

CHAPTER THREE

Tale of the Bell Curve

The Israel test begins with the issue of anti-Semitism, which remains a global plague as persistent and metastatic and multifarious, and as baffling in its etiology, as cancer.

The most compelling book on anti-Semitism that I have encountered is *Why The Jews? The Reason for Antisemitism* by Dennis Prager and Joseph Telushkin. I read the first edition when it was published in 1983 and then the new edition in 2003. It is lucidly written, intelligent, fervent, and historically sophisticated. It conveys the earnest, wise, and often ironical voice of its Los Angeles talk-radio-star coauthor, Prager. Although suffused with indignation and a tragic sense of life, it is clear-eyed and dispassionate on the critical issues. What's not to like?

Prager and Telushkin insist that anti-Semitism is "unique." It cannot be comprehended as a form of racism, neurosis, anti-nationalism, envy, ethnic hostility, religious bigotry, or resentment of success. They contend that "modern attempts to dejudaize Jew-hatred, to attribute it to economic, social, and political factors and universalize it into merely another instance of bigotry are as opposed to the facts of Jewish history as they are to the historical Jewish understanding of anti-Semitism . . ."

Prager and Telushkin recount many chilling and telling tales of anti-Semitic horror reaching far back into history, long before the modern forms of Jew-hatred could have emerged from current economic and political conditions. They show anti-Semitism stretching forward into the most refined centers of culture and the most learned redoubts of academic intellect—pantheons such as Harvard and the Council on Foreign Relations, both old haunts of mine—where any other form of racism would be socially leprous and outré. Our authors tout anti-Semitism's universality, its persistence, its protean irrepressibility, its grisly shapes, its ghastly violence, its frequent respectability, its secular animus, and its religious fanaticism as evidence for its monstrous and inexorable uniqueness.

"Anti-Semites have not hated Jews," they write, "because Jews are affluent—poor Jews have always been as hated; or strong—weak Jews have simply invited anti-Semitic bullies; or because Jews may have unpleasant personalities—genocide is not personality generated; or because ruling classes focus worker discontent onto Jews—precapitalist and noncapitalist societies, such as the former Soviet Union, other Communist states, and various third world countries, have been considerably more anti-Semitic than capitalist societies. . . ."

They conclude: "Anti-Semites have hated Jews because Jews are Jewish . . ."—essentially for the Jewish belief in their chosenness, in their own national identity, and in the universal reach of their one God and his moral law. Moreover, to spit in the wound of anti-Semitic humiliation, practicing Jews enjoy the best revenge. They live well, leading "demonstrably higher-quality lives" than others who do not believe and practice these things. According to our authors, it is these specific characteristics of religious Jews that cause anti-Semitism, not the widespread human sins of racism, envy, nationalism, and ethnic hostility.

Opening the book is a quote from the National Conference of Catholic Bishops that sums up the Prager-Telushkin view: "It was Judaism that brought the concept of a God-given universal moral law into the world. . . . The Jew carries the burden of God in history [and] for this has never been forgiven."

Jewish ethical monotheism and its propagation is a primary gift and goad to gentiles and Jews alike who have accepted a relativist morality and philosophy that condones sexual immorality, abortion, and other forms of convenient hedonism. Ethical monotheism is a cherished contribution to humankind and a resented standard of unreachable righteousness. By evoking faith in the meaning and regularity of the cosmos, it is crucial to Jewish science and business and indeed to all human achievement. As Prager and Telushkin finally contend, it may be the solution to the problem of anti-Semitism. But it is not, as they also contend, its cause.

The world tolerates all sorts and conditions of religious observance, from the Amish to Jehovah's Witnesses, from the Mormons to the Scientologists, and on and on. Many of these faiths include apocalyptic prophecies of the incineration of all their enemies and the survival of a chosen remnant. Some of these faiths evoke scorn, some laughter, most indifference.

Benzion Netanyahu, the historian father of Israeli Prime Minister Benjamin Netanyahu, has demonstrated in an awesome 500 thousand-word tome, *The Origins of the Inquisition in Fifteenth-Century Spain,* that the most vicious anti-Jewish pogroms not only preceded the emergence of Christianity but also represented a reaction against the *secular* power achieved by Jews. He vividly describes the ineffably horrific pogrom in Alexandria that was conducted by Hellenistic Egyptians in 38 C. E. Netanyahu concludes: "We agree with that clear-sighted scholar who said, unreservedly, in plain language: 'Anti-Semitism was born in Egypt.'" His book shows that motivating the Inquisition in Spain was not hostility to Jewish religion but rage against the superior effectiveness and ascendancy of Jews outperforming established clerics as *Christians*. "New Christians," mostly Jewish, were taking over the Spanish church by being more learned, eloquent, devout, resourceful, and charismatic than Christian leaders. As Netanyahu writes, "The struggle against the Jews was essentially motivated by social and economic, rather than religious considerations . . ."

All the sage observations by Prager and Telushkin miss the heart of the matter, which is Jewish intellectual and entrepreneurial superiority. As eminent Russian pro-Semite writer Maxim Gorky put it: "Whatever nonsense the anti-Semites may talk, they dislike the Jew only because he is obviously better, more adroit, and more capable of work than they are." Whether driven by culture or genes—or, like most behavior, an inextricable mix—the fact of Jewish genius is demonstrable. It can be gainsaid only by people who do not expect to be believed. The source of anti-Semitism is Jewish superiority and excellence.

The entire debate over Israel currently rides on a tacit subtext of crucial matters that cannot be discussed, such as the central contributions of Jews to global science, technology, art, and prosperity; proprieties that cannot be transgressed, such as pointing to the comparative brutality and barrenness of its adversaries; and immense realities that cannot be broached, such as the manifest supremacy of Jews over all other ethnic groups in nearly every intellectual, commercial, and cultural endeavor.

In *The Bell Curve* Charles Murray and Richard Herrnstein pointed to the massive superiority in IQs of Ashkenazi (Eastern European) Jews over all other genetically identifiable groups. The upside tail of the curve is massively Jewish.

As Murray later distilled the evidence in *Commentary*, the Jewish mean intelligence quotient is 110, ten points over the norm. This strikingly higher average intelligence, however, is not the decisive factor in overall Jewish achievement. As recently as 1999, Israelis of all races failed *on average* to outperform Americans in international tests of eighth-grade math and science skills. In math, Israelis ranked just behind Thailand and Moldova and one place ahead of Tunisia. Israel lagged nine places behind the United States, whose performance is usually deemed miserably far behind the leading Asian and European performers. In science, the numbers were similar.

What matters in human accomplishment is not the average performance but the treatment of exceptional performance and the cultivation of genius. The commanding lesson of Jewish accomplishment is that genius trumps everything else. As Murray explains, "The key indicator for predicting *exceptional* accomplishment (like winning a Nobel Prize) is the incidence of exceptional intelligence. . . . The proportion of Jews with IQs of 140 or higher is somewhere around six times the proportion of everyone else. . . ." This proportion rises at still higher IQs. Murray reports a study taken in 1954 of IQs in the New York public school system that showed Jews with some 85 percent of IQs over 170 (twenty-four out of twenty-eight). This superiority in IQ also manifested itself in excellence in games that demand exceptional intelligence. Since the 1880s, nearly half of all the world chess champions have been of Jewish heritage.

Such stunning findings in *The Bell Curve* aroused little comment. Respondents focused instead on a few provocative lines on the possible influence of genetic endowment in the IQs of blacks, though the margin of Jewish superiority over other whites was at least as large as the white edge over blacks and less amenable to sociological extenuation.

This reaction is typical of the great error of contemporary social thought: that poverty results not from the behavior or lesser capabilities of the poor, or the corruptions of failed cultures, but from "discrimination." In the current era, Jews will always tend to be overrepresented at the pinnacles of intellectual excellence. Therefore an ideological belief that nature favors equal outcomes fosters hostility to capitalism and leads directly and inexorably to anti-Semitism. These egalitarian attitudes are the chief source of poverty in the world.

Poverty needs no explanation. It has been the usual condition of nearly all human beings throughout all history. When poverty occurs in modern capitalist societies it is invariably a result of cultural collapse, typically represented by the American ghetto or Gaza or the West Bank or southern Lebanon, because young men are deprived of productive models of masculinity. What is precious and in need of explanation and nurture is the special configuration of cultural and intellectual aptitudes and practices—the differences, the inequalities—that under some rare and miraculous conditions have produced wealth for the world. Inequality is the answer, not the problem.

Murray's later work, *Human Accomplishment*, focused on the fact that, as judged by Murray's complex calculus fed by a database of historians, the Jewish three-tenths of 1 percent of world population has contributed some 25 percent of recent notable human-intellectual accomplishment in the modern period. Murray cites the historical record: "In the first half of the twentieth century, despite pervasive and continuing social discrimination against Jews throughout the Western world, despite the retraction of legal rights, and despite the Holocaust, Jews won 14 percent of Nobel Prizes in literature, chemistry, physics, and medicine/physiology." He then proceeds to more recent data: "In the second half of the twentieth century, when Nobel Prizes began to be awarded to people from all over the world, that figure [of Jews awarded Nobel Prizes] rose to 29 percent. So far in the twenty-first century, it has been 32 percent."

From the day Heinrich Hertz, whose father was a Jew, first demonstrated electromagnetic waves and Albert Michelson conducted the key experiments underlying Einstein's theory of relativity, the achievements of modern science are largely the expression of Jewish genius and ingenuity. If 26 percent of Nobel Prizes do not suffice to make the case, it is confirmed by 51 percent of the Wolf Foundation Prizes in Physics, 28 percent of the Max Planck Medailles and 38 percent of the Dirac Medals for Theoretical Physics, 37 percent of the Heineman Prizes for Mathematical Physics, and 53 percent of the Enrico Fermi Awards.

Jews are not only superior in abstruse intellectual pursuits, such as quantum physics and nuclear science, however. They are also heavily overrepresented among entrepreneurs of the technological businesses that lead and leaven the global economy. Social psychologist David McClelland, author of *The Achieving Society*, found that entrepreneurs are identified by a greater "need for achievement" than are other groups. There is little doubt, he concluded, explaining the disproportionate representation of Jews among entrepreneurs, that in the United States the average need for achievement is higher among Jews than for the general population.

"Need for achievement" alone, however, will not enable a person to start and run a successful technological company. That takes a combination of technological mastery, business prowess, and leadership skills that is not evenly distributed even among elite scientists and engineers. Edward B. Roberts of Massachusetts Institute of Technology's Sloan School of Management compared MIT graduates who launched new technological companies with a control group of graduates who pursued other careers. The largest factor in predicting an entrepreneurial career in technology was an entrepreneurial father. Controlling for this factor, he discovered that Jews were *five times* more likely to start technological enterprises than other MIT graduates.

These remarkable facts and their powerful implications have evoked surprisingly little discussion. But a book such as Prager and Telushkin's *Why the Jews?* on anti-Semitism that fails to come to terms with the raw facts of Jewish intellectual superiority will fail to persuade its readers, who will sense that the argument cannot bear the weight it is asked to carry. Yes, there is a religious component in anti-Semitism, but there is also a political and economic element, reflected in the objective anti-Semitism of Karl Marx, Noam Chomsky, Friedrich Engels, Howard Zinn, Naomi Klein, and other Jewish leftists who above all abhor capitalism. Jews, amazingly, excel so readily in all intellectual fields that they outperform all rivals even in the arena of anti-Semitism.

For all its special features and extreme manifestations, anti-Semitism is a reflection of the hatred toward successful middlemen, entrepreneurs, shopkeepers, lenders, bankers, financiers, and other capitalists that is visible everywhere whenever an identifiable set of outsiders outperforms the rest of the population in the economy. This is true whether the offending excellence comes from the Kikuyu in Kenya, the Ibo and the Yoruba in Nigeria, the overseas Indians and whites in Uganda and Zimbabwe, the Lebanese in West Africa, South America, and around the world, the Parsis in India, the Indian Gujaratis in South and East Africa, the Armenians in the Ottoman Empire, and above all—the over 30 million overseas Chinese in Indonesia, Malaysia, and elsewhere in Southeast Asia.

Thomas Sowell of the Hoover Institution reports that in Indonesia overseas Chinese constituted 5 percent of the population, but they controlled 70 percent of private domestic capital and ran three-quarters of the nation's top two hundred businesses. Their economic dominance—and their repeated victimization in ghastly massacres—prompts Sowell to comment: "Although the overseas Chinese have long been known as the 'Jews of Southeast Asia,' perhaps Jews might more aptly be called the overseas Chinese of Europe."

Sowell has written several books that document this pattern of hostility toward "middleman minorities" in fascinating detail and explain its causes and effects with convincing authority. The role of wealth creation and trade, with its rigorous disciplines, linguistic virtuosity, and accounting prowess, means that "middleman minorities must be very different from their customers." These groups, "their wealth inexplicable, their superiority intolerable," typically arouse hatred from competing intellectuals. "It is not usually the masses of the people who most resent the more productive people in their midst. More commonly, it is the intelligentsia, who may with sufficiently sustained effort spread their own resentments to others."

The culture of economic advance "and the social withdrawal needed to preserve this differentness in their children," Sowell writes, "leave the middleman minorities vulnerable to charges of 'clannishness' by political and other demagogues. . . . These accusations can exploit racial, religious, or other differences, but this is not to say that such differences are the fundamental reason for the hostility."

It is a mistake for Prager and Telushkin to ignore the persistence and universality of this phenomenon and to claim some special, more exalted, and elusive source of anti-Semitism, while half-denying the obvious and massively disproportionate representation of Jews in almost every index of human achievement. This evasive argument may reduce the number of available allies and divert attention from the real problem.

Prager and Telushkin are so immersed in the world of the Left and its perspectives that their economic analysis treats wealth or capitalist prowess as negatives, as potential sources of anti-Semitism from labor movements and the poor and their advocates, rather than as the best remedies for anti-Semitism.

Capitalism overthrows theories of zero-sum economics and dog-eat-cat survival of the fittest. Thus, as in the United States (outside the academic Darwinian arena, where professors angle for grants from above), anti-Semitism withers in wealthy capitalist countries. It waxes in Socialist regimes where Jews may arouse resentment by their agility in finding economic niches among the interstices of bureaucracies, tax collections, political pork fests, and crony capitalism. As the elder Netanyahu's great history shows, an oft-repeated pattern has the Jews serving as the most skilled and trusted servants of the central (or even absentee) government. Then, as the power of hated king or conqueror wanes, he abandons the Jews, who are left to the mercies of the enraged mob.

Static Socialist or feudalistic systems, particularly when oil-rich and politically controlled, favor a conspiratorial view of history and economics. Anti-Semitism is chiefly a zero-sum disease.

Christians may well gag at Prager and Telushkin's accounts of the depraved anti-Semitism of Martin Luther and various miscreant cardinals and rabid crusaders, as capitalists will retch at the views of Henry Ford. And all the charges are true. But, putting it as gently as I can, I would demur at the retrospective application of modern standards of morality to the long history of the human parade through the treacherous and bloodthirsty epochs of war, poverty, religious feuds, plagues, famines, and vicious ethnic struggles. The world has been at war for millennia, with hatred and death pandemic on all sides. During World War I, an entire generation comprising approximately 20 million young European men was lost. After World War I, 29 million more Europeans died of a flu epidemic alone. Until the ascent of capitalism and trade, there was no alternative to joining in the zero-sum struggles for existence against enemies everywhere.

Feminists look back on that appalling panorama and see nothing but misogynist oppression, rape, and murder. Blacks look back and see virtually nothing but lynching and slavery. American Indians see nothing but genocidal aggression by whites. Third worlders everywhere see a history of colonialist and imperialist depredations. Armenians and Kurds give harrowing accounts of a history of murderous attacks that killed millions. The Irish see an inexorable saga of predatory and vicious Englishmen, callously starving their forbears to death. American Southerners tell of the loss of a generation of young men and the devastation of Dixie in the "War between the States." The Muslims tell of rampant brutalities of the crusades. All of them cherish their own acute grievances and sagas of victimization. All now have been taught to couch their historic suffering, whenever possible and often when implausible, in the terms of "genocide."

It is unseemly, as well as tactically questionable, for American Jews, the richest people on earth, to grapple with Armenians and Rwandan Tutsis, Palestinian Arabs and U.S. blacks, Sudanese, and American Indians to corner the trump cards of victimization. Although Jews are objectively correct that the Holocaust was unique in its diabolical details and genocidal reach, current-day Jews will get nowhere pointing to the suffering of their forebears.

Every ethnic group has its own tale of woe, because the entire history of the world is woebegone. For most of human history, average longevity was less than thirty years. For the vast majority of humans of all ethnic groups, nearly all previous history seemed essentially hopeless in any terms except the physical struggles for Darwinian group survival. You hated your enemies from other groups because most of the time they sought to kill you. You had no vision of the successes of others as your own opportunity.

Until the dominance of capitalism, with its positive spirals of mutual gain, the prevailing regime was a Darwinian zero-sum game in which groups fought for survival against their neighbors. As Walter Lippmann eloquently explained in *The Good Society*, capitalism for the first time opened a vista of mutually enriching enterprise, with the good fortune of others opening opportunities for all. The Golden Rule, he said, was transformed from an idealistic vision of heaven into a practical agenda. From *Poor Richard's Almanack* to rich Andrew Carnegie's autobiographical parables, all were rediscovering the edifying insights of the Author of Proverbs.

Yes, "Jew-hatred is unique," as Prager and Telushkin's first chapter proclaims. Jews are unique. Anti-semitism subjects this uniquely gifted people to a crude and particularly incendiary manifestation of the immemorial hatreds that have afflicted the world for millennia. Judaism, however, perhaps more than any other religion, favors capitalist activity and provides a rigorous moral framework for it. It is based on a monotheistic affirmation that God is good and will prevail through transcending envy and hatred and zero-sum fantasies. Judaism can be plausibly interpreted as affirming the possibilities of creativity and collaboration on the frontiers of a capitalist economy.

The facts are clear. What makes Jews unique is their excellence. The solution is also clear. As Prager and Telushkin acknowledge, almost in passing, Jews do better under capitalism than under any other system. Anti-Semitism tends to wane under a growing and expanding capitalist system. Other consequences of Jewish superiority are also evident. On a planet where human life subsists upon the achievements of human intellect and enterprise, Jews are crucial to the future of the race.

The Holocaust was not simply an unspeakable catastrophe for Jews. It was incomparably more destructive than other modern genocidal acts not because of the diabolical evil of the Nazis but because of the unique virtues and genius of its victims. It was an irretrievable loss and catastrophe for all humanity, depleting the entire species of intellectual resources that will be critical to survival on an ever-threatened planet. Ironically, the rest of the world suffers far more than Jews from this loss of wealth-creating entrepreneurs and inventors.

The incontestable facts of Jewish excellence constitute a universal test not only for anti-Semitism but also for liberty and the justice of the civil order. The success or failure of Jews in a given country is the best index of its freedoms. In any free society, Jews will tend to be represented disproportionately in the highest ranks of both its culture and its commerce. Americans should not conceal the triumphs of Jews on our shores but celebrate them as evidence of the superior freedoms of the U.S. economy and culture.

The real case for Israel is incomparably more potent and important than the sentimental and self-serving mush usually mustered on its behalf. It has little or nothing to do with Israel's murky politics, its frequently malfunctioning democracy, its restraint in the face of constant provocations from its seething circle of demented neighbors, its clement treatment of gays or Palestinians or women or ethnic minorities, or its maddening indulgence of the Socialist sophistries of its critics and casuistically captious friends at Harvard, the *Atlantic*, and the *New Republic*.

The prevailing muddle of sentimentality and pettifoggery only obscures the actual eminently practical case for supporting Israel, for as long as it may take, without apology or deceit or waffles, without deception or obsequious self-denial. It is the case for Israel as the leader of human civilization, technological progress, and scientific advance. It is the case for Israel as a military spearhead of the culture of freedom and faith—the bastion of American progress and prosperity, and beyond America, for the progress and prosperity of all the people of the planet. The reason America should continue to "prop up" Israel is that Israel itself is a crucial prop of American wealth, freedom, and power.

In a dangerous world, faced with an array of perils, the Israel test asks whether the world can suppress envy and recognize its dependence on the outstanding performance of relatively few men and women. The world does not subsist on zero-sum legal niceties. It subsists on hard and possibly reversible accomplishments in technology, pharmacology, science, engineering, and enterprise. It thrives not on forcibly reallocating land and resources but on releasing human creativity in a way that exploits land and resources most productively. Survival of the race depends on recognizing excellence wherever it appears and nurturing it until it prevails. It relies on a vanguard of visionary creators on the frontiers of knowledge and truth. It depends on passing the Israel test.

Critics will call this a culpably Judeo-centric argument, missing lots of subtleties and complexities that shrewd, tough-loving critics of Israel cherish in their long catalog of its flaws. Olmert had the best answer, barking to Jeffrey Goldberg that he did not care about the flaws. Regardless of flaws—and Israel has fewer flaws than perhaps any other nation—Israel is the pivot, the axis, the litmus, the trial. Are you for civilization or barbarism, life or death, wealth or envy? Are you an exponent of excellence and accomplishment or of a leveling creed of troglodytic frenzy and hatred?

CHAPTER FOUR

The Palestinian Economy

S tranded between jungle and desert on a planet in peril, human life subsists on the feats of extraordinary men. The world does not run on cultural egalitarianism. Human civilization is always in jeopardy. The only way the world can survive the challenges of the coming century is by recognizing and promoting a culture of ingenuity and genius, excellence and accomplishment. That is to say, by passing the Israel test.

The test of a culture is what it accomplishes in advancing the human cause—what it creates rather than what it claims. There are similar numbers of Jews and Arabs in Israel and the territories, around five and a half million of each. Though numerous in the area for a longer period, the Palestinians had accomplished little by the time the Jews arrived in Palestine in large numbers after World War II. There was no self-conscious Palestinian nation, no industrial base, and virtually no exports.

Many people imagine that the Jews did something wrong during this early phase of Israeli history. What they chiefly did was purchase land, launch development projects, and build a country. Then they went to work on it, creating economic opportunities that attracted neighboring Arabs pouring across the bridges into Palestine. With the Arab population growing apace with the Jewish population in most neighborhoods, and faster in some, there was no displacement. What happened was enrichment and Arab migration toward it. When Zionist migration began in the 1930s, around 800 thousand Arabs lived in the area. By 1948 the number of Jews had grown to 650 thousand. Meanwhile, the number of Arabs had surged to 1.35 million (before the civil war flight), the most there had ever been in the history of the region. They were concentrated mostly in neighborhoods abutting the Zionist settlements. Only invasion by five Arab armies—and a desperate Israeli self-defense—drove out many of the native Arabs, some 700 thousand. Many Palestinian Arabs fled, chiefly evicted or urged to flee by Arab leaders in 1948 in a war that the Jews neither wanted nor invited.

After 1948, the history of Palestinian Arabs breaks down into three eras, each roughly two decades long. The statistical details remain cloudy and have provoked scores of academic brawls and millipedes of footnotes. But capturing the historic dynamics of population, economic growth, and foreign aid is a matter not of statistical minutiae but of orders of magnitude—general dimensions and relations between numbers. The orders of magnitude are clear and tell a story that is stunningly contrary to the conventional wisdom. Throughout the three eras, economic growth rose in proportion to the pace of Israeli settlement. Both Israelis and Arabs prospered until the eruption of the intifada near the end of the second era that ran from 1967 to 1993. The massive foreign aid associated with the so-called Peace Process in the early 1990s changed the Palestinians from workers and entrepreneurs into battling contenders for foreign money and attention.

Increasing flows of unearned outside funds have made the Palestinian areas the world's leading long-term recipients of foreign aid per capita for the last fifteen years and along with the associated violence destroyed their economy. The PLO and its codependent international-aid apparatus transformed the Palestinians into a ghetto of violent male gangs and welfare queens.

The late Lord Peter Bauer devoted much of his distinguished career to the study of the mostly erosive effects of foreign aid. What might be termed a "Bauer syndrome" prevailed nearly everywhere that foreign aid became the chief source of incremental income. Foreign aid normally flows to governments and tends to increase the power of government in relation to the private sector. Thus foreign aid fosters socialism, including, should the regime be so inclined, national socialism. As foreign aid eclipses entrepreneurial achievement as the dominant source of new income in a society, politics looms ever larger in the national life. A theater of grievance replaces a culture of economic advance. Rewards for violence eclipse the quest for profits. Displacing the peaceful outreach of commerce are seething concerns about international conspiracies, tribal loyalties, and betrayals.

Under the Bauer syndrome, elections sort out not merely who administers the country's laws and policies but who joins a gravy train and who gets thrown under it. Elections determine not just political power but economic success and status: who eats and who goes hungry. They determine whether a particular group or tribe ascends to relative luxury or suffers exclusion from the pipelines of wealth. In poor countries, access to the aid flows can become a matter of life and death. The more critical foreign aid becomes, the more it tends to foster violence between ethnic groups and political factions.

The first era of Palestinian economic history spanned the period between 1948 and 1967. During this period the Jordanians controlled the West Bank and the Egyptians controlled Gaza. In 1948, a total of nearly 600 thousand Arabs lived in these Palestinian territories (not including those who remained in Israel proper). The most significant of these territories, the West Bank of the Jordan River (also called Judea and Samaria), covers some 2,000 square miles of land. More than 500 thousand Arabs lived in the West Bank in 1948. Gaza, the other territory, is a strip of land on the Mediterranean contiguous with Egypt, which is approximately 25 miles long (40 kilometers) and 6 miles wide (10 kilometers) and hosted almost eighty thousand Arabs in 1948. As Hillel Halkin observed, "Jordan, Israel's main military adversary in 1948, saw to it that the West Bank it annexed had not a Jew in it." Similarly, Egypt would not tolerate Jews in Gaza.

In this first phase, under Jordanian control, the Arab population of the West Bank increased by 20 percent, to some 600 thousand by 1967, and the economy showed modest growth, with per-capita income around $800. The population of Gaza rose fivefold to some 400 thousand, while the economy in Gaza stagnated under unofficial Egyptian rule and an influx of Palestinian war refugees and UN programs. For the time, both Egypt and Jordan were substantial recipients of foreign aid, but it failed to enhance the environment for commerce in Gaza.

Many leading Palestinian entrepreneurs fled to Amman, Damascus, or Beirut, where they set up formidable machine shops and even banking and insurance firms. There are wealthy ex-Palestinians scattered throughout the Middle East. If economies are driven by the efforts of a relatively few exceptional entrepreneurs, most of the Palestinian "few" ended up outside Palestine. Growth in the West Bank and Gaza was sluggish at best.

The second era began after the 1967 war, when Israel routed four hostile armies in six days. During this second period, Israel took over the West Bank and Gaza and administered its economy.

During these twenty years under Israeli management until the First Intifada of 1987, the West Bank and Gaza comprised one of the most dynamic economies on earth, with a decade of growth at a rate of roughly 30 percent per year from 1969 to 1979. Annual investment in constant dollars soared from under $10 million in 1969 to some $600 million in 1991, rising from 10 percent of GDP to around 30 percent in 1987 (maintained through 1991). The Arab population rose from roughly 1 million in 1967 to almost 3 million in some 261 new towns. Despite the nearly triple growth in population, per-capita income tripled in the West Bank and in Gaza rose from $80 to $1,706 from 1967 to 1987. Meanwhile, the number of Jewish settlers in the territories rose to merely 250 thousand. During this period when the West Bank and Gaza were run by Israel, the territories received little foreign aid, the economy boomed, and the Palestinians increased their business activity and their standard of living dramatically.

Efraim Karsh tells the details:

"At the inception of the occupation, conditions in the territories were quite dire. Life expectancy was low; malnutrition, infectious diseases, and child mortality were rife; and the level of education was very poor. Prior to the 1967 war, fewer than 60 percent of all male adults had been employed, with unemployment among refugees running as high as 83 percent. Within a brief period after the war, Israeli occupation had led to dramatic improvements. . . . [T]he number of Palestinians working in Israel rose from zero in 1967 . . . to 109 thousand by 1986, accounting for 35 percent of the employed population of the West Bank and 45 percent in Gaza. Close to two thousand industrial plants, employing almost half of the work force, were established in the territories under Israeli rule.

"During the 1970s, the West Bank and Gaza constituted the

fourth fastest-growing economy in the world . . . with per capita GDP expanding tenfold between 1968 and 1991 . . . Life expectancy rose from 48 years in 1967 to 72 in 2000 . . . By 1986, 92.8 percent of the population . . . had electricity around the clock, as compared to 20.5 percent in 1967 . . . [Similar advances occurred in hygiene, healthcare, child mortality, immunizations, and communications, which all rose to levels equal or exceeding other Middle Eastern countries]. The number of schoolchildren . . . grew by 102 percent . . . Even more dramatic was the progress in higher education. [From zero in 1967] by the early 1990s, there were seven [universities] boasting some 16,500 students."

This second era of Palestinian progress and prosperity began to dwindle in 1987, with the outbreak of the First Intifada, when Palestinian Arabs launched systematic attacks on Israeli targets, putting economic growth into reverse.

In 1993, impelled by the urgencies of the Oslo Peace Process and a massive influx of foreign aid, the PLO was recognized as the representative of the Palestinian people and official manager of the territory, commencing the third era.

As Oussama Kanaan wrote in the International Monetary Fund Report, *Uncertainty Deters Private Investment in the West Bank and Gaza Strip* (1998), "The Peace Process . . . had the potential to yield substantial welfare gains, largely through rapid growth in private investment . . . However, a look at the evolution of private investment since 1993 reveals a radically different and disturbing picture. . . . In 1993–97 real private investment is estimated to have declined by an average of 10 percent per year and private investment's share in GDP to have declined from 19 percent of GDP in 1993 to 10 percent of GDP in 1997. What went wrong?"

The IMF report presents a raft of data from the dismal science to document the collapse. Military measures to suppress the intifada restricted economic activity, and most analyses focus on the exigencies of the conflict. But the real underlying story is the Bauer syndrome.

Rehabilitated by the Oslo Peace Process, Arafat returned from his exile in Tunisia in July of 1994, where he had fled from Lebanon in 1982. With massive aid flowing to his regime and Nobel laureate honors on the way, Arafat over time shifted the Palestinian economy from its growth dynamic led by entrepreneurs complementing Israel next door to a dynamic of terror and foreign aid led by the PLO.

In white papers and research tomes, UN subgroups and other international quasi-governmental organizations ("quangos") supplied a stream of sophisticated critiques of what was termed the "false" or "morbid" or "dependent" or "unbalanced" prosperity of the previous era. Quango PhDs supplied rationalizations for separating the Palestinian economy from Israel and then blaming Israel for the collapse of growth. Under PLO control, the Palestinian Arabs received more foreign aid per capita over the years than any other people on the face of the earth and became arguably the world's most twisted welfare culture of violence and demoralization. The PLO led the third world club of nations, with leadership based entirely on terrorism and hatred and international grievance mongering.

Previously, under the Israeli regime, the Palestinians in the West Bank and Gaza were oriented toward the possibilities of enterprise and organic economic growth complementing Israel's own economy. For a decade, the territories actually grew faster than Israel did. With Yasser Arafat banished, the Palestinians in the West Bank and Gaza enjoyed rapid economic growth in a climate of minimal violence.

With the ascendancy of the PLO beginning in 1993, however, the United States and the United Nations essentially gave

Arafat the store. All the power—and money—flowed to the PLO apparatus. With foreign aid pouring in by the billions to the terrorist leaders, the result was the emergence of Hamas, battling Arafat's Fatah organization for power and perks and mobilizing the forces in Palestine out of favor with the PLO. Violence became pandemic.

The increase in foreign aid after 1993 was associated with a 40 percent decline in per-capita income in the first half of this decade together with mounting terrorism and anti-Semitic animus. As aid soared, so did Palestinian violence. As the PLO focused on politics and sedition, the Palestinian economy shrank, and dependence on foreign aid increased along with constant complaints about its inadequacy. In this environment, Palestinian entrepreneurship collapsed amid much talk of the "humiliation" of working for Jews.

From the outset early in the twentieth century, Palestinian nationalism itself was an artificial construct mostly evoked by external politics of international organizations, from the United Nations to the Arab League, marked by their hostility toward Jews and capitalism. Palestinian political leaders were indifferent to enterprise and hostile to repeated international schemes for joint Arab–Israeli development of the Jordan River basin. Palestinian political behavior was so obnoxious that their leaders were rejected by every Arab state in which they sought refuge, including the contiguous state of Jordan when it ruled the West Bank between 1948 and 1967. But after 1967, and under Israeli rule, the Palestinians proved that by focusing on enterprise complementing the Israeli economy they could become prosperous.

• • •

In the face of this history, international organizations, from the World Bank to the United Nations Conference on Trade and Development (UNCTAD), have performed a series of further analyses of the Palestinian economy, including the experience of the Arabs within Israel. Their consensus is that foreign aid has been inadequate to meet the acute needs of the Palestinian Arabs. Meanwhile, the growth of the Israeli economy is ascribed largely to exploitation of the Palestinians.

In essence, the growth of the Israeli economy emerges in these studies as a gigantic "imbalance" in the region. This imbalance is seen to perpetrate huge "gaps." Contemplating this weighty matter, academic and political sages imagine that a more "balanced" outcome, gapwise, would be "a convergence of Israeli and Arab incomes in the area." The absence of such a convergence is somehow Israel's fault, or, for the more globally oriented, the fault of world capitalism.

In 1948, when Arabs comprised roughly 66 percent of Palestine under the British mandate, their share of a national income of perhaps $2–$3 billion dollars was 40 percent. To an observer who views economic advance as a good thing, both enriching its protagonists and providing economic opportunities for neighboring areas, the contributions of Zionism to the region would bespeak a need for yet more Zionist enterprise. This boon, in fact, occurred.

By 1992, the economy of Israel, including the Palestinian territories of the West Bank and Gaza, had grown to some $130 billion (in constant inflation-adjusted dollars). This fortyfold rise was accompanied by a near tenfold rise in the output of the territories, to some $11 billion in constant dollars. By almost any standard, a tenfold rise in real output over forty-three years is a considerable achievement, made to seem modest only by the extraordinary success of Israel.

In the early 1990s came a resurgence of suicide bombings,

kidnappings, and missile attacks on Israel. Alas, 1992 would turn out to be the peak year for the Palestinian economy. The economic deterioration that began with the institutionalization of the PLO after Oslo became real collapse with the so-called "second intifada" beginning in 2000. By the estimate of the World Bank, the economy of the territories had shrunk by some 40 percent in the first half decade of the new century. This acute downsizing occurred despite a continued influx of foreign aid from international bodies at an annual rate of some $4 billion, a 20 percent rise in remissions from overseas Palestinians, and Israeli support and subsidies for the Palestinian Monetary Authority that was charged with upgrading banking in the Palestinian territories. Despite all the aid, however, per-capita income in the territories has continued to stagnate.

To the sages in the UN and academic think tanks, the shrinkage was a result not of Palestinian violence under its saber-rattling leaders but of Israeli restrictions on free movement of Palestinians and impediments on their "access to natural resources." That might well happen to people who use their access to resources to lob missiles into Israeli villages and infiltrate suicide bombers onto buses and into cafés.

However, the most revealing gauge of the impact of the Israeli economy on Arabs—as opposed to self-inflicted disruption of terrorism—is the performance of the one-fifth of Palestinian Arabs who live in Israel as citizens. A recent thicket of sociology was planted on the subject by UN economist Raja Khalidi in the *Journal of Palestine Studies* published by the University of California Press in Berkeley, California, and edited by Khalidi's brother Rashid. Rashid Khalidi became briefly famous during Barack Obama's presidential campaign in 2008 for his "consistent reminders to me," as the presidential candidate said, "of my own blind spots and my own biases" related to Palestinian suffering. In his article, Raja Khalidi's view "pits a discriminatory and hegemonic Jewish state (and economy) against an ethno-national minority unable to access its fair share of national resources."

"The losing struggle to maintain access to natural resources," as Khalidi writes, "plays out in persistent gaps and imbalances in Arab educational advancement, occupational progress, and capital accumulation. It also entails an overall deterioration of terms of trade (labor, goods, and services) between the Arab ('regional') economy and the Jewish ('national') economy."

Concludes the UN guru: "The marginalization of Arabs in Israel is not unrelated to the state's Jewish character and its Zionist development policy preferences and priorities . . . [These] political, economic, and social processes . . . began well before 1948 and continue today to lock in and further degrade the position of Arabs [in Israel] . . ."

"These gaps are not coincidences of history . . . rather, they emanate from distinct external processes that impede the free operation of theoretically perfect (but actually imperfect) markets. Although economic convergence in the long term is promised . . ." it requires "leveling the playing field" . . . both "between developed and developing countries" and in Israel.

There you have it all—"gaps" and "imbalances"; "economic convergence"; access to "natural resources"; unequal educational attainment; capital accumulation; playing-field leveling— and the old UN favorite since the days of Secretary General Raúl Prebisch of UNCTAD—deterioration of the "terms of trade" (the relative value of the goods and services exchanged between two political entities). The idea is that manual labor and primitive handicrafts produced by poor people have increased in value less than the design and production of new semiconductor capital goods, microchips, complex medical instruments, and bioengineered pharmaceuticals produced by the graduates of the Technion (Israel Institute of Technology), the Weizmann Institute of Science, Bar-Ilan University, or the Jerusalem College of Technology. Why we are supposed to regret this state of affairs is hardly evident.

In the tragic calculus of anti-Semitism anything Jews do well is deemed regrettable. But the terms-of-trade concept, which implies the need for Socialist remedies, works both ways. Over the last decade, after all, the terms of trade have shifted massively in favor of cartelized and nationalized oil and commodity producers, mostly in fashionably anti-Semitic third world countries.

Globally, few countries are more "deprived of natural resources" than Israel, and the ethnic group most endowed with these benefactions includes among its members Arab oil barons and their tribal followers. So the United Nations has less to say on the subject these days, except as the concern applies within Israel itself. In Israel's case, the terms of trade have supposedly shifted against Arabs peculiarly denied "access to natural resources," chiefly land, after they sold it to Israelis and suffered sellers' remorse. Apparently, they did not anticipate that the land (these "natural resources") could yield the region's most fertile farms and could give birth to skyscrapers and high-technology factories. Why didn't anyone tell them? Now they want it back, along with the skyscrapers and factories.

In any case, the formidable successes of Palestinians working with Israel fail to impress Khalidi. According to him, Israel's own data on the Arab-Israeli economy "paint a dismal picture of the results of sixty years of failed integration (and Arab exclusion)." To rectify it requires "sustained policy intervention."

There, too, you have the Socialist remedy: "sustained policy intervention," if not by missiles and suicide bombers, then by the equally devastating ministrations from UN development officials. And you have the perennial Socialist invocation of "imperfections" in "theoretically perfect markets" to justify eclipse of the market by managerial global bureaucrats and politicians.

This entire argument itself suffers from a huge gap—namely, the absence of evidence that Arabs anywhere in the world outside of the United States have performed as well economically as Arabs in Israel. Contrary to the claims of deterioration and "lock in," the Arab average annual per-capita income in Israel is $600 per month (i.e., an annual household income of $14,400 for a family of four). This compares with an average annual per-capita income of $9,400 for a family of four in Jordan, which roughly matches the average across the Arab world. This compares with an average annual per-capita income of some $9,500 for a family of four in Jordan, which roughly matches the average across the Arab world. Moreover, while Palestinians in the disputed territories have undergone a catastrophic drop in income since the PLO's resurgence, the income gap between Israel's Palestinian Arab population and Jewish population has actually been decreasing.

As it is, the income gap is significantly an effect of the extreme youth of the Arab population—a median age of about twenty, almost ten years younger than the Israeli national median. The high birth rate of the Arabs, nearly double the national rate, plus the influence of Muslim culture, means that drastically fewer Arab women than Jewish women enter the work force. Jewish households thus have more income earners and work many more hours. Arabs in Israel live roughly as long as, or longer than, Arabs anywhere else on earth. The life expectancy of the Arabs in Israel has grown over the past forty years from about fifty-two years to over seventy-three years.

Moreover, any income gap between the Jewish and Arab populations of Israel is clearly attributable to the prowess of Jewish entrepreneurs and other professionals, whose excellence produces similar gaps in every free country on earth with significant numbers of Jews. Jews, for example, outearn other Caucasians in the United States by an even larger margin than they outearn Arabs in Israel. This probably reflects the fact that the United States used to have a freer economy, by most standards, than Israel.

Amid all the dismal talk of lock in and privation, even the UN guru Khalidi does acknowledge that "proximity to the more advanced Jewish economy has allowed for 'gains' [quotes are Khalidi's] that many Palestinians living under occupation or in exile would envy." But to the UN economist, who wants to have it every which way, the so-called economic gains mask a "degradation of *social capital*" [emphasis added] because successful Arabs in Israel may be lured away from the jihad. The discreetly bloodthirsty UN sage thinks that what would help more than wealth and longevity is for the "Palestinian minority" to "succeed in mobilizing itself and its full weight within the Israeli-Palestinian-Arab conflict."

Khalidi's gingerly suspicion toward successful Arabs in Israel who may not share his political obsessions reflects the unwillingness of the quango economic establishment to recognize the obvious fact that looms over all the data. Arabs constitute roughly 50 percent of the population of the entire Israeli-Palestinian area but contribute only 11 percent of its output, mostly in public-sector employment. Per-capita income of Palestinians outside of Israel is roughly one-fourth that of their counterparts' within Israel. Following the surging growth of the Palestinian economy during the second era under Israeli auspices, these numbers on the performance of Israeli Arabs suggest that nothing would benefit Palestinian Arabs more than an Israeli takeover of the entire country from the Jordan to the sea.

More important than all the legal debates, though, is the attitude toward achievement that is expressed in the literature of

Palestinian apologetics. Most of it echoes the view of Arab leader Musa Alami, meeting with Ben-Gurion in 1934. When Ben-Gurion told him that Zionism "would bring a blessing to the Arabs of Palestine, and they have no good cause to oppose us" Alami retorted, "I would prefer that the country remain impoverished and barren for another hundred years, until we ourselves are able to develop it on our own." This sentiment continues today under Hamas. In 2005, when Israelis actually relinquished their advanced greenhouses and irrigation equipment in Gaza, the leaders of Hamas ordered many of these facilities destroyed.

This concept of economic autarky is the chief cause of poverty in the world. No one can be rich alone. Wealth is an effect of sharing and collaboration between an elite of capitalists and the insurgent new businesses rising up around them. It is an effect of the willingness of the young and less educated or less talented to work for the educated and able. It is a product of apprenticeship and learning followed by entrepreneurial rivalry. The success of the Israeli economy is not an imbalance that creates invidious gaps. It is a gap that summons new energies and new wealth.

All capitalist advance generates imbalances and disequilibrium. Growth is an effect of the disequilibrating activities of entrepreneurs, the creative destruction unleashed by rare feats of excellence. It is the fallacy of perfect competition and convergence that leads most of the global media and academic establishments to interpret as gaps and imbalances what in fact represents luminous achievement and creativity.

Now emerging is a fourth era for the Palestinian economy. The immediate prospects seem grim. After the Gaza war of early 2009, the response of the international community was to mobilize some $4 billion in new foreign aid, including $900 million from the United States. Most of the money will tend to gravitate toward governmental institutions, increasing their relative power and depleting the private economy of entrepreneurial energies. Dominant in Gaza and bristling with weapons, Hamas will manage to capture the bulk of these funds, regardless of how they are initially distributed. Hamas accepts the money as a well-earned reward for its missile attacks on Israel and will bask in their glow as the cycle of appeasement and pelf for terrorists continues.

Nonetheless, the long-term possibilities illuminated during the second era of Palestinian prosperity between 1967 and 1987 have become even more inviting with the new global ascendancy of the Israeli economy. Israel's current administration, under the business-savvy leadership of Benjamin Netanyahu, is committed to the economics of collaboration and prosperity. When the violence abates, he is resolved to open up new opportunities for Palestinian entrepreneurship and growth.

So, as always, the choice remains clear between the ascent of capitalism and freedom and the economics of dependency and national socialism.

CHAPTER FIVE

The Economics of Hate

I n a great prophetic work, "A Draft of Guidelines for the Reconstruction of Austria," written in May 1940 as a report for Otto von Hapsburg, the former archduke of Austria, economist Ludwig von Mises predicted the effects of the banishment of Jews from Austria after the Nazi annexation in 1938. By implication, he also explained the predicament of the Palestinians today.

Presenting the facts of life for small countries without oil or other valuable natural endowment, von Mises wrote: "As a mountainous country with poor soil and few natural resources, Austria must rely on industrial activity to feed a population of six and a half million people. As an agrarian nation, [it] could at best eke out enough food for a population of one to two million. . . . To be an industrial country requires being predominantly an importer of raw materials and food and an exporter of industrial products. . . .

"The mainstays of such an organism," von Mises pointed out, "are the entrepreneurs of the export industry who have the know-how to produce [competitive] goods for the world market. The industrial and commercial genius of these entrepreneurs creates work and livelihood for all the other citizens. . . ."

By von Mises' estimate, "Old Austria produced about one thousand men of this kind." Von Mises recognized what David C. McClelland saw in America in his *Achieving Society* and what Edward Roberts and Charles Eesley discovered in "Entrepreneurial Impact" among MIT graduates. The leading entrepreneurial talent of the world is disproportionately Jewish. As von Mises observed about the entrepreneurs of the once-flourishing Austrian economy: "At least two-thirds of these one thousand men were Jews. . . . They are gone, scattered around the world, and trying to start again from scratch."

Not only Jewish entrepreneurs were driven out of the economy. The hatred of Jews epitomizes a general resentment of excellence and creativity. "Tax offices [as instruments of redistribution] were filled with a blind hate against 'plutocrats'" of all races and creeds. Moreover, technical talent and middle management are a crucial complement to entrepreneurial genius. Much of the most productive middle management of Austrian companies was also Jewish. Of the some 250 *thousand* Jews in Austria in 1938, according to von Mises, only *216* individuals survived the war without leaving the country.

Von Mises concludes: "The so-called Aryanization of firms was based on the Marxist idea that capital (resources and equipment) and labor . . . were the only vital ingredients of an enterprise, whereas the entrepreneur was an exploiter. An enterprise without entrepreneurial spirit and creativity, however, is nothing more than a pile of rubbish and old iron." Austria was left with many piles of rubbish and old iron. Its newly *Judenrein* industrial economy, once an economic miracle of export-led growth and a paragon of European commerce, would never recover its leading role.

Growing up in Austria during the period described by von Mises was Adolf Hitler, whose original surname was Schicklgruber. Explaining this Austrian catastrophe and similar disasters in

Hungary is the set of ideas and assumptions in Hitler's personal manifesto, *Mein Kampf*. Autobiography, creedal testament, anti-Jewish *cri de coeur*, and National Socialist agenda, Hitler's book is a dense, tortuous, and repetitive screed, suitable for consignment to the dustbins of history like its demonic author.

Mein Kampf, however, is anything but a historical relic. Banned by the Israelis when they ruled the West Bank, it became popular there when the Palestinian Authority took over. With every new Arabic edition it crops up on best-seller lists and bookstore displays across the Middle East. It loomed in menacing piles in the airport bookstore in Jordan. Israeli soldiers rooting through Arafat's possessions abandoned in southern Lebanon in 1982 discovered many copies at all his base camps. Its rhetorical idiom of "pigs" . . . "jackals" . . . "bacteria" . . . "vampires" . . . "parasites" . . . "vermin" . . . and "vultures" recurs in the speeches of Osama bin Laden, of al-Qaida, Iranian President Mahmoud Ahmadinejad, former Malaysian premier Mahathir Mohamad, and thousands of imams throughout Islamic lands.

As familiar and consequential as this book is, it is strangely misunderstood. It has been reviewed thousands of times without any grasp of the central theme of its case against the Jews. Critics notice the references to Jews as "an inferior race . . . the incarnation of Satan and the symbol of evil." Cited are Hitler's references to the Jewish mastery of the press, manipulation of propaganda and public opinion, and the Jew's devious "benevolence" and charity as "manure" applied as fertilizer for "future produce." Critics comment upon Hitler's celebration of the *Protocols of the Learned Elders of Zion*, now ubiquitous in the Arab world, and that book's claims of an insidious Masonic conspiracy controlled by Jews throughout history and around the world. Hitler's antipathy toward the Jews is presented as a bizarre and phantasmagorical obsession, as a demented chimera, or as a paranoid fantasy unrelated to the sophisticated attitudes toward Israel and Jews now widely upheld in faculty lounges, international organizations, television talk shows, and noted journals of opinion and newspapers of record.

To Hitler, however, Jews are anathema, not chiefly because of such exotic figments as their alleged racial inferiority or their demonic Satanism or their perennial Masonic intrigues, but because of a far more common and fashionable complaint still widely voiced at Harvard, Berkeley, and around the globe. Hitler's case against the Jews focuses on their mastery of capitalism.

As von Mises observed, more than two-thirds of the leading entrepreneurs in Austria at the time were Jewish. The focus of Hitler's racial theory in chapters ten and eleven of *Mein Kampf* is his resentment and paranoia toward Jewish prowess in finance and enterprise. The Jew's "commercial cunning . . . made him superior in this field to the Aryans," he wrote, and turned "finance and trade" into "his complete monopoly . . . The Jew . . . organized capitalistic methods of exploitation to their ultimate degree of efficiency."

In a theme later adopted by Osama bin Laden, Hitler asserts that the key to initial Jewish success was "his usurious rate of interest." He cites the immemorial notion that Jews gain an economic foothold by mulcting others through their prowess as shysters and shylocks, ensnaring "ingenuous" Aryans in webs of debt. Blind to the nature of capitalism, Hitler condemns interest as illegitimate gain, the embezzled returns of dispensable middlemen. Then he makes an elaborate case that Jews parlay their insidious middleman strategy into a broader economic dominance, first in banking and finance and then in all commerce and industry. He implies that their resulting affluence and ostentation will ultimately bring them down. Projecting on others his own revulsion, Hitler contended: "The increasing impudence which the

Jew began to manifest all round stirred up popular indignation, while his display of wealth gave rise to popular envy."

Adumbrating Mearsheimer and Walt on Jewish lobbying prowess, Hitler spoke of the Jew as an "eternal profiteer," mitigating popular hostility by paying "court to governments with servile flattery [and] used his money to ingratiate himself further . . ."

While sneering at Jewish lack of connection to the soil, Hitler wrote: "The cup of [Jewish] iniquity became full to the brim when he included landed property among his commercial wares and degraded the soil to the level of a market commodity. Since he himself never cultivated the soil but considered it as an object to be exploited, on which the peasant may still remain but only on condition that he submits to the most heartless exactions of his new master." This theme now pervades facile journalist coverage of the Palestinian territories, where water for agriculture is allocated chiefly to Jewish farms that pay for it by profitable use of the irrigated land.

Referring to Zionism, Hitler wrote, "They have not the slightest intention of building up a Jewish State in Palestine so as to live in it. What they really are aiming at is to establish a central organization for their international swindling and cheating," which is Hitler's characterization of Jewish enterprise.

Continuing his crude Marxist narrative, Hitler argues that as the Jews compiled wealth, "they bought up stock" in companies and had "predominance in the stock exchange." They "thus pushed [their] influence into the circuit of national production, making this . . . an object of buying and selling on the stock exchange . . . thus ruining the basis on which personal proprietorship alone is possible . . . [and creating] that feeling of estrangement between employers and employees . . . which led at a later date to the political class struggle."

This vision of a voracious and amoral capitalism that debauches moral codes, exploits the environment, and degrades the relations between workers and employers is a central theme of leftist economics today. Familiar, too, is the idea that stock and bond markets enable mostly Jewish middlemen and entrepreneurs, greenmailers and junk bond manipulators to seize companies from honest and stable management for financial exploitation. Change the wording by deleting the references to Jews and inserting the names of financiers, such as Michael Milken, Carl Icahn, George Soros, Henry Kravis, Gary Winnick, et al., or even such categories as "junk bond kings" and "private equity predators," and present it all under the name of, say, Schicklgruber, and you will have an exemplary book for public consumption at American universities. Unfortunately for some of the above, these anti-capitalist prejudices, with their often inadvertently anti-Semitic undercurrents, also made their way from the American media into U.S. courts. Michael Milken, for example, was accused of being a Ponzi schemer and predator, but within two decades the companies he financed were worth more than a trillion dollars. He was forced to plead guilty to a series of trivial clerical offenses by the prosecutor's threat to indict his totally innocent brother Lowell. The idea that behind every great fortune is a great crime joins anti-Semitism and anti-capitalism in the moralistic embrace that Hitler pioneered and epitomized.

Hitler's complaint probes still more deeply, however. He charges Jews with violating the deepest mandates of the Darwinian law of nature. The heart of Hitler's case against the Jews is that through their superiority over Aryans in capitalist finance and trade, they were cheating the law of survival of the fittest. They had found an individualist route to power without making the sacrifices necessary to achieve collective strength as warriors.

They were circumventing the mandate of nature that requires all creatures to gang together and fight for their own survival.

This is Hitler's concept of the key conflict in economies and societies. It is the division between Darwinian nature, governed by the survival of the physically fit and feral, and the effete and intellectual artifice of devious individualist entrepreneurs.

"Here we meet the insolent objection, which is Jewish in its inspiration and is typical of the modern pacifist. It says: 'Man can control even Nature.' There are millions who repeat by rote that piece of Jewish babble.

"Wherever [men] have reached a superior level of existence, it was not the result of following the ideas of crazy visionaries but by acknowledging and rigorously observing the iron laws of Nature."

This is the Hitler vision of the split between devious individuals (to him, Jewish) who gain power by prevailing in economic rivalry and groups that gain power by blood sacrifice in the perennial and always ultimately violent struggle for survival. It is the division between those who imagine that humans can manipulate nature and create new things under conditions of peace and those who believe that the greatest attainments come from solidarity and sacrifice in war.

As Hitler presents the law of nature in this way: "He who would live must fight. He who does not wish to fight in this world, where permanent struggle is the law of life, has not the right to exist."

As his devout jihadi followers do today, Hitler recognized that violence can trump economic exchange and progress. Against Jewish dominance in the stock market, he counterpoised his Hitlerjugend, or Hitler Youth movement, with its anti–Semitic lust for blood and its dominance in the streets. Just as the jihadis in their *madrasahs* today muster and indoctrinate a new generation of Islamic young males into Wahhabi codes of hatred and violence and suicidal martyrdom, Hitler's Brown Shirts espoused a solidarity of violence and sacrifice. Under a regime of "survival of the fittest," Hitler celebrated a sacrificial solidarity and drive to war that could thwart the capitalist enrichment of Jews.

At the same time, to justify his own plans for mass exterminations, he blamed the Jews in Russia for perpetrating the starvation and massacre of 30 million Ukrainians, Kulaks, shopkeepers, and other "class enemies." (Reaching for the ultimate affront, he even charged: "The Jews were responsible for bringing Negroes into the Rhineland.")

Hitler portrayed envy and resentment of Jewish achievement as a campaign of vengeance and social justice. True "social justice," according to Hitler, "is a typical Aryan characteristic." Individualist to the core, Jews merely pretend to support equality and social justice. Marxism, for Hitler, is ersatz socialism contrived by Jews to mobilize the workers against the enemies of the Jews, such as his own impending National Socialist regime. But the deeper Jewish offenses that he primarily details and denounces in *Mein Kampf*—usury, stock manipulation, exploitation of the land, cunning in finance and trade—are all expressions not of cultural inferiority or Marxist machinations but of capitalist superiority.

When the Arab leader Musa Alami in 1934 told Ben-Gurion that he would prefer Palestine remain a wasteland for a hundred years than permit the Israelis to develop it, he was echoing Hitler's position.

The fundamental conflict in the world pits the advocates of capitalist freedom, economic growth, and property against the exponents of blood and soil and violence. Capitalism requires peace. A real capitalist can want war only against threats to international peace and trade.

Although everyone benefits from capitalist prosperity, it inexorably produces "gaps" between rich and poor. It necessarily requires toleration of superior entrepreneurs who can make the system work. A free regime will always tend to favor peoples who excel in commerce and industry. For centuries, Jews have been disproportionately represented among these entrepreneurs and inventors, scientists and creators. Even though Jews are a tiny minority of less than a tenth of 1 percent of the world's people, they comprise perhaps a quarter of the world's paramount capitalists and entrepreneurs. This was true at Hitler's time and it is true today.

As in Hitler's time, demagogues tend to target successful capitalists for envy, resentment, and violence. They rant against the "rich" and wish to confiscate their wealth. They celebrate a cult of nature and land. In Thomas Friedman's felicitous metaphor, they cling to the olive tree and resent the Lexus. They hate capitalism and resent capitalists.

The ultimate source of their resentment is that, under capitalism, success does not normally go to the "best" or the naturally fittest as identified by physical strength or beauty or by the established criteria of virtue. Even the best in academic credentials do not prevail. To Hitler, "The Aryan . . . is the Prometheus of mankind, from whose shining brow the divine spark of genius has at all times flashed forth, always kindling anew that fire, which in the form of knowledge, illuminated the dark night by drawing aside the veil of mystery and thus showing man how to rise and become master over all the other beings on the earth." And so on. But if the Aryan's design of a Mercedes-Benz does not satisfy customers, he will not prevail over a member of the inferior Japanese race—making a Honda or a Toyota. If the Aryan's business choices do not prosper in the market, they will not succeed against the enterprises of Jewish entrepreneurs.

Under capitalism, Jews often prevail. Until the dominance of capitalism, Goths and Vandals and Teutons prevailed. Hitler preferred the previous regime. Hitler's followers in the Middle East now wish to restore it.

CHAPTER SIX

The Archetype and the Algorithm

The twentieth-century fall of middle Europe into anti-Semitic rage and plutophobia brought down the Austrian and Hungarian economies and centers of culture. It built up the awesome animus and momentum of the Axis armies. It unleashed the frenzies of the Holocaust and the Stalinist pogroms and finally brought forth a new global empire and apparat of Communist movements and powers. Then the forces mobilized by the Western democracies managed to turn back the totalitarian tide.

How did victory happen?

To observers who focus on politics and statecraft, the central history of the era follows the feats and follies of generals and dictators, politicians and demagogues. In many accounts, Roosevelt, Churchill, and Stalin, Eisenhower and Montgomery may seem to have defeated Hitler. But there is another way to tell the history of the time. All of these political and military leaders were utterly dependent upon the achievements of science and technology for success. At the same time that Hitler and Stalin, Roosevelt and Churchill were striding the stages of statecraft and war, other more singular and cerebral forces were more quietly released into the world. They launched a contrary tide that ultimately prevailed against Nazism and communism.

Pushing this contrary tide was the Jewish diaspora. Flowing around the globe, devoid of the repulsive force of nationality, the largely homeless Jewish intellectuals honed in like neutrons into the nuclei of the most receptive centers of Western science and technology. There they galvanized the energies that won the war, shaped the peace, and transformed the global economy and the scientific culture of the age.

The turning point came early in the twentieth century. Before quantum theory, science was chiefly an enterprise of gentile Europeans—men like Isaac Newton, James Clerk Maxwell, Lord Kelvin, Ernest Rutherford, and Max Planck. With the rise of quantum theory came the ascendancy of Jews in science, led by Albert Einstein, Niels Bohr, Wolfgang Pauli, and Max Born. In the post-World War II era, Richard Feynman became the paramount teacher and interpreter of quantum theory.

The twenty-first-century world emerged chiefly from this microcosm: the new revelation of the early twentieth century that matter consisted not of unbreakable solids but of enigmatic waves of energy, largely governed by information. From quantum theory ultimately issued IBM, Intel, Microsoft, Google, Sony, and Qualcomm. From quantum theory, too, would spring forth—from the wretched wastes of communism and feudal paralysis—the vast new energies of China, India, and the rest of increasingly capitalist Asia.

These developments originated in Europe early in the twentieth century, with events in Budapest and Vienna first rocking and then overturning the cradle of the new science and industry. The history of Budapest echoed the history of Vienna. In both great cities of the Hapsburg Empire, Jewish entrepreneurs led an economic miracle. But in science, Budapest was preeminent. From quantum mechanics to nuclear weapons to computer technology, information theory, and holography, Hungarian Jews bestrode the history of the twentieth century, from the pinnacles of research to the practical triumphs of Silicon Valley.

Paramount among these Hungarian Jews were Eugene Wigner, Edward Teller, and Leó Szilárd, who all played vital roles in the creation of nuclear weapons; Dennis Gabor, the Nobel laureate who invented holography; Michael Polanyi, the eminent chemist-philosopher who inspired a school of followers around the globe; and Arthur Koestler, the scientist-historian who wrote *Darkness at Noon* and edited *The God That Failed*, two books vital to the defeat of communism among intellectuals.

Of all the Jews who emerged from the anti-Semitic turmoil of Europe during World War II, however, none had more impact on the history of the epoch than the son of a marriage between Budapest banker Max Neumann and scion of finance Margit Kann. Adding an aristocratic "von" from the title Max Neumann purchased in 1913 but never used himself, his son John's name became von Neumann and it looms over our history. Born on December 28, 1903, John von Neumann epitomizes the role of the Jews in the twentieth century and foreshadows their role in the twenty-first.

Von Neumann's record of accomplishment is as stunning as his ubiquity across the sciences of his era. But this record, like the ubiquity, can be deceptive. Von Neumann's work intrudes widely not so much because he was a man of many ideas but because he was a man of one idea, or perhaps one idea about ideas.

Assuming an intellectual position more exalted in the hierarchy of knowledge than perhaps any of his peers, he successively imposed his synoptic mastery of abstraction in mathematics, quantum mechanics, nuclear weapons, computer science, game theory, and information theory—all through his charismatic powers of organization and persuasion. Bringing all these sciences and capabilities to bear, by himself almost, he could be said to have tipped the balance in the cause of freedom. But as Eugene Wigner wrote in his autobiography, "Despite the variety, all of his very great achievements rose from a single coherent view of life." Since his childhood, von Neumann was a master of the ladders of abstraction, from physical data through number and symbol to set and group, all unified by the concept of the algorithm.

An algorithm can be thought of as any stepwise set of instructions that is sufficiently precise to produce a determined outcome in every iteration without additional human intervention. Any machine from which its human tenders can walk away while it does its job is driven by an algorithm, which can be abstracted from the machine itself. Men make algorithms, but they also discover them in the process of exploring the physical world. Not every human endeavor is algorithmic. The design of a pitching machine made by men is algorithmic; the prowess of a Major League Baseball pitcher is not. Not every natural process is or can be described algorithmically: the human genome is revealed increasingly as being within the algorithmic realm; along with many other complex and chaotic processes, global-weather patterns still seem to lie outside it.

The algorithmic realm can be thought of as comprising all phenomena that can be satisfactorily governed or analyzed by some system of logic, from the somewhat stilted but still recognizably human language of much modern computer programming to the highest abstractions of mathematics. The progress of science and technology into the algorithmic realm has depended on progress into the quantum realm. It was von Neumann, more than any other man of his era, who joined the two.

The step into the quantum realm, the microcosm, both

fulfills and frustrates the "dream of science" since the Pythagorean cult—to see the world as made of numbers. By delving down deep in the atom we rise up to a level of mathematical abstraction only glimpsed in the previous experimental science of the visible world.

But we do not, as von Neumann supremely understood, rise all the way up. As Kurt Gödel demonstrated in the early twentieth century, and von Neumann, as Gödel's first interpreter and greatest prophet, repeatedly showed, the symbolic logic driving both math and science—the computer and the quantum—is ultimately axiomatic. It cannot prove itself in its own terms but must rely on a set of assumptions outside the system.

Though it frustrated many, von Neumann found this result both liberating and exhilarating. It would all be up to him. Gödel's incompleteness theorem makes logic a more powerful tool for reifying theory into practice, science into technology. The limits of logic—the futility of the German titan David Hilbert's quest for a hermetically sealed universal theory—would liberate humans as creators. Not only could humans discover algorithms, they also could compose them. This loophole in the mathematical logic of the universe would make von Neumann the most practically influential of all the great scientists of the twentieth century.

Created was not only a new science but a new economy that, more than any other previous human achievement, affirmed the core of all capitalist morality and the basis of all sound political economy: wealth springs from the minds of men, and, above all, from the minds of the relatively few men who operate at the nexus of word and world—on the borders of math and manufacture—in the realm of the algorithm. The struggle against Marx and Hitler, as between the West and the jihad today, is best understood as a war between the denizens of the new realm and the rage of its enemies. Hitler's claim in *Mein Kampf* that the Jews used commerce to cheat nature and deprive Aryans of the status due the warrior is a rant against the need to compete in the algorithmic realm. Fittingly, "Jewish science," in Hitler's derisive term, would be the decisive weapon in the struggle, as it remains today.

Despite the enormous and indispensable role of non-Jews in the new realm, Hitler's jibe was on target. The most valorous feats of Jews and the vilest slanders against them arise from this recognition: as the level of abstraction rises in any arena of competition so does relative Jewish achievement. It is easier to observe this anomaly than to explain it. Surely IQ, which mostly gauges the ability to perform abstract thought, is part of the explanation. But just as surely figuring in the causes is the diaspora's long history of exclusion from the "real" economy (as the materialists have always seen it), shunting Jews to the manipulative realms of trade, bookkeeping, shopkeeping, and finance. In any economy operating at its highest realm of abstraction, the allocation of capital can be among the most valuable kinds of work.

Or is it simply that the Jews have known from before the fatherhood of Abraham that it was the word that made the world—the ultimate assertion of algorithmic power?

Norman Macrae's intense and inspirational biography of von Neumann tells the tortured story of the Budapest from which he emerged early in the century. As Macrae describes it: "In the three and a half decades before Johnny's birth in 1903, Budapest had been the fastest-growing big city in Europe—next to New York and Chicago, possibly the fastest in the world. . . . [in just eight years] freight traffic on Hungary's railroads rose from 3 million tons in 1886 to 275 million in 1894 and passenger traffic multiplied nearly seventeenfold." At the time of von Neumann's youth, industry was flourishing, with the number of industrial workers surging from 63,000 in 1896 to 177,000 by 1910. Between 1867 and 1903, the population of Budapest rose from 280,000 to more than 800,000, surpassing such cities as Rome, Madrid, Brussels, and Amsterdam.

Vienna's twin in the Hapsburg Empire, Budapest achieved these feats chiefly through the expedient of openness to Jewish immigration. With virtually no Jews as late as 1867, Hungary accepted hundreds of thousands by the time of von Neumann's birth. At the time von Neumann entered the elite Lutheran High School in Budapest, 52 percent of the students were listed as Jewish. Perhaps two-thirds of the leading citizens of Budapest, outside the government—bankers, lawyers, industrialists, musicians, scientists, artists—were Jewish. Although they made up only 5 percent of the Hungarian population, they became the vanguard of Hungarian economy and culture.

Steve J. Heims's fascinating joint biography of von Neumann and his MIT rival Norbert Wiener expresses the fashionable view that the huge success of Jews in Hungary "often involved repudiation of their own origins and their less fortunate brothers . . . and was often achieved at great psychological cost." This psycho-sanctimony has become familiar on ivied campuses. But there is no evidence whatsoever that the success of the Jews who revitalized Hungary came at the expense of anyone else. In sophisticated form, Heims is expressing the usual cankered incomprehension of capitalism common among intellectuals everywhere, and, in cruder form, flagrant among other citizens as well, including many leftist Jews. It was such blindness to the wide benefits of Jewish achievement—and the resulting lethal resentment of Jewish wealth—that ultimately would drive the Jews away, bringing down the Hungarian economic boom along with the simultaneous, though less spectacular, economic rise in Austria.

Nonetheless, for most of Johnny's youth, Budapest thrived. To eminent business families like the von Neumanns and Kanns, Johnny's forebears, the city must have seemed even more secure and idyllic than Beirut seemed to Christians before the eruption of its fifteen-year civil war, triggered by Arafat's choice of Lebanon as the new operating base and refuge for his PLO.

The idyll came to an end after Hungary engaged on the losing side in World War I and lost two-thirds of its territory. Capitalist progress depends on long time horizons of stability and peace. In early 1918, inspired in part by the Leninist Russian Revolution, Hungarian leftists launched two general strikes, followed by the rise of a feckless Socialist government amid much carnage. In 1919, a brutal Communist regime took over. Its ruthless poet leader, Béla Kun, a secular Jew from Hungary, cherished a letter of advice from Lenin: "Make these promises to the peasants . . . Make these pledges to the proletariat . . . Give these assurances to the bourgeoisie . . . Do not feel in any way bound by these promises, pledges and assurances."

With Jewish Communist henchmen numbering some 161 out of the top 202 officials in his government, Kun killed six thousand "class enemies," focusing on bankers and financiers, many of them Jews, but missed von Neumann's family, which rushed off to a vacation in their summer home and then to Vienna. Kun's Leninist-certified methods, for all their violence, failed to establish his regime. Within months, a new Fascist leader, Admiral Miklós Horthy, took over and perpetrated mass murders of his own, punishing Communist Jews while inviting useful bankers such as Max [von] Neumann back to Budapest to revive the economy. But conditions in Hungary had taken an irretrievable dive.

A new law, then unique to Europe, barred all but 5 percent

of the slots in universities to Jews. The general turmoil, together with the flight of much of the professional and business class of Hungary, plunged the country into chaos, poverty, and crime. As many tyrants before and after, Horthy attempted to capture the means of production and discovered that they were merely so much iron and dirt without the men of production who make them work. As unemployment soared to over 30 percent, the chief victims of the Jewish flight were the poor and peasants of these countries.

Von Neumann, though, learned a redemptive lesson about the world. Never would he imagine that wealth and security were stable and predictable. Never would he drop his guard before the evil and treachery of humankind. As he told his friend and colleague Eugene Wigner many years later: "It is just as foolish to complain that people are selfish and treacherous as it is to complain that the magnetic field does not increase unless the electric field has a curl. Both are laws of nature."

Accompanying his sense of the downsides of history, however, was von Neumann's vision of the hierarchies of knowledge and aspiration. He could climb up from the morass of *mittel* European politics on the abstract ladders of mathematics and philosophy. As epitomized by von Neumann and Einstein, European Jewish scientists of the time possessed a passionate faith in the coherence of the cosmos. Underlying, suffusing, informing, and structuring the universe, so both believed, is rationality and meaning. In its way, it was a religious faith as formidably fecund as the Jewish monotheism of the Torah from which it ultimately stemmed, and it found its liturgy in the logic of mathematics.

Einstein's greatest attainments, general relativity and the equivalence of energy and mass ($E = MC^2$), were expressions above all of his monotheistic faith, more intense than any rabbi's, that the entire universe epitomized a profound inner consistency and logic, embodied most purely in the aesthetic beauty and wholeness of mathematics.

This faith, the algorithmic faith, ultimately would save the West. When Budapest collapsed into anti-Semitic furies, von Neumann escaped harm mostly through his supreme prowess in mathematics. Introduced by an inspiring teacher, Laszlo Ratz, to the great mathematician Michael Fekete, von Neumann by his senior year in high school already had published a significant original paper on the set theory of Georg Cantor. Above the abstraction of particular numbers themselves, set theory addresses a higher level of abstraction in algebraic symbols of numbers, then moves on up to yet a third level of abstraction: groups of numbers with common logical characteristics. Algorithms on algorithms, their study illuminates issues of the foundations of mathematics.

This set theory paper signified that by age fourteen or so, von Neumann was already delving beyond the superficial craft and processes of mathematics toward the ultimate truths beyond. He then went to Germany to study chemical engineering, for protective coloring in a practical science useful to the Reich, while keeping a position in the embattled PhD program in math in Budapest.

In Germany, von Neumann became a protégé of the venerable David Hilbert at the legendary University of Göttingen, a relationship that would shape von Neumann's first great ambition and achievement. Between 1772 and 1788, Joseph Lagrange translated Isaac Newton's mechanics into coherent mathematics. As Heims explained: "It was von Neumann's deep insight in 1926 that if he was to be the Lagrange of quantum mechanics" it would be his task to extend to physics the axiomatic regime Hilbert was imparting to mathematics.

Reaching back to his own previous work in axiomatic set

theory, von Neumann succeeded, providing a unified axiomatic foundation for all forms of quantum mechanics, showing how quantum theory reflected a deeper stratum of mathematical logic.

With Budapest childhood friend Eugene Wigner, he elaborated on his insights, writing four important papers extending quantum theory from the simple lines of the hydrogen spectrum pioneered by Niels Bohr to the thousands of lines of more complex atoms. This feat was regarded by atomic physicist Hans Bethe as von Neumann's supreme moment.

In this pioneering work on quantum theory as throughout his later career, wherever he operated in the domains of logical systems, von Neumann triumphed in part by his embrace of Gödel's incompleteness law. Whether in Cantor sets, quantum mechanics, logical systems, pure games, computer science, or information theory, every system, algorithm, computer, or information scheme would depend on assumptions outside the particular system and irreducible to it. Mathematics ultimately would repose on a foundation of faith. The universe rests on a logical coherence that cannot be proven but to which men must commit if they are to create.

Early in the century, von Neumann recognized where science could achieve completeness and where it could not, how logic could be embodied in machines, and what were its limits. These insights into the powers and borders of axiomatic thinking made von Neumann at once the most visionary and the most practical of scientists and leaders.

Von Neumann's contribution to quantum theory was made at the age of twenty-three. He followed a long passage from that moment of intellectual preeminence in physics through a role as protagonist in several other disciplines. In the end, von Neumann's genius was part of a movement of mind that rescued Western civilization from the chaos and violence of his time.

. . .

Perhaps the decisive event of the twentieth century was the Manhattan Project. If Nazis or Communists had been first to achieve nuclear weapons, the triumph of the West would have been impossible. Von Neumann was a major player in the creation of the bomb. As Kati Marton wrote in *The Great Escape*, her incandescent history of Budapest's "Zion on the Danube" and its dissolution, "Johnny enjoyed special status [in the Manhattan Project]. He came and went as he pleased, equally respected by the scientists and the military. When people at Los Alamos heard von Neumann was coming they would line up all their advanced mathematical problems. 'Then, he would arrive,' physicist Ralph Lapp [his Los Alamos roommate] remembered, 'and systematically topple them over.'"

Von Neumann's most specific contribution to the creation of the atomic bomb was to solve "the plutonium problem." Because the separation of fissile uranium-235 from uranium-238 was a slow process performed by hand, this source could sustain creation of only one bomb, which no one could be sure would work, or how well, and which the Japanese could imagine was the only one available. To build more bombs would entail using the more readily available element plutonium. But no one knew for sure how to trigger a reaction in plutonium. Von Neumann's proposal was an implosive process. Using any available computing equipment to calculate the complex non-linearities, von Neumann ended up specifying the process for unleashing a shock wave optimally shaped to compress a fissile mass. Spurring the project by some twelve months, this breakthrough enabled the team to produce the 60 percent more powerful Nagasaki bomb in time to end the Pacific War.

The Manhattan Project imposed a fateful Israel test. Capable of anti-Semitic sneers, particularly toward the mercurial Leó Szilárd, General Leslie Groves seems an improbable hero in this story. A stiff and conventional military man and a Christian of the sort most disdained by intellectuals, Groves represented the "authoritarian personality" that critics of bourgeois capitalism such as Theodor Adorno believed to explain the rise of the Nazis in Europe.

As Kati Marton explained, however, "General Groves, a deeply suspicious person, trusted Johnny more than he did most of the other scientists and relied on him for advice that went well beyond mathematics and physics to the strategic." Perhaps, as some have speculated, Groves did not regard von Neumann as a Jew. A superb judge of men, however, Groves was alert to genius. In selecting a director for the Manhattan Project, Groves faced a choice between the stolid and conservative Nobel laureate Ernest Lawrence, who was widely favored for the job, and Robert Oppenheimer, with all his Communist associations. In an act that may well have been decisive in the war, Groves chose Oppenheimer. The general explained, "While Lawrence is very bright, he is not a genius . . . J. Robert Oppenheimer is a real genius . . . he knows about everything." By relying on Oppenheimer and von Neumann, Groves passed his Israel test. He enabled Los Alamos to assemble and compress in the desert a critical mass of genius and ingenuity that propelled the Manhattan Project to triumph.

Always von Neumann's vantage point was the algorithmic realm, the center of the sphere, from which opportunities open up in all directions. This was also the vantage point of Einstein, who famously refused to contemplate the empirical data until he had deduced and perfected the logical structure of his findings.

Neither was religious in any traditional way, but both reflected the Jewish insight of monotheism: a universe ruled by a single mind lending it order and significance.

Heims explains von Neumann's strategy: "It became [von Neumann's] mathematical and scientific style to push the use of formal logic and mathematics to the very limit, even into domains others felt to be beyond their reach" regarding the empirical world, "probably even life and mind, as comprehensible in terms of abstract formal structure."

Bottom-up induction, stemming from empirical measurements alone, occurs not at the center but on the surface of the sphere. Induction requires theories—every experiment entails a concept to guide it—but the theories at the heart of scientific progress are often unacknowledged and mostly undeveloped. This inductive approach has ruled much of late twentieth-century science, driving it to an inexorable instinct for the capillaries. The unacknowledged governing idea is that the smaller an entity, particle, or string—and the larger and more costly the apparatus needed to conjure it up—the more important the entity is. By rejecting this approach von Neumann left as his greatest legacy the most ubiquitous, powerful, adaptable scientific "apparatus" humanity has ever known—and it made a new world.

• • •

Today, essentially every practical computer in the world is based on the "von Neumann architecture." As early on as von Neumann's return across the ocean from wartime Britain to the United States in 1943, he had declared himself "obscenely interested" in computing machines. He soon managed to transmit his obsession to the Manhattan Project, to missile research, to game theory, and to the modeling of economic activity. As he told a friend: "I am thinking about something much more important than bombs. I am thinking about computers." What he was thinking would thrust mankind more deeply than ever before into the algorithmic realm, the computer era, the information age.

A crux of the information age is the law of separation: separation of logic from material substrate, content from conduit, algorithm from machine, genetic message from DNA molecule. In biology, Francis Crick dubbed this proposition the Central Dogma: information can flow from the genetic message to its embodiment in proteins—from word to flesh—but not the other direction. In communications, any contrary flow of influence, from the physical carrier to the content of the message, is termed noise. The purpose of transmission is to eliminate or transcend it.

The governing scheme of all communication and computational systems is top-down. Applying to everything from the human body to the cosmos, hierarchical systems proceed from creative content through logical structure or algorithm, and then to the physical substrate or material embodiment, which is independent of the higher layers. The von Neumann architecture would be the expression in computer science of this hierarchy and separation.

Just as von Neumann insisted that the axiomatic content of quantum theory be separate from particular physical models, he resolved that his computing machines be independent of vacuum tubes or relays or magnetic domains or any other material embodiment. He wanted a general-purpose computing machine with a design so scalable and adaptable that it could survive the spiraling advance of the technology.

The crucial step to achieving adaptability was separation. Von Neumann would separate the physical memory from the physical processor and then keep both the data, and, crucially, the software instructions in memory, fully abstracted from the "mechanics" of the processor. This separation distinguishes a general purpose from a special-purpose computer.

A mechanical device physically embodies its algorithm, its "instruction set," in the material form of the machine. But this embodiment makes the one captive to the other: one machine, one algorithm. A vivid example is a classic Swiss watch, a special-purpose computer that achieves its goal only by a fantastically precise mechanical rendering of a single algorithm. If computers were built like Swiss watches—a dead-end toward which computer science actually did proceed for a time—each one would be a multimillion-dollar device good for one and only one function.

By separating memory from processor, and maintaining the processor's instruction set not in the mechanics of the device but in its fully abstract, algorithmic form as software in memory, a von Neumann machine would be able to perform an infinite number of algorithms or programs, ushering in the computer age.

Von Neumann was the first man to see that "in a few years" it would be possible to create computing machines that could operate "a billion times faster" than existing technology. Vindicating his vision, the von Neumann architecture freed the industry from contriving an ever-changing panoply of special-purpose machines and enabled engineers to focus on building speed and capacity in devices, such as memories and microprocessors, whose essential designs have been unchanged for decades.

The von Neumann machine assumed its first physical form at the Institute for Advanced Study (IAS) in Princeton, to which von Neumann moved in 1930 from the increasingly treacherous politics and parlous economics of Europe. All around the globe, scientists used the von Neumann architecture, embodied in the IAS computer, as a model for their own machines. Expounded in a major paper penned in 1945, the von Neumann architecture provided the basis first for some thirty von Neumann machines following the specific "Princestitute" architecture and then supplied the essential logic for all the computers to come.

After World War II, on the advisory committee of the Weizmann Institute in Rehovot, Israel, sat both Albert Einstein and John von Neumann. At a meeting in July 1947, the presence of these contending masses in orbit at the pinnacles of their prestige must have palpably distended the geometry of the room.

The two men clashed on the issue of whether the embryonic state of Israel could use what at that time was considered to be a giant computer. Its architecture would repeat the von Neumann design, created at the Institute for Advanced Study.

Einstein had long been happy to perform gedanken experiments that juggled whole universes in his head, while calling in associates for any necessary computing assistance. He could see no reason for the tiny embattled agricultural country to acquire a computing machine that could consume 20 percent of the Weizmann Institute's annual budget.

"Who would use it?" he asked. "Who would maintain it?" He implied that the machine was a golden calf in the desert, suitable for worship by miscreant militarists and a distraction from the pure tablets of true science.

Recalling this debate is Igal Talmi, an Israeli nuclear physicist still at Weizmann, who pioneered a deeper understanding of the "shell" of the nucleus. Under Einstein's influence, Talmi made two predictions about WEIZAC (Weizmann Automatic Computer). The first was that "it could never be built because of the limitations of Israeli technology. The second was that if it worked it would be used only an hour a week or so." Talmi was "very happy to be wrong on both points."

Right was John von Neumann, who was not as Olympian or

as visionary as Einstein, but was more insightful on such practical matters as building an atomic bomb or a computer. To Einstein, he responded that there would be no problem in constructing the machine, or finding uses for it. His former associate at the Institute of Advanced Study, Gerald Estrin, would build the machine and the software engineer and project manager would be von Neumann protégé Chaim Pekeris. Pekeris specialized in such fields as global weather and oceans and interstellar energy patterns that could not be explored experimentally, even perhaps in Einstein's capacious brain. "Even if no one else goes near the thing, Pekeris will keep it going full time," retorted von Neumann.

A tacit undercurrent of this exchange was a dispute between Einstein and von Neumann over whether Israel should develop nuclear weapons. While von Neumann had served in the Manhattan Project and was sure of its virtue, Einstein was wracked with second thoughts and regrets. He once called his letter to Franklin D. Roosevelt urging the construction of an atomic bomb "the worst mistake of my life." After the war, he downplayed the Soviet threat and at times believed that the greatest danger to the world was posed by Fascist Argentina and Spain. When McCarthyism erupted in the United States, Einstein at first imagined that it portended a new American Fascism echoing Nazi Germany.

As the inventor of game theory, widely used to model arms races, von Neumann understood that a U.S. or Israeli decision to forgo nuclear weapons would hugely increase the incentive for all other countries to build them. The smaller the nuclear capability maintained by the United States, the more tempting for enemies to seek nuclear dominance. In a region full of proven enemies, an Israel without nuclear weapons would not be viable.

In this confrontation of titans, as in other disputes, von Neumann was far more adept at politics and persuasion. He prevailed, and one of the first von Neumann machines in the world was built at Weizmann. The machine soon justified his confidence. The Pekeris team conducted complex non-linear computations that identified and simulated for the first time the amphidromic spot in the Atlantic where the tides so precisely balanced that there was no movement. The team won the Turing Award for this formidable global feat of research computation. At the same time, the Weizmann Institute team fatefully began a program of calculations in nuclear fission that would prove crucial to Israel's survival.

Toward the end of his life, von Neumann was an intellectual leader in the development of the U.S. response to Soviet nuclear weapons and intercontinental missiles. It was von Neumann who shaped the strategy of deterrence, who defined the missile systems that enabled the deterrent, who, with Edward Teller, championed the movement to build a thermonuclear hydrogen bomb, who made possible U.S. air defense systems based on computers, and who provided the computational resources for the development of small warheads suitable for delivery on the missiles available to the United States. In general, he fostered and framed American weapons and deterrent strategy throughout the tempestuous postwar period.

As a commissioner of the Atomic Energy Commission, as head of countless commissions on ballistic missiles and nuclear weapons for the United States Air Force, U.S. Navy, and the Pentagon, as a research leader at Los Alamos, Aberdeen, and Sandia, as a valued voice at the CIA, as a consultant with the RAND Corporation, TRW, IBM, and other critical defense contractors, von Neumann was an imperious force bringing order and vision to the chaos of programs and military factions in the 1950s, even as the United States seemed to fall behind the Soviet Union in critical capabilities. Virtually the entire panoply of defense of the United States bore the imprint of von Neumann's brilliance.

Admiral Lewis Strauss, chairman of the United States Atomic Energy Commission and long an admirer of von Neumann, told the story of Johnny dying of cancer at age fifty-three in Walter Reed Hospital in Washington, DC—dying, in all likelihood, of his exposure to radiation while observing nuclear tests. "Gathered round his bedside, and attentive to his last words of advice and wisdom, were the Secretary of Defense and his deputies, the Secretaries of the Army, Navy, and Air Force, and all the military Chiefs of Staff. . . . I have never witnessed a more dramatic scene or a more moving tribute to a great intelligence." They all realized, within the aura of his presence, that they were near to the center of the sphere.

After World War II, the most transformative development in science and technology was the emergence of information technology. As Edward Teller sagely observed, it was information technology—the rise of computer capabilities and their miniaturization on microchips, nearly all following the von Neumann architecture—that saved U.S. technical leadership during the cold war when the United States seemed to slip behind even the Soviet Union.

In government-run bureaucracies, swathed in secrecy, riddled with espionage, and paralyzed by pettifoggery and credentialism, U.S. science and technology could not even outperform the equally secret and bureaucratic programs of the Soviet Union. The Soviets developed more powerful bombs and missiles after World War II than did the United States. They launched Sputnik. They built nuclear weapons and exploded a hydrogen bomb.

What saved the United States were not the secret programs of the Pentagon or Los Alamos and other laboratories but the open enterprises of the computer industry. Created by scores of Silicon Valley companies, full of immigrants from Europe, microchips enabled the United States to miniaturize all the control functions in the payloads of their smaller missiles and to create the MIRV (multiple independently targeted reentry vehicles) system that secured the U.S. lead.

Anticipated in part by Einstein, fiber optics and lasers from Corning and Bell Labs gave computers the bandwidth to interconnect around the globe. The rise of information technology in the United States also revitalized the U.S. economy, yielding the resources necessary to win the cold war while endowing an ever-growing population with an expanding array of goods and services based on electronics.

In touting the twentieth century as an era of Jewish science, I am resorting to a heuristic device. With some daunting difficulty and awesome ellipses, one could even write a history that left out Einstein, Bohr, Pauli, von Neumann, Feynman, and all the other great Jewish figures. Rutherford, Planck, Schrödinger, Heisenberg, de Broglie, von Laue, Fermi, Dirac, Tomonaga, and especially Gödel, Turing, and Shannon, all gentiles, played essential roles in the evolution of twentieth-century science and technology. In recent decades, from Silicon Valley to China, Carver Mead of Caltech became a polymathic figure arguably as influential in the science and technology of his own time as von Neumann in his.

Science is a collaborative effort. The Jewish contribution, while crucial and vastly out of proportion to the number of Jews in the population, was not self-sufficient or even always paramount. Nonetheless, Jews were especially central to advances in mathematics and algorithms. Once in 1934, David Hilbert, who had brought von Neumann to the great German University of Göttingen, found himself seated at a dinner next to Hitler aide

Bernhard Rust. The Nazi education minister turned to Hilbert and asked pleasantly: "How is mathematics in Göttingen, now that it has been freed of the Jewish influence?" Hilbert replied: "Mathematics in Göttingen? There is really none any more."

Von Neumann did not make as significant contributions to quantum theory as Schrödinger, or greater contributions to the atomic bomb than Fermi; neither did he have more important insights into computer science than Turing, nor on information theory than Shannon. Nonetheless, an objective observer must acknowledge that without the constant contributions of Einstein, von Neumann, and their many associates—without what the Nazis insisted was "Jewish science"—there might be a mathematician or two in Göttingen, but "there would not," as Churchill said, "be a free man in Europe."

Twentieth-century science was not a racial competition. But twentieth-century history was engulfed in a racial war against Jewish scientists and capitalists, and their flight to the West was indispensable to the Western triumph. Von Neumann remains the only figure to bridge all the most critical physical sciences, technologies, and policy decisions of the era. Von Neumann was the unelected avatar and epitome of the Jewish triumph and the Israel test.

Now, in an era long after von Neumann, we face a new Israel test, based on yet another war against wealth and individual genius. Israel is at the forefront of the next generation of technology and on the front lines of a new racial war against capitalism and Jewish individuality and genius. Israel is not a peripheral player or a superficial issue of Middle Eastern history and politics. It is at the center of the sphere.

PART TWO

Israel Inside

CHAPTER SEVEN

From Last to First

M y interest in Israeli innovations all began in the late 1990s with the exotic yet familiar technology of free-space optics—what most of us call *light*. As a writer on technology and an investor in technology companies, I was long intrigued with the idea of taking the devices perfected for sending light thousands of miles over fiber-optics lines in the global Internet and using them to send light hundreds of meters through the air across crowded city streets. Already fully developed and tested for application in glass fibers, lasers sending pulses of photons through the air could eliminate the need for fiber lines in the last hundred yards to urban buildings, by orders of magnitude the most expensive hundred yards in any fiber network.

Making final connections to customers' computers often now means a prolonged process of sorting out mazes of property rights and political interests under urban streets, digging trenches and laying cables and making campaign "contributions" that in some bureaucratic cities end up costing more than laying fiber across the entire country. By transmitting billions of bits through the open air on benign low-power streams of light, engineers could luminously leap over this obstacle to the consummation of a broadband Internet, for cumulative savings of many billions of dollars across a national network.

The first company I pursued in this field was Terabeam in Seattle, which I proclaimed as launching the "Terabeam Era." But as I continued to investigate this venture, I received a life-changing jolt from Israel.

It turned out that an Israeli company called Jerusalem Optical Link Technologies (JOLT) had already demonstrated an effective free-space optics system. Its founder was a physicist named David Medved, who had made *aliya* ("immigration to Israel") late in life and would live in Jerusalem until his death early in March 2009. I learned that David was not only a physicist-engineer but also an octogenarian philosopher who seemingly never flagged in his output of new ideas and intriguing reflections. His latest surprise in 2008 was a treatise on science and religion, *Hidden Light: Science Secrets of the Bible*, which demonstrates an inextricable weave of concepts pervading the two domains in physics, chemistry, and theology. According to Medved, the Bible is not a science book, but it offers hidden light that illuminates the great issues of birth and death for both human beings and the cosmos.

I had predicted for nearly two decades that the Internet would move to "worldwide webs of glass and light," with the entire world economy pervaded by the hidden light of fiber-optics communications. In 1998 I invited Medved to speak at an event I ran, the Gilder–Forbes Telecosm Conference, held that year near Lake Tahoe in California. He described the promise of free-space optics for many high-end applications linking corporate buildings and campuses and even spoke of air force experiments in Israel that used the still higher frequencies and shorter waves of ultraviolet light for battlefield communications. His speech intrigued me with its message that some of the most important explorations of electromagnetic technology were happening in Israel.

In the telecom crash of 2000, Terabeam ended up going out of business and JOLT was forced to retrench its goals. But by the time I visited Jerusalem a few years later in 2007, JOLT was still alive and had been purchased for $80 million in stock by MRV Communications, Inc. of the United States. Medved became the head of MRV Jerusalem.

In the first decade of the twenty-first century, the ultimate fate of these particular free-space optical systems remains in doubt. But beyond doubt is the increasing role of Israel as a prime source of innovations vital to the United States and to the world.

In 2007 in Jerusalem, David Medved introduced me to his son Jonathan, a pioneering Israeli venture capitalist. In his offices high over Jerusalem, the burly and engaging, devout and visionary younger Medved told me the startling tale of Israel's ten-year rise to worldwide preeminence in high technology.

I had long known of Israel as a site of laboratories and design centers for American microchip companies. I knew that in a real sense much of American technology could reasonably bear the emblem *Israel Inside*. I was familiar with a few prominent Israeli start-ups, such as *Wired* magazine cover boy Shai Agassi's famed démarche in modular electric cars that boldly bypassed the entire world auto industry in redesigning the automobile from scratch. I was amazed by Gavriel Iddan's company Given Imaging, with its digestible camera in a capsule for doing endoscopies and colonoscopies. Rather than swallowing gallons of emetic fluids to clean out his system, the patient merely consumes a single capsule, the size of a pill, containing a camera and a wireless transmitter. This device takes as many as two thousand high-resolution pictures a minute and sends them wirelessly for the physician's scrutiny. From Jonathan I heard that his own venture-finance group had ruefully passed on Given but had backed an array of other intriguing Israeli technologies, including his own current video "ringtone" venture Vringo that aims to bring full-imaging capabilities to the cell phone.

In Jerusalem, however, Jonathan Medved was making a case not merely for Israel as a site for research and outsourcing and the occasional conceptual coup, but for Israel as the world leader outside the United States in launching new companies and technologies. I was surprised at the idea of this tiny embattled country, smaller than most American states, outperforming European and Asian Goliaths ten to a hundred times larger, deploying hundreds of billions of dollars in multi-state research-and-development subsidies, venture funds, and technology programs, and led by national-champion titans such as Roche and Huawei Technologies, STMicroelectronics and NEC Corporation.

Medved presented voluminous evidence in slide after slide of data showing Israeli outperformance of Europe and Asia. During my visit to his office, for example, he pointed to a watershed moment for the country: Israel had recently passed Canada as the home of the most foreign companies on the technology-heavy NASDAQ index and was launching far more high-tech companies per year than any country in Europe.

Medved told me that Israel was a prime source not only of fiber optics and free-space optics but also of another form of hidden light: what is called ultra-wideband (UWB) technology. These are wireless transmissions, not millions of hertz-wide at relatively high power like cell-phone signals, but billions of hertz—gigahertz—at power so low as to be undetectable by ordinary wireless antennas.

In a usual application, a company called Wisair, headquartered high in an office building in Tel Aviv, uses UWB for wireless interconnection of high-definition images and audio on computers and set-top boxes in homes. But more surprising, Israeli venturer Pini Lozowick, a founder of U.S. chip giant Broadcom, told me of another pioneer of ultra wideband called Camero.

This company in Netanya, Israel, has invented an ingenious ultra-wideband device that enables anti-terrorist fighters and police to see through walls and identify armed men and other threats within. An easily portable box about the size and weight of a laptop computer, Camero's Xaver 400 could suffuse an urban battlefield with hidden light that would penetrate walls and bunkers and be detectable only by its users. Such inventions are changing the balance of power in urban guerrilla and anti-terrorist warfare—a development from Israel that could be important to U.S. security.

As I investigated such Israeli companies, it became clear to me that this country had achieved an economic miracle that was important to the United States and to the world. Before July of 1985, Israel was a basket case with wage and price controls making everything scarce. Inflation rates were spiking from 400 percent to nearly 1000 percent by early 1985. As recently as 1990, Israel was a relatively insignificant technology force outside of a few military and agricultural initiatives, such as world leadership in targeted irrigation and desalinization facilities. Somehow, in little over a decade, it had become an engine of global-technology advance. How did it happen? Surely this lesson would be relevant to countries around the world.

Still more important, the technology leadership of Israel made the country a vital ally of the United States in its confrontation with a global movement of jihadist terror. Israel is not a charity; it is a central node in the fabric of Western power as it faces the onset of what Norman Podhoretz has long prophetically described as World War IV, following the cold war with a global engagement against the enemies of capitalism and civilization.

• • •

With the history of twentieth-century science and technology largely a saga of Jewish accomplishment, in retrospect it might seem foreordained that after World War II the rising Jewish nation in the Middle East would emerge not only as a financial power but also as a scientific and technological leader.

Yet surprisingly, for all the talk of deserts in bloom, the predictable miracle did not occur. Forty some years on, Israel by 1990 was still mostly barren of technology and finance. Apart from military breakthroughs, the scores of thousands of brilliant Jews assembled in Israel generated few significant companies or technologies, no significant financial institutions, and little important science. U.S. states such as California or New York, Massachusetts or even New Jersey far excelled all the accomplishments of Israeli enterprise. Jews outside Israel far outperformed Jews in Israel. Writing in 1990, Michael Porter in his famously definitive tome *The Competitive Advantage of Nations* mentioned Israel only once: "In Israel . . . principal clusters [of innovation] are related to agriculture (crops, fertilizers, irrigation equipment, other specialized equipment and machinery) and defense."

One measure of the creativity of an economy is its research-and-development activities. In general, public research is far less productive than private research. In its early years, Israel's research effort was mostly public, devoted to defense, and was paltry by any standard. As late as 1965, the ratio of research-and-development spending in Israel to its output of gross domestic product was under 1 percent, near the lowest in the entire

Organization for Economic Cooperation and Development (OECD), behind only Italy. In the proportion of engineers among all its employees, at one-tenth of 1 percent, Israel ranked far behind the United States and even Sweden (each with between two and three times as many engineers per capita). In the early years, wars and heavy defense burdens as well as an agrarian Socialist ideology provided an excuse for relatively poor economic and entrepreneurial performance.

The dominance of Jews in intellectual life and enterprise is not a necessary or inevitable phenomenon. Before the twentieth-century's efflorescence of technological capitalism, the global influence of Jews was chiefly restricted to the Christian religion, which in some perverse strains was hostile to Jews, as Jews were hostile to it. When Dr. Chaim Weizmann addressed a Zionist conference in Britain in 1909 on behalf of the establishment of the university now called the Technion-Israel Institute of Technology, in Haifa, he lamented the scarcity of distinguished Jewish professors who might teach at the new institution. Ignorant of Albert Einstein's *Annus Mirabilis* in 1905, Weizmann declared his opinion that "only two Jews had made major contributions to human thought, Baruch Spinoza and Karl Marx," both in speculative fields. "In the world of practical science," wrote the eminent journalist and academic Carl Alpert, "there had not yet been one outstanding Jew."

Located on the top of a hill overlooking Haifa, the Technion went on to become one of the world's supreme institutions of practical science and the chief contribution of the founders of Israel to its later preeminence in technology. It currently sprawls over its spectacular site with a massive maze of concrete institutional architecture—labs, auditoria, nuclear facilities, giant telescopes, and research monoliths, mostly named for American Jewish tycoons—as formidable as MIT. But, despite the Technion, nearly an entire century would pass, with Jews around the world forging the science of the age in an intellectual efflorescence unparalleled in human history, without any exceptional contributions from Israel. This failure came despite heroic efforts in the 1950s by Nathan Rosen, Einstein's collaborator on his most quoted paper, EPR (Einstein, Podolsky, Rosen), who chaired the physics department and became dean of the university. Under Rosen, the Technion was more a *pied à plage* for foreign scientists than a powerhouse of new technology.

The great irony of Israel is that for much of its short history it has failed the Israel test. It has been a reactionary force, upholding the same philosophy of victimization and Socialist redistribution that has been a leading enemy and obstacle for Jewish accomplishment throughout the ages. As a Jewish country, Israel should have arisen rapidly after the war as a center of Jewish achievement. Instead, its leftist assumptions actually inclined it toward the Soviet model.

A team of American economic consultants in 1957 described a "lack of managerial and supervisory skill . . . lack of experience in many fields . . . and a lack of appreciation of the deficiencies. High labor costs . . . reflected the high degree of job security . . . [and] the absence of adequate incentive to or rewards for superior efficiency or performance. In part, high-wage rates represented an effort on the part of labor to capture an amount of product that the economy simply was not producing.

"The absence of competition was a result in part of the virtually complete protection from foreign competition afforded by import and exchange controls . . . In part, it was the result of a widespread practice . . . operating 'cartel' agreements and other similar arrangement to prevent price and other competition and to restrict production. . . ."

The economists concluded: "In fact, these arrangements . . .

reflected the reluctance of the society to penalize inefficiency or to put a premium on aggressive effort."

Professor A. J. Meyer of the Harvard Center for Middle Eastern Studies in 1959 noted "uncertainty in the minds of many industrial producers [in Israel] that theirs is the 'good' occupation or that society really gives them credit—financially and in status—for their efforts." He cited "welfare state concepts [that] often dictate that incompetent workers stay on payrolls." These Jews, as the American sage Midge Decter described them, "were coming into the country armed with their socialism and their ideologies of labor and a Jewish return to the soil."

Imagine it, urban Socialists trying to reclaim their past glory and save themselves in a hostile world by returning to the soil in a desert. Once it was the Nazis who sought to confine them to the earth; now it was their own Marxist intellectuals. Fleeing oppression in Europe, they buried their heads deeply into the sands of delusional ideologies. They created fatuous communal experiments called kibbutzim and put intellectuals to work with hoes and shovels for all the world like a voluntary version of Chairman Mao's Cultural Revolution. In a truly menacing démarche of ideological madness, they attempted to abolish the family and private property.

Panicked by the Jewish caricatures and stereotypes wielded by their enemies, they resolved to become mendicant nebbishes even in banking and finance. They toured the centers of Western money and industry with tin cans in hand. They assigned close to a third of the economy to the ownership of Histadrut, a Socialist workers' organization prone to threatening nationwide strikes, always "helpful" in a nascent and embattled country. Under Histadrut pressure, they created minimum-wage levels that stifled employment for decades and propelled inflation, as much a phenomenon of depressed productivity as excessive credit, as high as

400 percent for a period of months in the first half of 1984. Then they imposed more controls on wages and prices and rents, making everything scarce.

In a general enthusiasm for public ownership of the means of production and finance, the government through the 1990s owned four major banks, two hundred corporations, and much of the land. Stifling any private initiatives that might miss these sieves of socialism, Israel's taxes rose to a confiscatory 56 percent of total earnings, close to the highest in the world. Erecting barriers of bureaucracy, sentiment, and culture, Israeli leaders balked the entrepreneurs and inventors who gathered there, creating a country as inhospitable to Jewish genius as any anti-Semite could contrive.

Israel's redemption from its misbegotten beginnings came from unexpected directions. In the mid-1980s, Yitzhak Shamir's Likud government, with Bibi Netanyahu as its Reaganite UN ambassador in New York, deployed tax-rate reductions that, if short of Reaganesque, increased the rewards of work and investment by some 30 percent and dramatically boosted economic growth and reduced inflation. At least as important to Israel's technology sector, however, was the fact that beginning in the late 1980s, the country committed itself to absorb close to a million immigrants, chiefly from the former Union of Soviet Socialist Republics (USSR). Impelled by constant harassment from the U.S. government responding to Senator Henry "Scoop" Jackson's emancipation amendment attached to any U.S. legislation of interest to the USSR, the Soviet government finally agreed to a frontal lobotomy of its economy. Under Gorbachev, the USSR released the bulk of the Soviet Jews who, despite constant oppression, continued to supply most of the technical skills that kept the Soviet Union afloat.

This influx of Russian Jews into Israel represented a 25 percent population increase over a period of five years, a tsunami of new arrivals tantamount proportionately to the United States accepting the entire population of France. Largely barred in the USSR from owning land or business, many of them had honed their minds into keen instruments of algorithmic science, engineering, and mathematics. Most had desired to come to the United States but were diverted to Israel by an agreement between Israel and the U.S. government. Few knew Hebrew, or saw a need for it. At best, they were ambivalent Zionists. But many of them were ferociously smart, fervently anti-Communist, and cynically disdainful of their new countrymen-to-be.

At the same time as the flood of former-Soviet immigrants, a smaller but seminal wave of returnees arrived in Israel from such companies as IBM and Bell Laboratories, with a knowledge of Silicon Valley and an interest in opportunities in Israel. Capping off and capitalizing these catalytic outsiders were a generation of eminent American retirees, either making *aliya* in the late 1980s and early 1990s, or focusing on Israel after successful careers in U.S. business: Morry Blumenfeld from General Electric; Ed Mlavsky from Tyco; Alan "Ace" Greenberg who helped raise Israel's first venture-capital fund; physicist David Medved from Amoco; Yadin Kaufmann and Erel Margalit from U.S. venture-capital firms; biotech pioneer Martin Gerstel from ALZA Corporation; and even an eminent economist, Stanley Fischer from MIT, who became governor of the Bank of Israel. Collectively these newcomers wielded billions of dollars of available capital, petawatts of imperious brainpower, a practiced disdain for bureaucratic pettifogs, and Olympian confidence in their own judgment and capabilities.

Mix the leadership of these dynamic capitalist retirees, finding new birth in Israel, with a million restive and insurgent Russians in a tiny Mediterranean land, and the reaction was economically incandescent. Throw in natural leadership from the irrepressible Natan Sharansky, who had faced down confinement in the Gulag and formed a new political party in Israel to mobilize his Russian compatriots, and the impact reverberated through the social and political order as well.

Such an influx could not be clamped or channeled, tapered or intimidated into the existing economic framework. These throngs were not all going to join the army, and as investor Tal Keinan remarks, "They could not all work for Intel," which had made large investments in the country. To deal with this overwhelming transformation of the human capital of Israel entailed radical entrepreneurial creativity and initiative. It required a vast ventilation and revamp of the Israeli economy.

This recognition did not come naturally to the Israeli leaders or to the existing population. Labor Party chief Shimon Peres declared: "I'm for the market, but the market does not absorb immigrants. The market is indifferent. Absorption has to be done by people. When you fight a war, the market doesn't fight. People do." Israeli politicians at first resisted the refractory insistence of the Russians on creating their own schools and media and only slowly learning the national language. The incumbent Israelis, unconsciously echoing anti-Semites everywhere, were known to grumble that the Russians thought they were better and smarter than Israelis and looked down on their hosts.

The absorption of immigrants, however, is not analogous to a war, which may initially entail mobilization of existing resources and industrial capacity. Immigrants provide a challenge and an opportunity to create new resources and capabilities. Many of the Russian newcomers commanded elite technical skills and scientific degrees. Such capabilities are best applied to innovation. Planned creativity and innovation are an oxymoron: creativity always comes as a surprise. If governments could plan innovations, the plans would constitute the innovation.

Until the early 1990s, Jews could succeed far more readily in the United States than in Israel. The Israel test gauges the freedom and equality of opportunity in a country by the success of Jews there. By this Israel test, the United States was far freer and more favorable to creativity and excellence, and thus to Jewish achievement, than the state of Israel itself.

Nonetheless, under the pressure of immigration and the emerging guidance of market-savvy politicians led by Benjamin Netanyahu, Israel accomplished what was the most overwhelming transformation in the history of economics. In a decade, it went from being a nondescript laggard in the industrial world to become a luminous first. Today, on a per-capita basis, Israel far leads the world in research and technological creativity. Between the years 1991 and 2000, Israel's annual venture-capital outlays, almost all private, rose nearly sixtyfold, from $58 million to $3.3 billion. From 100 venture-capitalized start-ups in 1991, Israel's venture funds launched some 800 companies in 2000. Israel's revenues in information technology rose from $1.6 billion in 1991 to $12.5 billion in 2000. By 1999, Israel ranked second only to the United States in invested private equity capital as a share of GDP. With 70 percent of its growth attributable to high-tech ventures, by this measure, Israel went in twenty years from last among all industrial countries to lead the world.

To a world transfixed by trillion-dollar bailouts of banker bureaucrats and crony capitalists, these numbers look small. But so it has always been. The same freedom and discipline that endow the seminal entrepreneurs of the era with mere hundreds of thousands or millions of dollars to start the companies that move the economy allow their stockholders and their children to accumulate hundreds of millions and billions.

The same forces and freedoms dictate as well that the resulting fortunes will disappear within a few generations. It is a rigid rule of capitalism that overfunded businesses, like overfunded banks, are disasters waiting to happen, while small sums in the hands of a few exceptional men can yield equally unexpected riches.

While the rest of the world slumped after the millennial telecom and dot-com crash, and Israel suffered an acute recession, its venture capitalists strengthened Israel's lead in technological enterprise. During the first five years of the twenty-first century, venture-capital outlays in Israel rivaled venture-capital outlays in all of the United States outside California, long the world's paramount source and sump of entrepreneurial activity in high technology.

In 2006, Israel's nearly eighty active venture funds raised $1.62 billion compared to $1.2 in 2005. The United States was the only country that raised more venture capital in 2006 than Israel, but in contrast, Israeli investments were at an earlier stage in their start-up development, making eventual returns higher. Although much of Israel's capital comes from the hugely greater American venture industry, Israeli companies are rapidly increasing their share.

A 2008 survey of the world's venture capitalists by Deloitte & Touche, the accounting consultancy, showed that in six key fields—telecom, microchips, software, biopharmaceuticals, medical devices, and clean energy—Israel ranked second only to the United States in technological innovation. Germany, ten times larger, roughly tied Israel. In 2008, Israel produced 483 venture-backed companies with just over $2 billion invested; Germany produces approximately a hundred venture-backed companies annually. With heavy government subsidies, Germany ranked decisively ahead of Israel in clean energy. In biopharma and medical devices Germany had a small edge in established companies, but Israel commanded some fifteen hundred biotech ventures, was well ahead in telecom, and clearly ahead also in microchips and software. These valuations registered absolute performance. Adjusted for its population, Israel ranked massively ahead of all other countries including the United States. Overall, Germany initiates a total of some hundred new venture-backed firms a year, while Israel launched 483 in 2008 alone.

As it approached the end of the first decade of the new century, Israel was a global center of microchip, telecom, optics, software, biotech, and medical-devices research, the country's development and entrepreneurship rivaled only by its partners in Silicon Valley. As one prominent U.S. engineer put it, "When I became VP of business development for ROW (rest of the world), it was obvious that Israel is now the capital of the rest of the world."

Venture capital is the most catalytic force in the world economy. In the United States, venture-backed companies produced nearly one-fifth of GDP in 2007. At a time when U.S. venture capital is flagging under the financial crisis, the emergence of a comparable venture scene in Israel, linked closely to Silicon Valley, is providential both for the American economy and its military defense. This development makes Israel one of America's most important economic allies. Israel's creativity now pervades many of the most powerful or popular new technologies, from personal computers to iPods, from the Internet to the medical center, from anti-missile defenses to the ascendant realms of "cloud" computing.

CHAPTER EIGHT

Inside the Computer Revolution

E arly in 2009, Intel Corporation launched a massive new advertising campaign to celebrate what it described as its most important advance since its initial invention of the microprocessor chip some forty years ago. It was its new "Core i7" device, code-named "Nehalem" ("stream" in Hebrew), which combined leading-edge computing power with unprecedented economy of energy use. Like many of the inventions that have made Intel the world's leading microchip company, the new chip was designed in Israel.

Today, in the spirit of the Intel advertising campaign in which it stamps *Intel Inside* on personal computers made by other companies but run by its microprocessor chips, Israel can claim to be "inside" many of the leading products of American technology. Most of Intel's key products could be stamped *Israel Inside*. So could leading routers from Cisco and Juniper Networks, leading disk-drive technologies from Seagate, leading FiOS broadband optics technologies from Verizon, leading

Global Positioning System (GPS) navigators inside many automobiles, leading imagers in digital cameras, and leading solid-state storage devices in iPods, cameras, and smartphones throughout the industry.

So what? Consumer electronics? Toys? Does civilization, or the security of America, depend on iPods?

Not directly. But above all, Israelis are leaders in the most important technology arena today, the ability of computers to accept and process information as quickly as modern transmission techniques—preeminently fiber-optics lines—can deliver it to the computer. Only by accepting and processing sensory data as fast or faster than the human brain processes the fantastically capacious and complex data set of a seaside sunset, replete with the sounds of sea and seabirds, the trade breezes and tropical aromas, or registers a glimpse of a known terrorist's face buried beneath $100,000 worth of plastic surgery will computers make the leap from being glorified adding machines to becoming indispensable allies against the forces of chaos and terror. Israel has become the epicenter of this effort.

Until the venture upsurge of the early 1990s, however, Israel was such a hostile environment for technology that most Israelis had to begin their technology companies in the United States, mainly in Silicon Valley, after stints in the Israeli military. The pivotal chip company of Silicon Valley and the global leader of the industry was Intel. In the 1970s, commanding a wide array of Jewish talent under the leadership of gentile-industry titans Robert Noyce and Gordon Moore, Intel launched all the key components that enabled creation of personal computers (PCs).

These components were dynamic random-access memory (DRAM) for the temporary working memory of the computer; the microprocessor computer-on-a-chip that performed the step-by-step processing; and the electrically erasable read-only memory (EPROM) that stored the on-chip software. These devices and their descendants still dominate the global microchip industry.

The pioneer was Dov Frohman, an Israeli studying at Berkeley, who began at Intel under the guidance of Andrew Grove. A Hungarian Jew who escaped after the 1956 Hungarian Revolution, Grove expounded his philosophy of business and life in his first non-technical book, *Only the Paranoid Survive*. His defining early achievement at Intel was taking the first Intel memory chip, DRAM, which at the time was its only significant product, through production in the face of a grave manufacturing crisis that reduced yields on the chip to close to zero. Over a career of more than forty years, Grove went on to become CEO of Intel in 1985 and a legendary figure in Silicon Valley. In 1997 he was named *Time*'s Man of the Year. But perhaps nothing he did was more important than hiring the Israeli Dov Frohman.

Frohman himself had to learn paranoia and survival with the best of them during World War II, when both his parents were dispatched to Auschwitz in 1943 and he was spirited away just-in-time at the age of four to a Christian family in Holland. Named Van Tilborgh, the family took him in and risked their own lives and the lives of their children by hiding and disguising Dov throughout the war. Frohman remains close to the Van Tilborghs and uses them as an example of heroic risk taking in his book, *Leadership: The Hard Way*. "Thanks to the help of people like the Van Tilborghs," he writes, "some sixteen thousand Jews who went into hiding [in Holland] survived the war."

"I also learned something else from the Van Tilborghs's behavior," he wrote. "If a leader is too focused on personal survival as head of the organization, he or she may end up, paradoxically, undermining the organization's long-term capacity to survive." It seemed to Frohman that the Van Tilborghs's decisiveness and confidence was more effective in saving the family, and him, than more timorous and evasive strategies would have been.

After helping Grove surmount the DRAM crisis, Frohman provided one of the two inventions that made Intel the world's leading microchip company. The first Intel invention, announced in 1971, was the microprocessor, which was largely designed and created by Federico Faggin, an Italian Jew who had also introduced the crucial technology of self-aligned silicon "gates" to the industry. Gates are the tiny switching "on-off" nodes that perform logical functions all across a chip. Replacing aluminum gates and gates deposited with exquisite accuracy on top of the chip, silicon gates were made of essentially the same substance as the rest of the chip. Simplifying radically the chemistry and mechanics of chip manufacture, this innovation provided the key logical switch underlying the industry's standard method for creating cheap digital products in huge volumes.

Also invented in 1971 was Frohman's contribution: the floating-gate electrically programmable read-only memory (EPROM). Unlike the DRAM and one hundred times slower than it, the EPROM offered the crucial capability of being nonvolatile: it could keep its contents when the power was turned off. Today, the early EPROM as conceived by Frohman seems like a kludge, a cockeyed Rube Goldberg way to achieve a goal. It actually had a plastic window on top of the chip. It stored bits of content by "tunneling" streams of electrons at high voltage onto insulated tiny repositories for electrical charge, called "floating gates." It erased the bits by a blast of ultraviolet light through the plastic window. It required two different power supplies, plus the light source. But, kludge or not, as holder of the vital software for booting up the computer, the EPROM contributed some 80 percent of Intel's profits over the next decade and sustained the company's growth to become the world's leading semiconductor company.

With the help of a company named Xicor, started by Israeli Raffi Klein, Frohman's EPROM soon dispensed with the ultraviolet erase technology and evolved into the Flash memories that today dominate the industry. Today, Flash memories in all their forms are a forte of the Israeli microchip industry and lie behind many of the miracles of miniaturization coming from American companies, from Apple's iPod nano to Hewlett-Packard's Mini netbooks.

After leaving Intel in 1974 for a charitable sojourn teaching electrical engineering in Ghana, Frohman returned to Israel to establish an Intel design center in Haifa. Again Grove saw the advantages of access to the human capital of Israel. This laboratory soon vindicated his judgment and Frohman's competence by conceiving the so-called 8088 microprocessor, which was incorporated into the first IBM personal computer. In 1979, also in Haifa, Frohman supervised the development of Intel's first mathematical floating-point coprocessor, the 8087, a critical element in most subsequent personal computers and workstations.

During the early 1980s, Frohman reached out to other Israelis by teaching a seminal course at Hebrew University in semiconductor electronics, with an accent on non-volatile memories. Among his students were Giora Yaron, founder of National Semiconductor Israel, and Yoav Nissan-Cohen, CEO of Tower Semiconductor, the only independent chip-manufacturing "foundry" in Israel. Another leading student and follower of Frohman was Boaz Eitan, a dauntless inventor and entrepreneurial force who has influenced the entire world of non-volatile memories. Born in Israel in 1948, he entered the military at age eighteen as a fighter pilot. Shot down over Syria in 1970, he spent three years in a Syrian jail. As a prisoner, Eitan began his study of physics with two other captured Israeli pilots, using books donated by the Red Cross. "Part of the difficulty in such a jail term as being a POW is that there's no definite end to it. You need something besides hope to wake up for," Eitan says. "In jail I found out that I could do well in physics and math. Before that my only dream was to be a pilot. I wasn't that hot a student in high school."

In 1973, Eitan and the two other pilots were exchanged for five Syrian prisoners captured by the Israelis. After working his way through school as a plumber, his father's trade, Eitan entered Hebrew University, gaining physics and math degrees. He achieved his master's and PhD under Frohman. Between 1981 and 1992, Eitan spent much of his time in the United States, working first at Intel and then defecting to WaferScale Integration (WSI), an ambitious effort to put entire computers not on chips on printed circuit boards but rather on relatively large silicon wafers, as many as four inches wide.

At WSI in Silicon Valley, Eitan worked closely with fellow Israeli Dov Moran, whom he intrigued with the role of nonvolatile memories. Moran became CEO of M-Systems, the acclaimed inventor of a disk-on-chip (or so-called "thumb drives") for mobile devices, the little dongle that you plug into the side of your computer or cell phone to gain access to huge amounts of information from a device the size of a key.

These dongles feed on an invention by Eitan: Flash memories that could put several bits in the gate of each memory cell. Eitan took the delicate and difficult floating gate of insulated charge, invented by Frohman, and replaced it with a new method of trapping charges on an entire layer of insulation blanketing the chip, a breakthrough crucial to the emergence of Flash memory in solid-state disk drives that can be put in an iPod, a nano, a netbook, or a key. To develop this concept, in 1997 he started

Saifun Semiconductors, whose name translated from Hebrew to English means "gladiola"—a flower sold by his uncle in the 1950s. Also a beneficiary of this technology was former Frohman student Eli Harari's SanDisk Corporation, one of the semiconductor industry's leading stock-market stars, which supplies storage for digital cameras and other devices. In 2006, SanDisk purchased M-Systems for $1.5 billion, and Moran left to launch Modu Corporation, devoted to creating the world's smallest cell phone.

All of these developments stemmed from Dov Frohman's invention. More significant than any particular device, however, was Frohman's conception of a way to get Intel and its culture more deeply inside Israel. He contrived a way to tap the genius of Jews for Intel while bypassing the rules and tolls and taxes that balked smaller Israeli companies in Israel.

It only began with the Haifa design center. Frohman knew that "the real action in the semiconductor industry was not just in chip design and product development but in manufacturing." Manufacturing chips then entailed a $150 million investment in a factory and an elaborate fabric of technical and chemical expertise and support services that could lift the capabilities of the entire Israeli economy beyond software algorithms and chip designs.

Frohman wanted Intel Israel to establish a semiconductor "fab," or factory, in Jerusalem. After a battle with Andy Grove over the costs of training Israelis to run the fab, Frohman managed to enlist $60 million in support from the Israeli government and led the project to completion within three and a half years. By the late 1980s, the Jerusalem fab, Intel's first outside the United States, was producing some 75 percent of the global output of Intel's flagship "386" microprocessor and was gearing up to produce the "486" as well.

Frohman later persuaded Grove to open production plants in Kiryat Gat in the Negev. During several phases of Intel's history, these wafer-fabrication factories produced the bulk of Intel's profits. Meanwhile, from Intel's Israeli design centers emerged several generations of the Pentium microprocessor and the Centrino low-power processor that integrated Wi-Fi wireless capabilities into portable PCs.

After developing the microchips that launched the personal computer era, Jews, many from Israel, turned to the challenge of linking them together on the Internet. Conceiving the key network packet-switched architectures for the net were Leonard Kleinrock of UCLA, Paul Baran of RAND Corporation, and Robert Kahn, who with non-Jew Vinton Cerf created the crucial TCP/IP network protocol for the Internet. Norman Abramson's ALOHAnet in Hawaii was an inspiration for Bob Metcalfe's industry-standard Ethernet while Metcalfe was with Xerox.

All these breakthroughs were achieved far from Israel during the period of the technology doldrums. But with the transformation of Israeli policy in the 1990s, which began more to favor economic freedom, the key Internet entrepreneurs began to create their companies in Israel. Following the inspiration of microprocessor developments at Intel Israel, Israeli companies took the lead in developing network processors, which play a role in switches and routers for the Internet comparable to the role that microprocessors play in personal computers. From putting *Israel Inside* the personal computer, Israeli engineers and inventors moved toward putting Israel "Inside the Internet" as well.

Von Neumann's final contribution in computer science was an effort to achieve an axiomatic model of brain functions, summed up in a posthumous book of lectures entitled *The Computer and the Brain* (1958). At first baffled by the mazes of apparently disordered brain connections, he contrived a statistical neural model with high levels of redundancy that guided his theory of how to make reliable machines or networks out of unreliable components. The von Neumann insight came to fruition in the works of Paul Baran and Leonard Kleinrock, which are regarded as the intellectual foundations of the Internet as a redundant system that could survive and circumvent major disruption.

Transforming the Internet from a robust and redundant but slow system into an all-purpose global net was the widespread deployment of fiber optics: strands of glass that could carry virtually unlimited volumes of data. This created a need for fiber-speed processors for the network, silicon chips that could function not at fingerspeed, the speed of your fingers on keyboards and touchpads, but at the speed of fiber lines transmitting floods of data at the speed of light. Targeting this goal were hundreds of companies in Silicon Valley and around the globe, including Intel, Alcatel, Motorola, Lucent, and IBM. During the first decade of the new millennium, however, it became clear that new Israeli companies would dominate this new frontier of chip design.

The new era would require the industry to transcend the central technology of the previous era: the von Neumann architecture of computing. All Intel microprocessors essentially followed a serial regime, step-by-step, getting instructions and data from memory, processing the operands one at a time, and sending the results back to memory. In these applications, von Neumann machines were so dominant that any other design was termed a "non-von."

Fiber-speed processing for the floods of data on the Internet would bog down this process. Von Neumann machines were optimal for performing mathematical functions and relatively simple step-wise algorithms for spreadsheets and word processors, but they could not address the famous supercomputer grand challenges of chaos and non-linearity, fluid flow and phase changes, weather modeling and molecular chemistry. They could not process vast quantities of data in real time to find bombs or missiles headed for a city or terrorists in an airport. They foundered at pattern recognition, vision, and haptics (touch), all functions that were characterized by the need to absorb large amounts of information in parallel.

W. Daniel Hillis was the creator of several formidable non-von architectures based on a massively parallel design called cellular automata. The irony is that cellular automata were also an idea of John von Neumann. In transcending von Neumann, it was often necessary to resort to other von Neumann inventions. In any case, Hillis described the problem of von Neumann's original step-by-step architecture as "the paradox of common sense," or why sense is not common in computer science.

Among humans, common sense springs from lots of knowledge about the details of the environment. In general, the more humans learn, the better they function. But in a computer, it is the opposite. The more it learns, the dumber it gets. The more knowledge that is put into a von Neumann computer, the bigger and more crowded its memory and the slower it functions. That is why your Google search engine runs not on one huge computer and one centralized database but on hundreds of thousands of networked small computers.

Hillis explained the problem in his book *The Connection Machine*: "As we build bigger machines with more silicon, or equivalently, as we squeeze more transistors into each unit of area, the machines have a larger ratio of memory to processing power and are consequently even less efficient. This inefficiency remains no matter how fast we make the processor, because the length of the computation becomes dominated by the time required to move data between processor and memory."

This time sump—the time required to move data between processor and memory—is called the "von Neumann bottleneck." To overcome it is the grail of much computer science to this day. The usual method is to remove the bottleneck by multiplying the processors and attaching memory to each one, distributed through the machine. This concept is called "massively parallel processing." Based in part on models of human brain functioning, the new designs eschew the step-by-step regime and adopt parallel methods that can simultaneously process scores or even thousands of bit streams.

Digital computers might be universal Turing machines that could simulate anything in the cosmos that could be programmed in numbers and algorithms. But digital computers could not interact with the real world. They were deaf, dumb, blind, and insensate. "Dumber than an airport urinal," as Nicholas Negroponte puts it, since the urinal these days at least knows you are there. Computers might be "general problem solvers," but they could never solve the problem of driving a car, taking a photograph, finding a missile in a crowded sky, or a terrorist in a crowded airport. All these functions depend on machines capable of processing billions of bits rushing at fiber speed across the room or across the globe. The von Neumann machine could never be equal to the task.

CHAPTER NINE

Inside the Internet

The leading company bringing Israel "Inside the Internet," transcending the limits of von Neumann machines, is a small venture that typifies the creativity of Israeli entrepreneurship. Its founder is Eli Fruchter, a kindly, tough, humble, inspiring man, with sandy hair above a broad, blunt, weather-beaten face.

In an unimpressive, gray, glass-clad multistory building by a pitted road on a hill in Yokneam, far from the centers of Israeli industry, with no architectural distinction or flourish, Fruchter has performed a miracle. But Eli does not preen as a miracle worker.

"I am not important," he told me as I opened the interview for this book.

Then he asked me about Einstein.

"You are going to put me in a book with Einstein?" the entrepreneur of EZchip Technologies asked incredulously.

"Yes," I said, "Einstein and Bohr and Pauli and von Neumann and Feynman. All those guys were just preparing the way for you, Eli, providing the theoretical foundations for network processors that can compute at the speed of fiber-optics communications, at the speed of light."

Eli peered back at me full of skepticism.

I tried to explain.

Science finds its test in engineering. The effort to transcend the von Neumann machine takes the best work of twentieth-century science—quantum chemistry and solid-state physics and optical engineering and computer science and information theory—and makes it into an entirely new device: a network processor that can apply programmable computer intelligence to millions of frames of data and packets of information traveling at rates of a hundred billion bits a second. That's one hundred gigabits a second, about twelve thousand books—each four hundred-pages in length—every page or so scanned and addressed and sorted, all sent together in one second to the right destination.

Crucially, when conditions on the network change, the network processor must be able to be reprogrammed rather than replaced. Computers were invented, originally, to do the same thing over and over again. Computers multiply by adding—very quickly. But for computers to become real partners for us, like us they must be able to change and adapt. A network processor must "touch" each data packet as many as eight times, classifying the packet, looking up addresses, finding the best route—parsing, searching, resolving, modifying, resetting the packet headers. That means not only trillions of operations per second but also millions of programmable operations per second, operations different from the trillions of operations per second the processor performed just a few seconds before.

Though a key to this effort is transcending the von Neumann architecture, it depends entirely on the unifying theme and achievement of von Neumann's career. No one has fully fathomed the quantum mysteries underlying modern electronics. The modern world depends on machines whose inmost nature we do not fully understand. But von Neumann was the paramount figure of twentieth-century science because he was the link between the pioneers of quantum theory and the machines that won World War II, that prevailed in the cold war, and that enabled the emergence of a global economy tied together and fructified by the Internet. The entire saga is one fabric, woven largely by Jews. Von Neumann was the man who outlined the path between the new quantum science of materials and the new computer science of information, and even as Eli Fruchter and others pass von Neumann, they walk the path he cleared.

I first heard Eli describe his plans for a network processor at a forum in Atlanta called NetWorld+Interop 2000. At the time, EZchip was one of at least fifty companies pursuing the technology, clearly the most challenging and imperative target for the next generation of microchips. For most of the decade of the 1990s, fiber optics—light transmitted down glass threads—grew in bandwidth and capability at a pace at least three times as fast as the pace of advance in electronics. The pace of advance in fiber optics has made Moore's law—the famous rule that computer technology doubles in cost effectiveness every eighteen months—look like a costly bottleneck.

The network processor has to bridge this gap. Just as the Pentium is one of the microprocessors that makes the PC work, the network processor has become the device that makes the next-generation Internet work—that does the vital routing and switching at network nodes on the net. The next-generation Internet, allowing "petaflops" (10 to the 15th) of real-time computational power to be deployed to virtually any point on the earth—or above it—will be not only the lever of global economic growth, it will be the indispensable shield protecting the law-abiding and productive from envy, terror, and rapine. It is both the next great machine of capitalism and the next great weapon in its defense.

As the PC, on a smaller scale, distributed intelligence to every desktop—only to see every desktop become a node in the network—the network processor will allow any permitted node on the network to access data and processing power exponentially greater than that incorporated in any PC or any single corporate data center. And it will do so in a way that can wipe away every current concern about privacy and security. It will be the key link holding together the economy of mind and holding off the economics of hate. And it will be created largely in Israel.

At the time Eli Fruchter was launching EZchip, the leaders in network processing were Motorola, Intel, IBM, TriMedia (now part of Alcatel), Cisco, Lucent, Texas Instruments, AMCC, Broadcom, and Agere Systems, most of them investing billions of dollars apiece in network-processor projects, summing to more than $20 billion into network-processor design and development over the last decade.

Surveying these companies, I realized that the most plausible, scalable design for a network processor was presented by Fruchter of EZchip, who alone among the presenters grasped that network processors would have to scale faster than computer technology, moving beyond the von Neumann computer architecture. Even massively parallel systems of von Neumann machines would be limited by the speed with which information could shuttle back and forth between memory and processor. It seemed to me that none of the existing network processors had addressed this challenge in a persuasive way.

Nonetheless at Interop, Motorola, Intel, AMCC, Agere, Bay Microsystems, and IBM, among others, were presenting programmable network processors that were available in the market and were being produced in volume in workable, programmable silicon devices.

Fruchter, meanwhile, was presenting a drastic, revolutionary, world-changing . . . PowerPoint presentation.

Fruchter had at least fifty competitors and no customers, no product, and at best a hundredth of the capital his rivals had invested.

Eight years later, Fruchter's EZchip would have more than fifty customers, six industry-leading products, and virtually no serious competitors, with all the large players—Intel, Motorola, IBM—having essentially left the field. Even after the crash of 2008, EZchip market capitalization ranged from a quarter of a billion dollars to almost half a billion.

Fruchter's story, like most Israeli stories, started in sin, amid the turbulence and terror of middle Europe in the 1930s, when his mother, a seventeen-year-old girl born in Poland in 1917, lied about her age. In those years you lied about your age not to cadge a beer but to board a boat to save your life. Creating documents affirming she was twenty-one and eligible for *aliya*, she gained passage in 1933 on a vessel headed for the embattled desert wasteland of the Yishuv. Her brother and her sister stayed behind: they were later dispatched to a camp and killed by the Nazis. In Haifa, she met Eli's father, who had similarly fled Hungary, and they began a family. Eli was born in Haifa in 1955, the youngest in the family. He grew up watching his father at work, creating orthodontic devices, sensing already a destiny of knowing and making.

In 1973, while Eli was a student in a technical high school, the Yom Kippur War erupted and took everyone by surprise. The lack of preparation by the government was a national scandal. Pulled from his classes, Eli was assigned to work in a bomb factory. With the end of the hostilities, he graduated in 1974 and entered the Israeli Air Force, where he joined a team of ground staff maintaining F-4E Phantom jet planes.

There he noticed that the most charismatic and brilliant of the pilots was taking some of the best-performing soldiers on flights in the Phantom. Eli qualified for the honor and ended up on an unforgettable ride in the jet, zooming up to fifty thousand feet, and plunging down fifty feet above cars on a road. Vomiting in his mask, he had to take it off, and couldn't speak. "Are you dead?" the pilot asked Eli. Almost a decade later, in 1981, the charismatic daredevil pilot was part of the team that made the attack on the Iraqi nuclear plant at Osirak.

After three years in the army and six months of preparatory courses, Eli entered the Technion in 1978. He spent four years studying electrical engineering and computer science and finished with an intimate knowledge of the IBM mainframe technology of the day, with its punch cards for programming and its dumb terminals that merely entered data for the mainframe. When Eli finished the Technion as a certified engineer and computer scientist, he applied to Rafael Advanced Defense Systems, the national-defense industry leader and then the leading employer of technical manpower in Israel. Rafael represented a secure career path in the heart of the Israeli industrial establishment, which was then dominated by the military and the government. He never got there, having been deflected by the economic crisis of the early 1980s and a hiring freeze at Rafael.

With marriage in prospect and his own finances in deficit, Eli took a job in one of the first entrepreneurial Israeli companies, Fibronics, a manufacturer of transceivers and cables for fiber-optics communications. One of the founders of Fibronics was Moti Gura, an engineer who was trained in an army unit that specialized in technology for intelligence operations. Fibronics used the glass threads of fiber optics, with their nearly unlimited potential capacity, to displace the ponderous metal coaxial cables that then ensnarled the computer networks of the world's businesses. To transmit and receive on the same optical channel entails canceling the echoes of the other transmission, preventing interference with the signal. Under the leadership of Gura, Israel's Fibronics developed the first solutions to this problem.

With the company growing rapidly as a complement to the industrial dominance of IBM's mainframes and terminals, Eli became one of Gura's trusted lieutenants, traveling the world in pursuit of markets for Fibronics. But Fibronics put its network nodes onto printed circuit boards, where the need to shuttle information from one logical node to another foreshadowed the same sort of agonizing bottleneck between memory and processor that would fundamentally challenge the von Neumann architecture.

In 1984, Gura came to Eli with the idea of founding a new company whose device would perform the same function as the Fibronics circuit boards but eliminate the bottlenecks by putting all the function on a single chip. Eli accepted. The company was called Adacom and the device was an application-specific integrated circuit (ASIC), one of the first in Israel and indeed in the world.

With the Adacom chip designed to support IBM mainframes and associated network architecture, and with IBM a virtual monopoly in business applications, Adacom enjoyed a meteoric success. But after a couple of years of ascendancy, IBM's standard began giving way to a form of Ethernet, a robust and reproducible technology invented by Robert Metcalfe and David Boggs at Xerox PARC in Palo Alto, California. Ethernet at the time interconnected powerful workstations and even nascent PCs rather than mainframes. It made steady gains as the PC prevailed, then took off in the mid-1980s when SynOptics Communications developed a technology implementing Ethernet over cheap copper wires.

Fruchter stayed with Gura at Adacom for five years, between 1984 and 1989 but felt the restiveness of the compulsive
entrepreneur as Adacom began running out of gas. With IBM
pushing its new challenge to Ethernet (in a local area networking system called Token Ring), Eli decided to launch a company that would both resolve a critical defect in IBM's
approach and ride the dreadnought's wake to success as Adacom had done.

Grasping that local area networks (LANs), whether Ethernet
or Token Ring, would soon have to interoperate with fiber optics, he called his new company LanOptics. One of the first
technology start-ups in Israel, LanOptics lacked all the supports
and cultural props that sustain the start-up culture in Silicon
Valley. There was virtually no venture capital, little "angel" capital from other companies, no friendly Silicon Valley Bank sym-
pathetic to the needs of a new technology company, no settled
procedures of due diligence that he could follow to qualify for
funds, and little readiness of workers to leave established businesses to enter the entrepreneurial fray. Nevertheless, with Adacom clearly fading, Eli succeeded in bringing several engineers
with him into LanOptics, including the crucial software de-
signer Eyal Choresh, who made many vital contributions to the
company's advances. With an improved Token Ring ready in
months, Fruchter set out to conquer Europe, then IBM and its
Token Ring territory.

Fruchter's first major project was the new Munich Airport in
Germany, where thousands of terminals were attached by Token
Ring. Deutsche Bank and Mercedes followed with major pur-
chases. By July 1990, five months after the launch, LanOptics
was profitable.

By November 1992, the company went public on NAS-
DAQ, raising some $15 million in an initial public offering at a

valuation of $60 million. Its board consisted of Eli Harry and three other founders who had gathered in a lawyer's office to launch the company in early 1990. With Fruchter and Harry owning 51 percent, the 49 percent owned by the three other founders yielded nearly one hundred dollars for every dollar of the $300 thousand total investment they had made.

This was the first big score by an Israeli company on NAS-DAQ. Fruchter attracted attention as a man with a natural gift for technological opportunities. But at the very moment of his triumph, he sensed that Token Ring, the one technology mastered by his company, was already dying. By 1995, Fruchter abandoned all Token Ring activity, and LanOptics went into swift decline. In late 1999, with LanOptics shares down to about a dollar apiece and the company bereft of cash, the LanOptics board met and resolved to sell the company for $5 million. At this, Fruchter, normally the most equable of men, lost his temper.

Stalking out of the room, he hurled back: "Sell your mother for $5 million if you want, but I am not going to sell this company."

It was no mere emotional release. Fruchter already knew where he wanted LanOptics to go. He would follow the trail that Adacom, and for that matter Intel itself, had blazed: reducing whole systems to a chip. Intel had "hollowed out" the personal computer by putting most of the key hardware functionality onto a single system-on-a-chip, a microprocessor, replacing scores of separate chips on a printed circuit board. Fruchter aimed to hollow out the network router and switch. He would put *Israel Inside* in most of the routers and switches across the Internet.

His immediate problem, however, was that LanOptics was hollowed out itself. It had become a shell. Fruchter decided to use the shell as a route to NASDAQ for his EZchip dream. EZchip would be a hermit crab, gaining access to public funds through the husk of LanOptics.

Eli decided that this was the time, at last, to resort to venture capital. Although there was only an embryonic venture community in Israel at that time, he had encountered various venture capitalists around the world: STAR Ventures of Germany and Apax Partners with offices in the United States. In early 2000, the market for technology stocks was stumbling after its vertiginous peak a year earlier in 1999. Eli realized that it might be now or never for his EZchip vision.

In February 2000, at the time of his board meeting, the value of LanOptics was $5 million. By March, as the market crumbled, he induced two venture capitalists to invest a couple million to keep the company going at a valuation of $18 million. By November he was already running out of money when he was approached by JK&B Capital from Chicago, a Goldman Sachs affiliate, whose team members were Israeli venture capitalists whom he had known for years.

Perhaps remembering his mother's lifesaving claim to be twenty-one, on which his entire existence was predicated, he told JK&B that he had a *serious* offer for the company at a valuation of $100 million.

Fruchter calculated that he needed this valuation to bring his network processor project to market. And he was talking to several venture capitalists about $100 million valuations (at least *he* was serious). He told JK&B that if they wanted to participate they would have to come to Israel for the closing of the deal in November with the board. All five partners of JK&B came to the meeting. After listening to Eli's case, they asked the LanOptics executives to leave the room. At the time, Eli assumed they would demand a lower valuation and more control. But within fifteen minutes, the JK&B partners called him back into the room and agreed to invest $13.5 million at a valuation of $100 million. EZchip was on its way.

Since that day in 2000, EZchip has had many ups and downs. But today it has flawlessly fulfilled its agenda of building network processors that can link the electronics of computers to the fiber optics of the Internet. It produces fiber-speed processors for Cisco, Juniper Networks, and scores of other router and switch companies, and its valuation has remained close to $400 million throughout much of the global recession in 2009. EZchip and Eli Fruchter are survivors, and the next generation of the Internet will have EZchips inside.

During my trip to Israel in 2008, Eli, Amir Eyal, and Guy Koren of EZchip took me out to dinner in Caesarea. The restaurant was on the Mediterranean beach. Above the beach were the ruins of Roman temples and terraces, theaters and arches, all surfaced with golden sandstone and carefully refurbished and illuminated. Decorously arrayed along the beach were shops and restaurants. The rush of water on the sands, the scent of fish in the air, the glow of sunset, and the lights on the Roman stone all lent the area a magical feeling of peace and prosperity. Inside the restaurant, the three men from EZchip told me of their plans for the future—how their network-processor architecture could be adapted for homes and entertainment centers and computer clouds in a new world of global networking.

This is the promise of Israel. To extend new technologies to the world and sustain an expanding capitalism with new opportunities opening up for people everywhere, new horizons as peaceful and prosperous as Caesarea and Tel Aviv to the south.

Then I thought of Gaza a few hundred miles farther south,

with similar beaches and balmy weather, and similar possibilities of human advance. Why could not the Gazans combine with the Israelis to create a Riviera on their exquisite beaches, their glowing sands?

But the people of Gaza were uninterested in the future. They lived in a world of zero-sum chimeras and fantasies of jihadist revenge and death.

Meanwhile, Israel was deep inside the United States and world economies.

CHAPTER TEN

The Next Generation

Eli Fruchter amused himself on more than one occasion by reciting to me a long list of Israeli entrepreneurs he claimed to be far more important than he was. But above all he told me repeatedly I must go see Zohar Zisapel.

I found him first inside a book, a coffee-table tome with a foreword by Rupert Murdoch of News Corp. celebrating the technological accomplishments of Israel. A smooth, handsome, friendly face, with twinkling eyes and an anchorman's gray coif, he evokes an Israeli Robert Noyce, founder of Intel.

When Zohar is asked why he does not relocate to the United States, where entrepreneurs like him are national heroes, Zohar says: "There are two reasons that motivate people to get involved in start-ups. One is because they want to deliver their own babies. The other is because they want to make money.

"In America making money is more important; in Israel, delivering your own baby is more important."

I doubt that, debating him in my head. But I let it pass. All entrepreneurs, particularly Israeli entrepreneurs when they ascend to the empyrean of legend like Zisapel, like to claim indifference to money, and all of them, in some sense, are telling the truth. They are unconsciously responding to the slander upon

Jews—emerging during centuries when Jews were often denied the right to secure property in land and in things—that they cared for nothing but money. Exchanging, arbitraging, seignior-aging, lending, factoring was all they were allowed to do. Thinking, computing, calculating, philosophizing. The world believed that the fruits of these activities were less real or durable than the ownership of land and physical capital. Finance, insurance, banking, the handling of money are among the world's most useful work, making economies flow and grow. But beneficiaries of this magic were inclined to impugn the morality of Jews. Jews sometimes respond by protesting too much their indifference to money.

True, if you fixate on money for yourself, it will elude you. You will mostly find poverty. Pursue innovation in a market system where others determine your success by committing their wealth in exchange for your product, and you will make money. Then, in the usual entrepreneurial cycle, most of the time you will reinvest it, and make more of it, until you find yourself in an "embarrassment of riches," richly embarrassed, accused of greed by nonprofit poseurs. You find yourself giving money away to fashionable charities and start denying its significance and begin posing for posterity in a garb of pecuniary sanctimony. Not to worry, within a couple of generations your heirs will dissipate your fortune and dissolve their burden of guilt, all too often in a seethe of resentment toward capitalism.

Money remains an indispensable measure of the value of what you do for others. Money is a measuring stick. And for opponents of capitalism a stick with which to beat Americans. But Zisapel is no cliché critic of the United States. He has more on his mind. "There is a third element in Israel: it's the feeling that, 'I'm doing something for the country, for Israel.' People respect you for that. I don't blame people who decide to go to America.

Everyone makes his own decision. But I was born in Israel and I will die in Israel."

Before he dies, though, he will offer a vision for Israeli technology of the new millennium. At first the vision may seem less than visionary.

"Computers will become connected to the television set-top box, to the DVD, to the DVR for downloading films on the Internet, to the digital camera." But haven't we heard this before; isn't it already happening; and most of all—does it really matter?

But he has more to say, and Eli has promised me it will be worth hearing. The pace at which information flows between all these devices is called bandwidth. Insufficient bandwidth is the plague of networks. But Zisapel wants us to think of it as abundant and uniform—"like electricity," he says.

"You receive electricity in your house. You might use it for lighting, for heating, for your television set, or your DVD player—no one asks what you use it for. In the future, people will receive broadband in their home and nobody will ask if it is used for television, telephone calls, or for the computer. Like electricity, you will use it as much as you want in any way that you want, and everything will be the same price."

What is the significance of this? Because if bandwidth becomes even more abundant, universal, and ubiquitous than electricity—more because it can be wireless—then all the data, all the intelligence, all the images on the network can be brought to bear at any point on the network all but indifferent to cost and speed. It is the ultimate solution to the von Neumann challenge—liberating machine intelligence from the machine. The "Arab–Israeli conflict" is almost everywhere understood (wrongly, in my view) as an impossibly embittered dispute over absurdly small patches of geography. The promise of a global network seamlessly providing near-infinite bandwidth indifferent to application is the promise, like almost every major economic advance for the past two hundred years, to render geography relatively trivial.

Only bandwidth in unprecedented volumes can enable electronics and optics to relieve the pressure on energy use—from global travel between Silicon Valley, Tel Aviv, and Taipei to pullulating Vegas conferences with millipede taxi queues and five gigawatts of air-conditioning pumps and sumps, with everyone seething *Hot, Flat and Crowded* with Tom Friedman, or swooshing on silver wings to intimate Aspen séances in the glittering dark with Amory Lovins, or jetting to Davos, Switzerland, for green rites and ruminations among many churning stomachs and ski lifts and freighted glimpses of Buffett and Gates, or zooming to Frankfurt industrial assemblies and book fairs, or flying at near-sonic speeds to animated and aerated auditoria in Vienna and Los Angeles and Geneva, stopping at domed stadia in San Diego and London and skyscraping offices in New York and Ramat Gan. The new technology of teleportation cannot displace, or even successfully complement, the old jet fuels and hotel follies without creating fully satisfying vessels of communication. The new technology must link people without ensnaring their feet and minds in thousands of entangled copper nooses and lassoes every time they boot it up and without entailing the aspiring communicators to become IT professionals.

The scandal of home and office electronics, personal and corporate computing is the mat—the tangle of connections behind the TV and workstation and the high-definition home theater and the set-top box and the network node and the game player and the residential gateway and the cell phone and the video teleconferencing center and the teleputer and the DVD machine and the intercom and the digital camera and the audio player and the fire and burglar alarms and the camcorder and the speakers and the microphones, and, so they say, the washing machine and the refrigerator and even the complex links to the antenna for the "wireless" transmissions of the phones and computers in the household, the Global Positioning System panel in the car and the DIRECTV dish on the roof.

When something goes awry, or someone steps on some wire or cable, finding the offending connector or dangling link or shorted power supply amid the haystack mazes of connections, many of them sealed behind the walls of the house, is a challenge for the most sophisticated technician. Most people just throw up their hands in despair.

It is an incredible morass and the next major challenge in home electronics. The solution for home and consumer electronics, necessarily being orders of magnitude cheaper and simpler than the Forbes 500's or Pentagon's or Israeli Defense Forces' solutions will ultimately dominate those markets as well. All the world's major electronics companies are on the case. But at the end of the first decade of the new millennium, Israeli firms are moving toward the lead.

This is a hard problem. What it requires is supplying levels of bandwidth or communications power comparable to the capabilities of a phone-company central office at a price point that families can afford for home equipment. Central offices use fiber-optics connections and high-end electronics from Alcatel and Cisco. But these solutions are too complex and fragile for the home. High-definition signals consume some 1.5 or more gigabits a second, more than one thousand times the capacity of the T1 lines that still connect most U.S. businesses to the Internet. When not only games and movies but also telephone connections come to function in high definition, the home will have to accommodate tens of gigabits of total bandwidth.

Aggravating the challenge is the multiplicity of different

connectors. Each form of high-definition image requires a different protocol, a different compression scheme, a different physical link, a specialized converter from analog to digital and back. While providing unprecedented bandwidth in homes, the industry will have to supply unprecedented intelligence and adaptability among the diverse devices.

An Israeli company AMIMON was the first to cut this Gordian knot of wires. It began by banishing all the different video compression standards and substituting uncompressed image streams. Offering "robust, wireless whole-home high-definition connectivity," as described on its Web site, AMIMON can deliver three-gigabit flows of HDTV at a range of over one hundred feet, or thirty meters, through multiple walls and with a latency of less than a millisecond (for human beings, latencies of a hundred milliseconds are scarcely detectable). In 2008, Sony, Mitsubishi, Samsung, Sharp, Hitachi, and Motorola all joined the AMIMON Wireless HD Interface standard (WHDI).

While AMIMON throws bandwidth at the problem—by replacing intelligence with raw pixel power—another Israeli company, Celeno, offers the alternative of marshaling "carrier-class" intelligence in complex trillionfold transistor circuitry. Carrier class is what the world's telecom companies require and supply. Celeno brings it into the home in systems on chips based on the Wi-Fi standard raised to gigabit levels.

To handle the multiplicity of standards and links, it supplies a core technology based on spatial radio switching (identifying where the signals go), combined with adaptive channel coding (changing the channel in response to different streams), dynamic space-time scheduling (adding to its spatial sensors a system of time slots), tight security, and multimedia Quality of Service (QoS).

These two companies seem to be on a collision path, but the

world will accommodate both for many years. AMIMON can handle all the links to theater screens and other digital HD devices, while Celeno can create the home network that brings all the other devices into the Internet wirelessly.

Meanwhile, Wisair has developed a chipset that provides the actual radio signals on which all these devices rely. Wisair uses a technology called Ultra Wideband (UWB), which transmits at extremely low power across relatively huge spans of bandwidth at relatively low-radio frequencies. Because the power is so low, Wisair systems can operate in parts of the spectrum already occupied by other devices that transmit at high power in narrow channels. Using the Universal Serial Bus (USB) standard common in all personal computer technology, Wisair's chipset will go into such appliances as digital video recorders, digital cameras, teleputers, televisions, camcorders, and game machines.

Also addressing the electronic Tower of Babel of industry standards, spectrum bands, and connector formats is another Israeli company called ASOCS. Headed by CEO Gilad Garon, it is focusing on the challenge of the wireless handset or teleputer that has to connect at one time with the Internet, cell-phone base stations, and Global Positioning System links. Working with Fujitsu's fabrication technologies, ASOCS has launched what it calls the first MultiComm processor that can run three air interfaces at once and has incorporated a software reconfigurable core that allows teleputer manufacturers of all kinds to move into the next generation of wireless, called 4G, using programmable software.

Taking a different approach to the new generation is a company called Provigent. With all these mobile devices multiplying across the network, the further challenge is to bring the signals back to the central office to be redistributed to the Internet or other cable and telephone systems. This challenge is called wireless backhaul. Based on insights in information theory, Provigent uses a series of unique compression tools and protocols to facilitate this backhaul process. Lowering the power for any given bandwidth or increasing the bandwidth at any given power, the company's chips radically improve the trade-offs and efficiencies in network designs for backhaul.

One of the surprises of the last decade has been the emergence of passive optical networks (PONs)—fiber-optics systems that operate at low power and require no amplification—not first in the backbones of the system but in the connections to homes and businesses. Scores of companies have been competing to supply these crucial chips that link video and other Internet content to fiber-optics lines at central offices and head-ends and then reconvert the signal at the other end for entry into the home or office.

The leader in supplying the technology that enables Verizon's FiOS last-mile broadband system is BroadLight. Its headquarters are high in an office tower in Ramat Gan, a coruscating new city near Tel Aviv. One of its leading rivals is also Israeli: Ethernity Networks, whose CEO is David Levi, founder of BroadLight. Ethernity is a configurable network-processor company, providing an entire passive optical network line-terminal card on a single chip.

Attempting to put all these capabilities into a new "convergence" architecture is Siverge Networks. Headed by former IBM executive Yuval Berger, Siverge has invented a unique engine core that can process multiple channels, ports, and protocols with scalable bandwidth, supporting many telecom interfaces, communications speeds, and networking standards.

The efflorescence of creativity in today's Israel resembles the early days of Silicon Valley, reproduced with technologies that work millions of times faster and more efficiently. Like the early Silicon Valley, the new Silicon Israel—or Silicon Wadi—is a global phenomenon, enriching New York and Los Angeles as much as Tel Aviv, and feeding on ideas from everywhere. But it finds its roots in the same essential culture of twentieth-century science, enabled by Jewish breakthroughs in quantum theory, optical engineering, algorithms, and information science. The current technological miracles in Israel merely represent a delayed homecoming and harvest of insights pioneered by Jews over the previous hundred years.

The next application of their algorithmic advances will come in biology, the final frontier outlined by John von Neumann—virtually on his deathbed.

CHAPTER ELEVEN

The Shoshana Algorithm

An algorithm, explains David Berlinski in his book, *The Advent of the Algorithm,* is a finite procedure written in symbols, governed by precise instructions, moving in discrete steps, automatically, to its conclusion. It is usually thought of as a set of steps, a subroutine, in a computer program. Linking a conceptual regime to a physical machine, software to hardware, symbols to materials, it is normally a human construct. Without mind and consciousness to give it significance, a symbol cannot have meaning.

Mathematics, computer science, economics, and all models and simulations are symbolic systems. Together they represent a crushing reply to the Marxist and Nazi claim, whether in the form of economic determinism or the blood claims of the fatherland, that matter must rule over mind: that the manipulators of symbols are mere dispensable middlemen, while muscle and machines and marching men make the world. The reign of the algorithm vindicates the monotheist—and capitalist—intuition that the world in the first instance is a manifestation of thought.

Without symbolic logic, no computer or algorithmic machine, no automated factory or modern automobile, no enterprise or engineering project is possible. The most portentous and radical discovery of the late twentieth century was the insight that human beings themselves are in part algorithmic machines. This is the message of DNA. Biological beings thus partake of the Gödel proof of the limitations of symbolic logic—its dependence on axioms that it cannot prove. Like mathematics, biological science depends on and transcends an orderly cosmos of monotheistic faith.

The discovery that biological systems are algorithmic opens the most promising frontier in the world economy. This opportunity is to model on computers the symbolic language and algorithmic structures inscribed in genetic systems and then to translate them into new pharmaceuticals and medical devices.

Engulfing science today is an avalanche of new genetic data. In computational terms, this genetic information (genes in the genome) is software, and it is stored in the DNA molecule in every human cell.

The DNA double helix is essentially a data-storage device. In the cell, the DNA system converts software instructions, such as the recipe for another protein, into RNA *transcripts* that resemble digital packets on a network. Like the packets processed by EZchip's network processors, the RNA packets contain an address and instructions that invoke other agents (enzymes), or processors necessary for a specified effect. Like Internet packets, the RNA transcripts move on to what might be termed a microprocessor: in biological terms the *ribosome*, which translates the information into a different form for final use.

The software of genes may be compared to a recipe in cooking. The central dogma of biology, as defined by Francis Crick, co-discoverer of the DNA double helix, declares that proteins cannot generate DNA any more than pudding can write a recipe. The genetic information flows in one direction only.

The computer and the biological information system differ in their final products. The computer puts out yet more processed information, while the ribosome is a factory creating an actual protein comprising hundreds of amino acids. In these tiny molecular factories, RNA transcripts guide the translation of the genes into the amino acids that form proteins. This process, however, turns out to be hugely more complex than originally understood by Crick, who believed that the links between DNA and proteins were simple and direct. In fact, the path of transformation breaks out into a maze of baffling twists and turns. That unexpected complexity turns out to provide a huge opportunity for Israel.

The shift of leading-edge science from modern physics to modern biology crosses a chasm from the intricate empirical enigmas of quantum theory to the radically different top-down algorithmic world of DNA. It is a move from material science to computer science. As Berlinski shows, these are separate domains. Although an algorithm must have a material carrier, the algorithm is entirely independent of its physical vehicle and cannot be reduced to it. A computer can be made of anything from matchsticks to magnetic domains, from LEGO blocks to beach sand.

Modern biology has more in common with John von Neumann than with James Watson, who saw biology through a chemical paradigm, as a science of materials rather than information. Science and technology are climbing a ladder from the experimental morass of physics and chemistry into the abstract domains of excellence in algorithms, with Israel ready to play a role comparable to its role in the era's other computational domains, where it stands second only to the United States.

A central figure in this Israeli ascent in computational biology is an American, Martin Gerstel, who made his *aliya* in 1994. Eight hundred on his math SAT, the outstanding chemistry student in Fairfield County, Connecticut (1959), star engineering graduate of Yale class of 1963, number-one MBA from Stanford Business School in 1968, eminent biotech executive for four decades, Martin Gerstel is a distinguished biological entity. Process the DNA and insert a social science algorithm (with Gerstel, everything is DNA and algorithms), and you get a typical Jewish American prince. Typical because there is a contrarian inverter in there somewhere as well; for more than three decades, Gerstel did not see himself as Jewish, or as a prince.

His Yale honors came after flunking out in his sophomore year. On the Jewish question, he would acknowledge only that his parents were Jewish. But he himself harbored no religious beliefs. He did not know his father, a deceased chemist from Norwalk Tire and Rubber Company, had a troubled relationship with his indigent and near-suicidal mother, and retained no links to his extended family.

As for Israel, he felt no special ties to the country and no particular interest in visiting it. An unemotional man, he had to struggle to show enthusiasm on the basketball court. A good player in high school and as a freshman at college, he was known for his ability to perform under pressure. "It made no difference to me," he says.

After Yale, he continued to outperform under pressure, leading his Stanford Business School class. Within days of his graduation he had vaulted to a pinnacle, alone on the cover of *Business Week*, which judged him the most promising of all the nation's MBAs.

He vindicated his laurels quickly with a mercurial career as the protégé of the biopharma pioneer Alejandro (Alex) Zaffaroni of Syntex Corporation, rich and famous from the birth control pill, who wanted Gerstel in his eponymous new company ALZA, headquartered next to Syntex in Silicon Valley. Devoted to the project of radically improving the processes of drug delivery, Zaffaroni was launching a new pharmaceutical company based not chiefly on chemistry, like the others, but on physics and engineering.

Alex Zaffaroni came on so strong that Gerstel accepted a job without knowing what it was. When he asked what he would be doing, Zaffaroni answered: "I'm going to be president and head of research, you can be anything else." For salary, Alex told him, "Take your three highest offers, add them up, and divide by three and that is your salary." As for his obligation to Cummins Engine Company that paid Gerstel's way through Stanford? "No problem, I'll take care of it," said Alex. Floating free of family and heritage, Gerstel rose up into a nirvana of polymathic merit. Into the capacious emptiness he felt at the heart of his personality, he attracted choirs of angels—tycoons and women, money and admiration.

The first new pharmaceutical company to go public, ALZA introduced Gerstel to the magic of equity finance, which he would exploit heavily in Israel. His ALZA options made Gerstel a multimillionaire on paper by the age of thirty.

ALZA had just one serious problem. The products didn't quite work. While the prototype devices developed by the engineering team functioned efficiently and well, the scientific advisory board required constant redesigns. The scientists wanted to conform the curve of release of an anti-glaucoma drug exactly to the curve of physical receptivity of the patient. Zaffaroni couldn't say no to Nobel laureates who had honored the company by serving on its advisory board, and nobody ever asked if the human eye could actually distinguish among small differences in the curves in the flow rate. The result was a complex and cumbersome multilayered glaucoma device that tended to fall out. It did not sell at all. With ALZA's new birth control device, the problem was worse, aggravated by the scandal three months before surrounding the Dalkon Shield IUD, which produced infections and hundreds of lawsuits. No one cared that ALZA's intrauterine device was different in almost every way.

Close to bankruptcy in 1977, ALZA's stock crashed. But Gerstel was enthusiastic about the prospects of a new line of patch products that would release drugs through the skin to targeted parts of the body. It was in the midst of the 1970s' energy crisis and economic slump. So he went out to persuade oil companies to invest.

"I found myself living at the Tehran Hilton for months soliciting the Shah of Iran and his wife, the Empress." At a loose end in Tehran in the winter of 1978, a non-Jewish friend in the CIA suggested they visit Israel. "In those days, EL AL flew nonstop between Tehran and Tel Aviv. . . ." He soon found himself standing on the tarmac at Ben-Gurion International Airport, with tears in his eyes and unruly emotions welling up in his chest.

He could not explain it at all. It was not like him and he did not like it. But there it was: the big guy, precocious exec, rich on paper, feeling himself pulled inexorably "inside the pale," into a puddle of messy primal feelings, merely by the touch of unseasonal breezes on his cheek and the scuff of possibly ancestral ground under his feet.

Months later, at the Hilton (now Crowne Plaza), Jerusalem's tallest building, overlooking the Knesset, the feelings would grow even more intense. What was it about this girl Shoshana? She was blonde, from Haifa, lithe and elegant as she moved across the tennis court and then scintillating as she climbed from the swimming pool. A physical therapist for the Hadassah Medical Organization, working in a hospital near Ethiopia Street near the summit of the city, she was perhaps Israel's most eminent nurse. When presidents of the country were hospitalized, they insisted on Shoshana. To Gerstel, her smile seemed to capture the entire panorama of his new emotional life.

• • •

Gerstel fell in love with Israel on his first trip and with Shoshana on the second. He was thirty-seven years old. When Shoshana invited him home for dinner to meet her mother, that first evening, he was captivated in a way that never happened in Palo Alto. She offered him history and heritage that could link him to an ancestral kingdom and find him a home in the world, fill up the void. It was strange and exhilarating—and troubling too. It was Martin Gerstel's first Israel test, and it left him in an emotional storm.

Over the following years, he and Shoshana would visit Israel regularly, but his career and their home were in Silicon Valley. Finally, in 1994, he retired, and then returned to Israel. As a consultant for American venture capitalists, he quickly found himself in the midst of a biotech start-up scene. His favorite project, then and now, was Compugen, an Israeli company that launched and dominated the field of computational biotechnology.

Compugen executes biogenetic algorithms on special-purpose computers that operate a thousand times faster than ordinary machines. Reverse engineering the beautiful and complex organisms of life, the company's scientists duplicate the governing logic *in silico*—in computers designed and optimized for biological research.

Building such "Bioaccelerator" computers in the early 1990s and selling the first one to Merck in 1994, Compugen's young Israeli scientists and engineers dominated the market for machines that could survey and simulate the informatics of the genome. This market, however, turned out to be small, numbering in the hundreds of units. Once most relevant universities, research institutes, government bodies, and major pharmaceutical and biotech companies had acquired their biocomputers for $100 thousand apiece, no further Compugen wares were needed. "They should have charged a million apiece," Gerstel remarks today. There was nothing to do but declare victory and withdraw from the industry.

Gerstel and his team, however, observed that in many cases the Compugen machines were merely processing garbage-in into garbage-out a thousand times faster. The researchers still did not fully grasp the relevant algorithms that convert DNA genes into messenger RNA transcripts and thence into amino acid, protein molecules, and useful peptides that could modulate or affect specific receptors in the body to remedy disease.

Under Gerstel's guidance, the company changed its strategy from building special-purpose computers for others into identifying and defining the algorithms that govern the genetic cascade all the way from the DNA "words" to the protein flesh.

From his days of teaching calculus as a high-schooler, Gerstel was always sensitive to the elegance of algorithms, whether for simulating a nuclear reaction as a Yale undergraduate computer prodigy or for projecting diesel-engine sales at Cummins Engine in Indiana. Under Gerstel's algorithmic touch, even accounting became elegant. Before graduation, he began teaching accounting at Stanford Business School as a system of equations. As he puts it, "The entire system of double-entry bookkeeping is a beautiful algorithmic machine." To Gerstel, math is a language, not a science. After mathematics, all languages paled, and he was never inclined to learn another.

In fifteen years in Israel he has yet to learn Hebrew. But following the von Neumann example, he learned to find the algorithmic language uniting apparently disparate fields, animate as well as inanimate. Biology is a set of living algorithmic entities. Compile the biological entities into a database and apply the algorithms, and you can find pathways to the inner logic of life: Shoshana by the pool in Jerusalem.

The algorithmic thinking that fuels such ventures comes naturally only to the gifted and diligent few. Without permitting the gifted and diligent to emerge, prevail, create, and ultimately rule the commanding heights, there is no way to have a successful system based on the algorithms of the new economy.

Gerstel traces the Israeli prowess in algorithms in large part to the military's explicitly elitist Talpiot program. With every Israeli youth required to serve in the military before entering college, the bright students were in danger of losing ground to students in other countries who went to college directly from school. In part to compensate for this disadvantage, the Israeli Defense Forces decided to put the smartest thirty-five or fifty candidates into engineering and math programs engaged in crucial military research. Over a six-month period, participants, known as "Talpions," study for fourteen hours a day on one subject at a time. Talpiot ended up creating a group unmatched anywhere in the world, its students designing systems for the military for ten years before entering college.

Indian prowess in software is based on similar merit-based programs that filter out a small elite of hundreds from the millions of students in Indian schools. The hundreds who graduate every year from Indian Institutes of Technology accumulate to the mere thousands of Indian engineers who have changed the world economy in much the way that the Talpions of Israel have opened up new opportunities both in Israel and in Silicon Valley.

With this Talpiot system, complemented by other elite military programs, the Israelis not only avoided the democratic temptation to level the pyramids of talent but also took advantage of the precocity of mathematical talent. In most of the world, students are not allowed to do original work in math and engineering until they are beyond the age when they are most capable of it. In Israel, these Talpiot teenagers address military problems under conditions of life-and-death exigency.

"The key capability that came out of this program was algorithms," Gerstel observes. "So much of military intelligence is related to having access to tremendous amounts of raw data from unmanned aircraft, spacecraft, fighting situations, battlefield surveillance, reconnaissance, all requiring real-time processing"—to get the answers before it is too late to respond. To deal with all this data creates a need for finding the intrinsic logical structures and patterns within it, "the algorithmic ability to take an enormous amount of raw information and interpret it in real time, to survey a vast stretch of land from afar and identify tanks and troops" before they go away or attack. "Not cars or trucks or pedestrians or postal-delivery vehicles, but tanks and troops."

"That is why there are certain technical problems that have only been solved by Israelis. Trying to determine whether a computer chip is 100 percent correct is similar." Millions of data points have to be subdued by algorithms to find the patterns of error in wiring links, "race conditions," or temperature hot spots. "Chip and printed circuit board inspection and measurement is an Israeli forte." Among the leaders are RAD, Camtek, Elbit, Valor, and Orbotech. "It's all algorithms and data. This is the reason why so much of this stuff comes from Israel." In later years, Talpions star in many kinds of Israeli high-tech businesses. Under Gerstel's guidance, twelve of them joined Compugen.

The idea for Compugen originated when Liat Mintz, the wife of Talpiot star Eli Mintz, came home from working on the Human Genome Project. As she described the morass of information flowing from her research, Eli Mintz saw the prospect of a computational solution. He got together with two other Talpiot engineers, CTO Simchon Faigler and software chief Amir Natan and began Compugen. Soon after they brought in Mor Amitai, another Talpiot friend, to become CEO. Introducing the Compugen team to Gerstel was venture capitalist Jonathan Medved.

According to Gerstel, Compugen still commands the most valuable algorithms in bioscience. The foundation is the human genome, comprising some three billion base pairs or "letters" inscribed in the DNA helix. These base pairs comprise some one billion codons—sixty-four different three-letter words redundantly symbolizing the twenty-three amino acids of which proteins are made. Because there are sixty-four codons and only twenty-three amino acids, the amino acids cannot specify the codons that program for them. The direction of influence, as the Central Dogma declares, is from the DNA to the amino acids and not the other way around. As Crick put it, "once the information gets into a protein, it cannot get back out."

The Compugen algorithms could translate the genome's DNA into messenger RNA transcripts. Echoing the DNA *genome*, Compugen calls this RNA library a *transcriptome*.

These transcripts, programmed for amino acids, enter the ribosome "factory" where they are ultimately translated into specific proteins. These proteins—amino-acid combinations—comprise what is called the *proteome*. All these one-way transmissions are governed by algorithms and thus are expressible in

Compugen's computational programs. The programs enable fast and accurate simulations of biological processes.

The goal of all the computations is the discovery of peptides—fragments of proteins—that can fit in the body's cell receptors and impart a medical effect. To find appropriate peptides, Compugen develops further algorithms to function as learning systems—algorithms with feedback loops that adapt and correct themselves. These learning systems are designed to scrutinize proteins for their cleavage points, which are vital to the creation of peptides.

Peptides—coherent components of proteins, crucial to some 50 percent of all drugs—can directly modulate receptors in the human body. All the databases from genome to proteome are climaxed by this *peptidome*. Possessing the genome and all these algorithms, Compugen can generate new drugs to spec on computers rather than discover them empirically.

These algorithms are based on a sophisticated new understanding of molecular biology. Although the Central Dogma itself remains intact and crucial, a simplistic "extended dogma" erroneously assumes a direct path of one gene, one transcript, one protein. Compugen's algorithms replace this direct path with scores of complex byways and alternative splicings. As Yale biologists Michael Seringhaus and Mark Gerstein put it, "To the modern genomics scientist, the classical image of a gene and the extended dogma associated with it are quaint."

Moving beyond the classical image, Gerstel offers a powerful vision of how Israel can parlay its current eminence in post–von Neumann computer architectures into pioneering leadership on the new frontiers of biotechnology. Just as quantum physics enabled the movement of science from the macrocosm of visible Newtonian objects into the microcosm of the invisible inner structures of matter, which in turn enabled the computer revolution, so, Gerstel believes, can deeper insights into genomic science enable a revolution in programmable biotech. The difference in biology is that all the devices, functions, and systems already exist in the form of *us* and our molecular components, organs, and neurological processes.

"It is as if an alien landed on earth after a natural disaster without much understanding of physics and tried to reproduce our current set of digital computing and networking systems." He would try to reverse-engineer them, to uncover their secrets. But without a mastery of twentieth-century physical and computer science, all the radios and antennas, microchips and optical networks, all the underlying and overarching algorithms of software would seem baffling and enigmatic.

The aliens would have to resort to trial and error—essentially random experiments—to determine how these objects function. Gerstel believes that this is how most biotech companies conduct research: by trial-and-error techniques of discovery. "There is no process for learning from errors, and in fact subsequent findings are more difficult than the early, more obvious discoveries." In this random process, there is no obvious learning curve.

Compugen, by contrast, continues to extend the power of the algorithms. The company's first breakthrough was the discovery of the significance of alternative splicings, a critical error in the prevailing assumption of "one gene to one protein." Although biologists recognized the phenomenon, they regarded multipath cascades as rare and anomalous events. The Compugen scientists discovered that alternative splicing is the way biological systems achieve redundancy and robustness. By creating the first robust implementation of the algorithms that govern alternative splicing, Compugen became the first company with a reliable model of the cascade of transmissions and translations between the genome and the peptidome. Thus uniquely they could find peptides that actually worked to modulate the receptors in the body and function as drugs.

Running their peptidome program in 2001, they discovered some thirty peptides that seemed able to perform this task effectively. Narrowing a universe of billions of peptides down to thirty contenders, the company had radically simplified the discovery of bio-based drugs. Out of these thirty, Compugen came up with eight working peptides. As Gerstel points out, "The usual rate of advance of the entire industry is two new peptides a year. We found eight in one computer run."

Gerstel now is struggling to explain why he is taking over as chief executive officer of Compugen. Once a stock market phenom, up to a near $400 million valuation after its IPO on NASDAQ in 2000, by the end of 2008 it was down more than thirtyfold to $14 million. It seemed to be losing altitude fast in the swirling markets of 2009. But Gerstel knew its real value was growing, as Merck and Teva confirmed within months.

In 2007, the international public research consortium that produced the ENCODE (*ENCyclopedia Of DNA Elements*) Project confirmed a further misconception of the extended dogma: the idea that all RNA transcripts express specific genes. As the Compugen algorithms assumed, the transcripts can include material from the large body of so-called "junk" DNA, which has been treated as dead and unusable. Combining alternative splicings with the new knowledge of junk DNA, Compugen can now push Israel to the forefront of a revolution in computational biology. The industry can move from being an experimental field, looking for algorithms, to become a predictive industry, using computers to execute the algorithms in order to uncover further algorithms that can be manipulated to cure diseases.

This is the promise of computational biotech, a new forte of the Israeli economy. Confirming the wide range of application of Compugen's technology are its spin-offs, such as Evogene in Rehovot, Israel. Aimed at exploiting Compugen's world-leading predictive-discovery capabilities in the agricultural biotechnology field, and run by executives and researchers from Compugen, Evogene commands biocomputers that have enabled a new way of creating and enhancing agricultural products through manipulating their DNA. Launched in 2002 and chaired by Gerstel, Evogene develops improved plants through the use of plant genomics. As Gerstel remarks, "The process is faster than for drugs because the plants don't have lawyers."

Evogene enhances plant characteristics, both for food and for fuel, and commands intellectual property pending for some three hundred novel genes and more than forty validated promoters. Among traits aided by the Evogene genetic processes are agricultural yield under normal conditions, yield under stress (such as drought), and receptivity to fertilizers. For meeting the global challenge of food production, Evogene is as valuable as Compugen for spurring the production of new drugs. A number of improved plant traits are in relatively advanced stages of development through deals and collaborations with world-leading companies such as Monsanto, Pioneer Hi-Bred, Bayer CropScience, and Syngenta. In August 2008, Monsanto also became an investor in Evogene, purchasing an $18 million equity stake in the company, with an agreement for $12 million more in the future.

Today, thirty years after the spectacular revival of ALZA based on the delivery of drugs through skin patches—a breakthrough in applied medicine—Gerstel is a rich and rooted man. He lives with Shoshana in a mansion of Jerusalem stone and filigreed arches on the same Ethiopia Street where they met, a vantage as lofty in repute and vista as Russian Hill in San Francisco. On the corner is a vast mansion owned by Ira Rennert, owner also of the largest house in the Hamptons on Long Island.

Nearby is the former home of famous pianist and political writer, the late David Bar-Ilan. In this historic district in the heart of Jerusalem, Gerstel seems fulfilled. When the intifada reached his part of town early in the decade and festered for a year and a half, he refused to change his habits in any way, striding confidently around the city. "It's just part of living in Israel," he says. "You have to accept it."

Chairman or founder of some fifteen companies in Israel, Gerstel is the driving force of the emergence of the country as a leader in biotech. In Israel, he is chairman not only of Compugen and Evogene but also a founder of Itamar Medical. Itamar has discovered a way to measure signals non-invasively from the autonomic nervous system that indicate heart problems long before they develop. Another device, its Watch-PAT200, can be worn around a patient's wrist to monitor sleep apnea as it occurs. Gerstel is also a director of Teva Pharmaceutical Industries, the world's leading generic drug company, and Yeda Research and Development, a technology-licensing vehicle for the Weizmann Institute of Science, which is responsible for dozens of Israeli biotech start-ups. Collectively, Gerstel's companies represent a new frontier of Israel's economy.

At the heart of this frontier are Israeli research universities. In the United States, inventor-prophet Ray Kurzweil has long predicted the development of nano-computers that can flow through the bloodstream, calculate imbalances, and emit the appropriate medicines. Ehud Shapiro of the Weizmann Institute has now created the first prototype, a new nano-computer based on DNA molecules. It is a new programmable machine that can be implanted into the body and address diseases before they show any symptoms. With a knack for publicity as strong as Kurzweil's, Shapiro has found his way into the *Guinness Book of World Records* for the smallest biocomputing device.

Professors Aaron Ciechanover and Avram Hershko, of the Technion, and Professor Irwin Rose of the University of California, Irvine, won the Nobel Prize in Chemistry in 2004 for their discovery of a new biological molecule so pervasive it is called Ubiquitin. It is responsible for breaking down proteins in cells and controlling many biological processes such as cell division, which fixes DNA and critical parts of the immune system. This molecule fits well into the Compugen model, as does Copaxone—a synthetic peptide developed by Weizmann Institute researchers to relieve the ravages of multiple sclerosis, and already generating revenues of some $600 million for Teva.

From Given Imaging's ingestible cameras to Compugen's peptidome, Israeli biotechnology and medical machines are a convergent harvest of the country's unique algorithmic sciences, all ultimately a spawn of von Neumann's gift to the world.

CHAPTER TWELVE

Hong Kong in the Desert

F inance feeds on the same resources as technological enterprise—the same infrastructure of educational institutions and of accounting and law, and the same agility of intellect. The successful allocation of capital, like the launch of a new technology, is an elegant expression of the capitalist law that mind rules and matter serves, just as the squandering of capital can create economic havoc far beyond that wrought by any supposedly critical scarcity of material goods.

In this most intellectual of capitalist endeavors Jews throughout history have excelled. And yet Israel until recently was almost entirely barren of financial industry. Through the 1950s, finance in Israel mimicked banking in the Soviet Union more than banking in the United States. Even until the 1990s, Israel was amazingly devoid of any capabilities in money management—with virtually no investment houses, deep capital markets, or venture capital. With performance fees barred, hedge funds were essentially illegal. Even into the early years of the twenty-first century, Israel remained a pathetic laggard in finance. As young Israeli financier Tal Keinan now tells the story, "All my Jewish friends were making their money at

Goldman Sachs, while Israel's finance was dominated by a heavily subsidized labor union."

A powerful motive of Zionism was to escape the Jewish archetypes of Europe—the image of shylocks and middlemen. Internalizing this most persistent and destructive of anti-Semitic slanders, Israelis long saw banks as a necessary evil. They wanted to stay as far away as possible from such industries as money lending, banking, trading, factoring, and arbitrage. To this day, most long-term retirement savings and insurance funds in Israel remain in the grip of Histadrut, under actuarial commitments that assure a real, inflation-adjusted, 6 percent yield guaranteed by the government. Despite this huge subsidy, Histadrut in its role as manager of a complex of largely government-owned businesses needs regular bailouts from the taxpayers.

The ideal of the more romantic, early brand of Israeli economics was a kibbutz with communal ownership, communal childrearing, and no private property (although the kibbutzim constantly proved the futility of these goals by giving them up in practice). For decades, Israelis doggedly shunned the processes of financial development that Ronald McKinnon of Stanford has shown are necessary for any enduring economic growth. Perhaps the most ironic symbol of this Israeli predicament is the Rothschild family's engagement in Israel. Although the Rothschilds were Europe's paramount banking family and in the late nineteenth century were prime supporters of Zionism, their only legacy in Israel is the founding of the modern Israeli wine industry.

Throughout the epoch of Israeli technological ascent, most of the money for Intel Israel and its followers came from the Israeli government or from U.S. technology companies. As Jonathan Medved observed, "What Israeli investors there were at the time were all trying to imitate U.S. venture capitalists." The pioneers were former Israeli Air Force commander Gideon Tolkowsky and Yadin Kaufmann of Athena Venture Partners. With U.S. partner, venture capitalist Fred Adler, the first venture-capital group in Israel was founded in 1985 with $29 million. Edward Mlavsky, who made *aliya* after leading Tyco through the go-go conglomerating years of the late 1960s and early 1970s, came to Israel to retire and launched the BIRD (Binational Industrial Research and Development) Foundation in the late 1970s for U.S.-Israeli R&D joint ventures. Then he began Gemini which eventually became the leading Israeli venture firm.

Aiding these early efforts were tax cuts undertaken in response to the economic crisis from 1980 and 1984, which saw inflation peak to nearly 1000 percent in 1984, even as the real economy contracted and tax receipts fell sharply. The tax cuts, modest compared to Bibi Netanyahu's more fundamental reforms in the 1990s, did reduce top personal tax rates of 60 percent down to 48 percent, as well as make significant if smaller reductions in business taxes. The results duplicated those of virtually every significant reduction in top marginal tax rates anywhere in the world for which we have decent data: economic growth surged, inflation fell (down to 11 percent by 1993), and tax receipts rose. And Netanyahu's reduction in personal tax rates continues—to a planned 39 percent by the year 2015.

A major driver of the ascent of Israeli venture capital was the Yozma program in 1993, which waived double taxation on foreign venture-capital investments in Israel and put up a matching fund of $100 million from the government. With overseas Jews from the United States and Russia immigrating to Israel, demand for the money was so intense that the government hiked the amount and doubled the matching-funds requirement. These moves helped spur the venture-capital upsurge in Israel.

Nonetheless, as the millennium dawned, Israel had still failed to create a financial services industry or wrest control of much of Israel's capital from the hands of Histadrut. When asked to address issues of finance, Israelis still wandered through the fogs of Socialist nostalgia with a handout and a "what-me-worry" look. Although the country managed to tap U.S. capital, it lacked the ability to mobilize capital in Israel. There were still no investment banks, or flexible capital markets, and few financial services firms to speak of. Israelis remained virtually the world's only Jews baffled by the prospect of handling money.

Without a financial industry, Israel would continue to be a charity case, dependent for funds on American Jewish organizations and individual Jews such as Mike Milken and Gary Winnick of Drexel Burnham back in the late 1980s. "We'd put up the money, but we'd never see any of it again," Winnick recalls. "I think the Israelis went off and spent it on matzos."

Getting the Israelis decisively out of their Socialist slough into the modern world of finance took the ingenuity of Benjamin Netanyahu, an indefatigable campaigner for allowing capitalist acts among consenting-adult Jews outside the United States. In the 1990s, climaxing during his administration as prime minister between 1996 and 1999, he promoted a supply-side program of tax-rate reductions, exemptions from double taxation for foreign investors, trade liberalization, and venture-capital programs. Netanyahu was as responsible as any other single man for the rousing Israeli economic revival of the 1990s, with every tax cut bringing in floods of new revenue.

Netanyahu's greatest achievements in his struggle to free the Israeli economy came during the first decade of the twenty-first century when he served as finance minister under Ariel Sharon. With his unique grasp of the intricacies of both the Israeli and the American political systems and his intimate connections in both countries, the MIT graduate and Boston Consulting Group alumnus took the opportunity to transform Israel's economy from a largely socialized domain dependent on foreign finance into one of the world's most open and flourishing financial systems. In the process he created what occasional advisor Tal Keinan calls "the greatest opportunity in our lifetimes."

During a financial crisis in 2003 and 2004 in the midst of the Palestinian intifada, Netanyahu proposed a series of radical reforms. Included were privatization of the banks and other major Israeli corporations, further reductions in tax rates for investment, and new laws authorizing investment banks and hedge funds.

As an Israeli supply-sider, Netanyahu faced the adamant opposition of Histadrut and its allies in the Knesset. Confronting an internal Israel test, Netanyahu finally managed to overcome the hostility to finance capitalism that had long hobbled the Israeli economy. But he could not do it without vital help from President George W. Bush and his treasury secretary John Snow.

With financial markets shaken by recent memories of bombs going off in buses and cafés and with the United Nations blaming Israel's conservative government under Ariel Sharon, the country could sell its government securities only with a punishing risk premium. This problem hit the Knesset politicians where they lived; if they could not issue government bonds, they would be largely out of business. Netanyahu sought a sovereign loan guarantee from the United States that would give Israeli bonds the full faith and credit of the United States Treasury, so they could issue bonds on the same terms as the world's leading economy. It was a bold request, but Israel was in dire straits, and the U.S. government wanted to help the country.

The United States, however, did not want to appear to be a patsy of Israel. Snow felt that he could not put the U.S. taxpayer on the line guaranteeing Israeli bonds without a major quid pro quo from Israel. What would that quid pro quo be? Well, Bush and Snow decided to be tough. They would have to hurl Netanyahu head over heels into the briar patch of a bristling battle with the Knesset over financial reform.

In exchange for the American guarantees, Snow stipulated that the Israeli finance minister secure from the Israeli parliament a series of drastic financial reforms that would forever change the nature of the Israeli economy. Israel would have to give up its nationalized banks and industries, its socialized insurance and pension systems, its sclerotic double and triple taxes on foreign investment, its bans on hedge funds, its sweetheart Histadrut labor bonds, and its handout "woe-is-me" culture. It could have been no coincidence that the massive reforms stipulated by Snow turned out to be exactly the reforms Netanyahu was already preparing for Israel's economy.

Under the pressure of the crisis of Israeli bonds, the Knesset was trapped. Sure enough, there were protests and complaints about the ruthless American conservatives and their Israeli patsies. But the Israeli legislators ultimately had to succumb.

As Netanyahu put it at the time: "By meeting the goals of the economic plan, we were able to receive U.S. government financial guarantees that helped us stabilize Israel's economy and reinforce faith in it. At the same time it should be noted that these guarantees were given gradually and that they are dependent on meticulous implementation of the reforms."

Enacted in late 2004, the Netanyahu–Snow agenda was put into effect on January 1, 2005. Jews in Israel could at last escape their captivity to the anti-capitalist prejudices they had absorbed from their persecutors.

First Histadrut had to give up its direct line to the Israeli treasury. The Histadrut bond would be entirely phased out over a period of twenty years. Starting immediately with the first 5 percent of its holdings, Histadrut would need to begin finding other ways to invest its $300 million per month of cash flow from the slowly expiring bond. Somehow a financial industry would have to arise in Israel to handle this huge trove of funds.

A second briar-patch reform demanded by Snow was immediate privatization of Israel's state-owned industries, reducing government ownership from 60 to 20 percent. Among the privatized ventures were nearly all the banks, the government oil refineries, the Bezeq telephone monopoly, and the EL AL national airline.

The third key reform that could make the others work was emancipation of the financial services industry, complete with legalization of investment banks, enablement of international private equity funds, performance fees for hedge funds, and elimination of double taxes not merely on investments in Israel but also on international investment activities by Israelis. For Israel to become a global financial center, it could not impose punitive tolls on all transactions in Israel.

At a time when U.S. finance is in chaos, this liberation of the Israeli economy represents one of the largest opportunities in the history of finance. Ready to seize it is Tal Keinan, a young Israeli financier, one of four brothers born and raised in the United States.

After studying Hebrew and Arabic at Georgetown University's School of Foreign Service, Keinan went to Tel Aviv University and fell in love with Israel. To this formidably brilliant, good-looking, and ardently articulate young American Jew, Israel possessed the excitement of a work in progress, on the cusp of history. He wanted to be part of it.

Serving as a fighter pilot in the Israeli Air Force, he ended up with the rank of major and became commander of the IAF

Combat Flight Instructor School. Until 2005, he was an active partner in Giza Venture Capital, one of Israel's leading venture-capital firms. From this vantage point he watched the opportunity in Israeli finance grow bigger and bigger by the month after the Netanyahu reforms were enacted, as Histadrut's bonds matured without being replaced, and the money piled up at the rate of some $300 million every thirty days. He was sure that other Israelis, older and more experienced, would rush in to provide the necessary services.

Finally, in September, he decided to act. He went to his venture partners at Giza and announced that he was leaving to form a new financial services firm in Israel. It would be called KCPS and Company, after the names of the founding partners. The business plan was to exploit the tremendous mismatch between the opportunity created by the emancipation of the Israeli economy and the huge untapped resource of pent-up Jewish financial talent.

Keinan began by calling friends in New York, one working with George Soros, another at Goldman Sachs, a third running his own hedge fund. Putting up $100 thousand apiece, they launched the new financial services company. Raising $26 million to invest, they were on their way. As word got out of this new venture in Israel, unexpected talent showed up. Morris Smith, who had run the Fidelity Magellan Fund, retired in Israel, moving to the occupied territories. He arrived at KCPS ready to go to work for no salary ("I'll eat what I kill"). Joining an advisory board was Jay Pomrenze, an industry leader and pioneer of the trading desk at Bankers Trust Company before it was purchased by Deutsche Bank. Pomrenze had made all the money that he wanted to make before the age of sixty, and his residual role had diminished to a seat on the Deutsche Bank board of directors. But he soon agreed to become CIO of KCPS.

Within two years of its founding, KCPS had thirty-eight traders and funds of $550 million under management. It is organized into two groups. One is devoted to fund management and includes a hedge fund of funds, a private equity operation, and a private wealth management team. The other group is a trading desk dealing in currencies and commodities. Some 80 percent of its customers and 30 percent of its investments are outside Israel.

Keinan's firm, emblematic of the new regime, is only one of many that will arise. Israel's transformation has just begun. With U.S. finance in chaos and operating under the threat of further regulation, Israel is moving in the opposite direction. Its increasingly free and creative financial markets can play an important role in preserving and expanding the capital of the West.

Crucial to Netanyahu's vision is the power of Israel as a global financial center to transform the economics of the Middle East. Israel can become the "Hong Kong of the Desert." Hong Kong ultimately reshaped the Chinese economy in its own image when Deng Xiaoping mimicked its free economics in his free-zone program. Even the conflict between Taiwan and Communist China became insignificant when China turned capitalist and most of Taiwan's investment moved to the mainland. Under Netanyahu, Israel can become a similar force for economic liberation in the Middle East, reaching out to Palestinians and other Arabs with the blandishments of commercial opportunity. After all, it has long been Israeli enterprise, the efflorescence of the desert that has attracted Arabs to the country. Netanyahu has long believed that the Peace Process as we have known it is irrelevant, focused on a handful of issues that could have been designed to breed anger and perpetuate conflict. Meanwhile, peace and the promise of a decent life lay waiting to be picked up by those Palestinians and Israelis who are willing and now increasingly able to invest in creation over destruction.

PART THREE

The Paradox
of Peace

CHAPTER THIRTEEN

Peace Now

Next to the Dan Hotel in Tel Aviv is the glittering Raphael Resto-Bistro, featuring culinary specialties from Morocco and Japan. Our host for the evening, Shaul Olmert, oldest son of then prime minister Ehud Olmert, takes us to a table in the middle facing a panoramic front window.

Named after a novel by the pioneering Zionist Theodor Herzl, Tel Aviv (*Hill of Spring*) is a grand modern city full of the feel and spirit of Silicon Valley's San Jose, with a beach. The Raphael overlooks Tel Aviv's seafront promenade. At sunset, as we sit down for dinner on a December day, a stream of joggers plods by across the sand with the sweaty seriousness of Californians.

Olmert has been a Californian, working in Irvine for MTV Corporation, adapting their TV properties to the digital-game industry. Now he has gone on to become a game-technology entrepreneur himself. As the son of the former prime minister, he saliently represents a new generation of Israelis, perhaps the most entrepreneurial cohort of all, offering new promise for the future of his country, and perhaps a portent of its still possible failure.

The Resto-Bistro chef is the young Olmert's pal and will ply his guests with suitably exotic fare—"don't bother about the menu," he says. "Do you want Israeli wine or Californian?" Then, sampling the best Israeli wines and hors d'oeuvres, Shaul will answer a question on the sources of Israeli entrepreneurship by talking about survival.

He recounts the astonishing trek of his grandparents Mordechai and Bella from the pogroms of Odessa in the Ukraine in the 1920s across the Russian steppes all the way to China, where they eke out a living for ten years in Harbin in the northeast, learn Mandarin, and briefly marry others before finally decamping to the wilderness of 1930s' Palestine. "They had to give up everything, all their possessions, every convenience, to make it happen," as Shaul puts it. "They were innovators, border crossers, rule breakers, entrepreneurs of survival. They were Zionists above all, but they were citizens of the world. Mordechai's last words were spoken in Mandarin."

He pauses. "Did you like those appetizers?"

"Yeah they're 'licious," I mumble through a mouthful of hummus, salmon, and wasabi.

In Palestine, the saga of the Olmert's grandparents became even more tempestuous. It was not simply entrepreneurship or nimble survival tactics. Mordechai joined the guerrilla group Irgun to fight against British limits on Jewish immigration to Palestine and against what he saw as the appeasement of Britain and the Arabs by David Ben-Gurion's Mapai Party and its military arm, Haganah. Called terrorists at the time and still today, and pursued by Haganah during the "Hunting Season" of 1945, the Irgun under Menachem Begin demonstrated that the British could not pursue their curious imperial romance with the Arabs without cost. As the Irgun argued, violence was "the new Esperanto" (the once fashionable "world language" created by the Jewish physician Ludwik Zamenhof).

At a time when Europe's death camps were in full operation, releasing Jewish refugees by the millions, and Arabs under the leadership of the British-appointed Grand Mufti Haj Amin al-Husseini were already avid for a new Holocaust, the British were actually cutting back drastically on immigration to Palestine. Appeasing the Arabs who had allied with the Nazis, rather than rewarding Jews who had fought them, the British were proposing to limit the numbers of Jewish immigrants to Palestine to seventy-five thousand over five years.

In the context of the time, the Irgun was fully understandable and may have played a key role in the formation of the new state. Irgun's most infamous terrorist act, the bombing of the British Army Headquarters at the King David Hotel, was preceded by three phone calls warning the occupants to evacuate. With the state on the way in 1948, Begin gave up all resistance. Mordechai Olmert lived to see the troubled caesarian birth of Israel. In the end, their son Ehud would grow up to become mayor of Jerusalem and then prime minister.

"In Israel," explains the young Shaul, "you keep coming up with ways that will allow you to survive and allow you to grow. This is why Israelis are so innovative. We have to be entrepreneurs, to survive."

"But it's not just survival," Olmert continues. "The second reason for Israeli innovation is . . . Look around you." He waves his arms toward other tables full of denim and suits and faces evocative of a similar scene in San Jose. "You see people that look like Russians, like British, like Iraqis, Ethiopians, different cultures, thrown here together at the same time, with the need to survive. Within three months in the States, you're an American. You feel like an American. But in Israel it's different. There are so many cultures, and no one culture defined Israel before that, so each one of us adopted some of the culture of the other.

This leads to tolerance of other cultures and a talent for dealing with them."

After stints of education in new media at Stuttgart and NYU, and employment in London, Los Angeles, Paris, and New York, and even some surfing in Huntington Beach, California, Olmert began thinking globally. He smiles: "When I was in the States, my friends at MTV used to say: '*You* go deal with the French people at Vivendi. We really don't *get* those guys. Those guys are impossible. You go to Paris and work it out.' As an Israeli you are a citizen of the world. You live your life adjusting who you are talking to and who you work with."

Now, as a serial entrepreneur of video-game companies, Shaul claims the world's first system for "streaming applications over the net," the world's first OS-neutral video-game player runtime engine, and the world's first set of in-game utilities to enhance the realism of the experience of massively parallel on-line multiplayer games such as World of Warcraft ("Look, Mom—no browser!") Here the great challenge of survival is to reach the next level of the game—whether it's "hyperspace" or a NASDAQ IPO.

"Nothing excites Israelis so much as the idea that something is impossible. Goes back to the fact that the whole being of this state of Israel is risky. The entire state is a new venture." As Fox pundit Dan Senor and Saul Singer of the *Jerusalem Post* write in their pioneering new book, Israel is the *Start-Up Nation*.

Olmert goes on: "If you want to send a space ship to Mars . . . next Thursday . . . you will get Israeli engineers to work on that project, and the spaceship will go out to Mars next Thursday . . . *but* it might *not* come back.

"If you want the spaceship to go to Mars *every* Thursday *and* come back you want American engineers. It will take longer but it *will* go to Mars every Thursday and it will come back.

"The Americans are good at systems and planning," he observed. "I wish the Israelis were better at planning. But they're not. But they are good at innovating."

Shaul is sure that Israel's test of survival, daily undergone, is the secret of Israeli enterprise. "When you're concerned about your survival, *every day*, you think outside of the box . . ."

As he says this he imagines that he has been doing it, thinking out there beyond the "pale of settlement," beyond the flapping tongues and flags of tradition. For all his talk of innovation and survival, Shaul is an utterly conventional follower of the Israeli Left.

He is uncertain how his wealth contributes to the world or to Israel. "Wealth is finite," he says. "If one side gets too much, the other side will suffer." As his colleague Itzik Ben-Bassat explains his game technology to me, Shaul looks off into the darker recesses of the restaurant with a look of anxiety, the features of his father imprinted on his handsome young countenance, but as if haunted by a harrowing memory or a portentous future lurking in the darkness. It seems as if all is not well with the rebel youth and his virtual games, as if from the kitchens of the seaside bistro may burst forth at any moment a Palestinian mob of busboys and waiters demanding a redistribution of the wealth, or an Arab capital in Tel Aviv, or as if his father might suddenly loom up out of the shadows and reproach the son for his globalist views and hedonist games. Shaul wants to move ahead with his company and his life. He is impatient with the perils and moral entanglements of his country. Playing it safe, he retains his apartment in New York and will send his children to summer camp in upper New York state. Like so many, he wants "Peace Now."

"I have never tried to run away from my Judaism," he explains. "As a Jew growing up I heard many stories about the sufferings of Jews, the fear, the Holocaust. As a Jew I'm obliged to be sensitive to the suffering of others. The occupation is making us less moral and less sensitive to the suffering of other people. I don't want to occupy other people. It is important for Americans to be good. I fear that Israelis are losing their moral bearings."

"I want the Palestinians to have a better life," he says. "The reality today is we're sitting here in this nice restaurant having a nice dinner and an interesting conversation while 4 million Palestinians live in misery.

"I support the Peace Process and the withdrawal from the territories."

I point out that withdrawal will not help the Palestinian Arabs. As Jonathan Adiri, a top advisor to President Shimon Peres, told us earlier that afternoon, it is not that simple. I recall standing on a promontory near Gilo in Jerusalem looking down across the valley into the West Bank at an elegant four-story mansion a few hundred yards away and from which a stream of bullets had issued during the intifada toward an apartment complex on the top of the hill. Pointing to the entangled weave of ethnic communities, Adiri told us of the failure of all efforts to separate the Palestinian Arabs from the Jews. "We expected the Palestinians to gravitate to their own communities but instead the prosperity and growth in the Jewish parts of Jerusalem acted like a magnet."

From the beginning, the Arabs have been attracted to parts of Palestine that the Jews have been enriching. They don't want to move toward the existing Palestinian communities. They vote with their feet. It is the Palestinians who would benefit from the overthrow of the leaders sacrificing them to the jihad—leaders who say they would rather their people suffer for "a hundred years" than prosper by working with Israelis.

I try a new tact. "Arafat died in a house with piles of *Mein Kampf*," I point out.

Olmert laughed bitterly and then launched a riff familiar on the Israeli Left: "Yes, I know we did a terrible job in picking our enemies. A lousy job. I apologize. Next time we should do better. We *will* do better. I promise. We'll audition them better. Find nicer guys to oppose us. I'll give it more thought."

Until then they would seek "Peace Now."

Before meeting him, I already knew that Shaul was not all fun and games. I had read of a petition that he had signed from a protest group urging Israel's reserve forces to refuse to serve in the "territories." I also learned of his famously lesbian sister Dana, who had joined a rowdy protest march against the Israel Defense Forces for their apparent responsibility for a deadly explosion on a beach in Gaza that accidentally killed eight members of a Palestinian family. "The Intifada Will Prevail," read a placard in the march.

The Olmert family accepted the rebellion of Dana, according to Shaul, and Shaul apologized for embarrassing his father. But they did not recant their positions. As Shaul explained: "My father is paying the price for being a liberal person. It kind of reminds me of this movie *Guess Who's Coming to Dinner*, this movie in which two parents raised their daughter to be very liberal and very open-minded and one day she comes home from college and brings her new boyfriend and they find out that he's an African American and they are trying to be very liberal and politically correct about it, but they're also kind of stunned by their daughter's choice.

"So I guess that my father was in a similar sort of internal debate throughout our childhood because we definitely used the freedom that we were granted and the encouragement to think for ourselves and develop our own views, and we developed our own views, which happen not to coincide with his."

Nonetheless, the Olmert kids were altogether too trigger-happy in blaming Israel first for violence instigated by enemies set on their country's destruction. In the end, he and his sister are privileged children assuming costly moral postures that are inevitably paid for by the less fortunate. Jihadists will inevitably see pacifism and other dissension in Israel's then "first family" as a sign of weakness. Conspicuous weakness is a prime cause of war.

Olmert reminded me of Bernard Avishai, a similarly impatient Israeli leftist who has published a passionate book entitled *The Hebrew Republic* in a kind of quest for a separate Peace Now. A shaggy professor with a plaintive manner of speech, as I recall from his editing one of my articles for the *Harvard Business Review* some twenty years ago, he has long seen Zionism as "a tragedy." Nothing that has happened in Israel in recent years has dissuaded him from the view that the country as currently constituted is a gigantic mistake. His catalog of complaints echoes Shaul Olmert's: discrimination against Arabs, sorely maldistributed wealth and income, a runaway engine of West Bank settlements that represent an imperial "occupation," and an impending demographic catastrophe caused less by the more procreative Arabs in Israel than by philoprogenitive Haredim and other ultra-Orthodox Jews. Over the last twenty years the Orthodox share of the population has risen from 10 percent to around 25 percent. By any reasonable standard, these defenders of the faith represent the answer to the demographic crunch caused by secular Israelis with their abortion culture and their gay-rights marches. Yet it is Orthodox population growth that disturbs the Israeli Left.

All in all, in Avishai's vision, Israel is a deeply flawed democracy twisted by special laws favoring Conservative religious Jews and Judaism, by racism and segregation, by the Law of Return, by a labyrinthine separatist wall, by an ethnocentric national anthem and a Davidic flag, and by other grievous offenses to Palestinian Arabs.

In his book, Avishai collects his petitions and amasses his complaints from the usual trio of eminent Israeli writers: Amos Oz, A. B. Yehoshua, and David Grossman. But he adds a variety of Palestinian Arab, Arab Israeli, and Christian Arab vendors of politically blighted belletristic angst, all seeking—with suitable ironic glosses and abraded sensibilities—to blame Israel first for a failure to achieve Peace Now.

The general posture of all these Israeli cosmopolitans is a belief that the conflict in the Mideast is somehow the fault of the Jews, who are too religious and too xenophobic and insufficiently democratic, tolerant, pacific, idealistic, sensitive, sacrificial, and visionary to negotiate a satisfactory peace.

Knowing that in general capitalism does not work amid violence, Avishai contends that the prime supporters of Peace Now should be venture capitalists and entrepreneurs. And indeed, like Shaul Olmert, many of them are. Avishai's prime source is none other than Dov Frohman, the inspired inventor and Intel executive whom we have met before. Now he fears that his proud new Intel Fab 18 at Kiryat Gat in the southern Israeli desert will be exposed to attack from the latest generation of rockets in Gaza.

Frohman has long been one of my heroes. He was the pioneering entrepreneur in Israel. But he now lives in the Dolomite mountains in northern Italy for much of the year and has absorbed the syndrome of Euro-pessimism about Israel.

"The vital signs seem okay," Frohman tells Avishai, "but we are really in the dumps, socially, morally, culturally, everything. This is a drugged democracy, which is worse than a dictatorship, because in a dictatorship you try to rebel—and in this place you don't do anything. We need some kind of catalyst to get people to the streets. We need to start talking about social issues—and without the generals doing the talking."

That will do it, I thought. That's just what Israel needs to rev up its economy and impress the jihad: more street protests and more talk about "social issues."

Frohman is glum even about the technologies he pioneered—which brought me to Israel—and are attracting entrepreneurs and investors from around the world. Told that Bibi Netanyahu deems Israel's increasing lead in technology as a durable basis of national strength, Frohman retorts: "This is bullshit. *Bullshit.* Investors will not come to us in a big way unless there is political stability . . . What Bibi says is demagoguery. He's done some of the right things, which in a healthy environment would have been pretty good. But before these policies can have an impact, we'll have more violence."

Frohman disparages the surge of investment in Israel during the first decade of the new century. "There is a lot of financial type of investment but little production type of investment—these are investments which can be taken out at will. And in the meantime, we are losing our reputation as a place for global companies to pioneer."

He asks Avishai: "What will make our entrepreneurs want to stay in Israel, if they don't have quality of life? There is continuous movement of people, they will want to stay elsewhere. . . . But the really critical thing is keeping our young people here. I don't need to do a poll to know that 50 percent of the young people would go."

Frohman and Avishai have absorbed the Peace Now mantra and message that Israel has become an aggressive and even imperialist power. They don't like the Orthodox religious forces in Israel that are the hope of the future demographically, the quarter of the population that bears most of its children. They don't like the politics with its multiple parties and interest groups. They don't like the culture that derided Dana Olmert's gay pride and resisted a planned march of gays, lesbians, bisexuals, transgenders, and such down by the Western Wall. They believe that both the gays and the Palestinians are essentially moral and right in their claims. If the Arabs take over Jerusalem, it may become less gay in the Old City, but the Olmerts will be long gone, and Avishai will be tending his garden in Wilmot, New Hampshire. All these Israeli dissidents can justify their multiple-passport lives by echoing the angst of the novelist protestors such as Amos Oz, who puts it as bluntly as any anti–Semite: "We're the Cossacks now, and the Arabs are the victims of the pogroms, yes, every day, every hour."

Is there something about novelists and intellectuals that makes them incapable of grasping the reality of enemies that want to destroy your country and you, enemies contemptuous of all your legal nuances, literary apercus, civil-liberties refinements, Booker Prizes, and generous globalist poses? Oz, Grossman, and A. B. ("Bulli") Yehoshua, all proud advocates of Peace Now, all want to give up the land of others—settlers—for what is called "peace."

It has long appeared to be a plausible strategy, upheld by each successive Israeli and U.S. administration and by many sophisticated observers and activist experts blind to the obduracy of Israel's opponents. Israel took land from the Palestinian Arabs in the wars of 1948 and 1967. "Now it is time to relinquish it for peace."

It makes sense. Why not Peace Now? *Shalom Achshav.*

In the end, Shaul and Dana won their debate with their father. Once assertive about Israel's right to settle in Judea, Samaria, and Gaza, Ehud Olmert concluded that because of the demographic trends, Arabs would come to dominate any Israeli state that included the territories. He became the single Israeli prime minister most avidly committed to achieving peace with the Palestinians, Syria, and Lebanon. He supported the withdrawal from Gaza and the removal of some twenty-five thousand Jewish settlers from there. In secret negotiations in 2008 with Mahmoud Abbas, the Palestinian Authority's president, he offered to withdraw from the territories, divide Jerusalem, and give scores of thousands of Palestinians the "right to return" to Israel. He declared the West Bank settlements illegal, attempted to uproot several of them, and was willing to remove all of them, a quarter-million people.

In this pursuit, he gained the support of the Bush administration, which dispatched Secretary of State Condoleezza Rice to the region sixteen times in twenty-one months to bring about peace and to arrange peace talks at Annapolis.

The conventional wisdom is that Olmert, Rice, and Bush were unlucky or maladroit in their negotiating tactics. Experts declared it "ironic" that this ardent pursuer of Peace Now found himself fighting two wars, one in 2006 with Hezbollah, and one in 2008 and 2009 with Hamas in Gaza. Following the withdrawal from Gaza, Israel won no plaudits or support from the international community and no respite from attacks. Since 2001, Hamas and its allies have targeted towns in southern Israel with more than four thousand rockets and thousands of mortar shells. After Israel withdrew entirely from the Gaza Strip in August 2005, rocket attacks increased fivefold.

Following the Hamas rockets came an Israel incursion into Gaza in the last month of 2008 and first month of 2009. Entitled crudely "Operation Cast Lead," it destroyed scores of arms-smuggling tunnels, dozens of ministry buildings and offices, police stations, military targets associated with Hamas, and several Hamas officials.

The result was a huge uproar from the United Nations and other bodies, widespread demands for a cease-fire, and pervasive denunciations of the "disproportionality" of the Israeli response. The *New York Times*, the *Economist*, and *Time* all treated the conflict as an opportunity to tote up the number of civilian casualties on the Gaza side. It was pointed out that the some four hundred Gazan civilians lost exceeded by a factor of one hundred the civilian deaths in Israel that provoked the incursion.

When Israel withdrew after twenty-two days amid Hamas' claims of victory, the United States promised some $900 million for Gaza, to be channeled through the United Nations. Since Hamas continues to control Gaza and to intimidate the UN officials who persisted in taking the Hamas side in the conflict, the chances of keeping the money out of Hamas' clutches seemed dim.

In exchange for expending a few million dollars on missiles, the jihadist group (or its Iranian sponsors) would eventually gain three times as much money from the United States ($900 million) as it has reportedly received from Iran. A week later some seventy countries and international organizations convened in the Red Sea resort of Sharm el-Sheikh and pledged an additional $4.48 billion, over $1.5 billion more than the Gazans had requested. Their cup runneth over. Again, the donors stressed that the money would all go to the Palestinian Authority, to Fatah rather than Hamas. But Hamas controls the territory, so it will extort a large proportion of the funds, regardless of contrary intentions. The clear lesson is that terrorism pays and pays. The donors will predictably get what they pay for. So what else is new?

Certainly this sequence of "Peace Now and Then War" was nothing new. It followed the previous even more avid pursuit of the Peace Now agenda by the Clinton administration, when Israel agreed to abandon 95 percent of the territories, financed a new PLO militia to keep order, and committed to a new Palestinian state and a divided Jerusalem. The world was euphoric again, in time with the Nobel Prizes awarded both to Arafat and to Yitzhak Rabin in 1994 for allegedly achieving peace.

The result was four years of intifada—suicide bombs and deadly attacks. But this, too, was nothing new. Similarly, after the 1967 war, in which Israel won a sweeping six-day victory, the country sought peace by proposing to give up its gain of territory. The result was repeated attacks by Nasser's Egyptian army at Suez and then the Arab–Israeli War of 1973, desecrating Israel's holiest day, Yom Kippur. With U.S. support, the Israelis managed to avoid defeat, consolidated their control of Sinai, and established thriving new settlements there. This, too, was nothing new.

Then in 1977, the supposedly bellicose Menachem Begin and the right-wing Likud Party displaced Ben-Gurion's Labor Party in Israel for the first time. The world was appalled. Around the globe and in Israel itself opinion leaders condemned the Israeli voters who, by electing a "former terrorist" to confront the urbane and civilized Egyptian leader Anwar Sadat, had effaced every moral distinction between the Arabs and Israelis. With Begin in power, war was believed to be inevitable.

The result, however, was again "ironic" and "baffling." Peace broke out. Not only did Sadat agree to talks, but he actually traveled to Israel, addressed the Knesset, and aroused the wild acclaim of Israeli crowds. As Ruth Wisse observed in her authoritative book *Jews and Power*, "The Israeli Hebrew press ran Arabic headlines to welcome the visitor, soccer fans proposed Israeli–Egyptian matches, Israeli radio played Egyptian music. The people of Israel 'fell in love with the enemy.'"

In the Camp David negotiations that followed, the reputedly pugnacious Begin succumbed to the Peace Now spirit. Under pressure from Sadat and then U.S. president and peace paladin Jimmy Carter, Begin gave up the Sinai and expelled the Jewish settlers. Israel might permit 15 percent of its population to be Arab, but the newly friendly Egyptians stopped well short of allowing a small but prosperous Jewish presence on their territory.

In conversation with Sadat, the former Israeli prime minister Golda Meir epitomized the Jewish stance, subordinating the pain of loss of Israeli soldiers to the pain of inflicting military losses: "We can forgive you for killing our sons, but we will never forgive you for making us kill yours." It's nice rhetoric, but in the usual liberal stance, she was elevating her own moral feelings above the practical effects of her actions.

As Wisse writes, "This point had been made long before by the foremost exegete Rashi . . . in his commentary on the passage of Genesis 32:4 . . . 'Jacob was very afraid and he was greatly distressed . . . lest he be killed by his brother Esau, but he was even more 'distressed' that in self-defense, he might have to kill Esau . . .' Whereas Rashi was expounding this high moral principle for his Jewish audience, Golda Meir was admitting it to an antagonist whose political traditions interpreted her confession as weakness. . . .

"Four years earlier, when Golda Meir had been prime minister, [Sadat] had coordinated with Syria the attack on Yom Kippur. . . . If he now came to Jerusalem to regain the territories lost by Egypt, it was not out of regret for having killed too many Jews but with the realization that he could not kill enough to defeat them."

Even so, his treaty with Israel, however favorable to his country, outraged the Arab League, which maintains a genocidal posture against Israel as its *raison d'être*. The league moved its headquarters out of Cairo to Tunis. Its hostility to Sadat continued until his assassination two years later by Hamas precursors from the Muslim Brotherhood.

But this was nothing new. When King Abdullah of Jordan

expressed his willingness to negotiate a treaty with Israel in 1951, he was assassinated by family members of the Grand Mufti of Jerusalem, Haj Amin al-Husseini, at the entrance of the al-Aqsa Mosque in the Holy City. That ended Jordanian moves for Peace Now. And this, too, was nothing new.

CHAPTER FOURTEEN

Games of War
and Holiness

Robert Aumann, a Nobel laureate economist, fled
Frankfurt with his parents in 1938 just two weeks
before Kristallnacht. A textile tycoon, the older
Aumann lost everything in his flight to New York and had to
scrounge for work. Aumann gained a clear notion from his father of the vulnerability of wealth and power.

From his point of view, the pattern of peace initiatives followed by war is neither "ironic" nor "baffling." It does not suggest that Israel somehow has failed to seek peace with sufficient
ardor and resourcefulness. It shows that by relentlessly seeking
Peace Now, Israel has predictably communicated to the Arabs
that terror and aggression work. By repeatedly informing the
Arabs that it wants peace more than it wants victory, Israel
evinces a short-term strategy that powerfully and consistently rewards bad behavior. As a result, Israel gets neither peace nor victory, and the Palestinians get neither economic growth nor
political progress. Peace Now is essentially a pursuit that gratifies
its preening pursuers and harrows everyone else.

Aumann's Center for the Study of Rationality at Hebrew

University is perched on Mount Scopus overlooking Jerusalem, and affords glimpses on good days of the mountains of Jordan and the Dead Sea. In 1999, Aumann became founder and first president of the Game Theory Society, and he has taught at Stanford, Princeton, State University of New York at Stony Brook, Berkeley, New York University, and Catholic University of Leuven in Belgium. He gains his insights as the leading living practitioner of the most austere and abstract of sciences: the game theory excogitated in a great synoptic burst by John von Neumann.

Originally based on simple games of strategy, such as poker, it applies to all situations of conflict and cooperation. After conceiving this discipline in a 1928 paper introducing the "Theory of Games," von Neumann developed its full mathematical foundations in stolen moments of collaboration with Oskar Morgenstern during World War II. Their masterpiece, the *Theory of Games and Economic Behavior*, published in 1944 by Princeton University Press, bristles with complex mathematics. Although it was one of the best-received books of the epoch, scrupulously weighed and fathomed by several current or future Nobel laureates among fifteen other major figures in economics and mathematics, it remained too formidable a restructuring of economics from the bottom up and too practical an application of pure mathematics from the top down to be readily absorbed by either of those disciplines. It caught on chiefly at the RAND Corporation, which was devoted to developing military strategies of nuclear deterrence after World War II.

Von Neumann was acting to save the social sciences from their towers of Babel—macro- and microeconomics, sociology and psychology, evolutionary biology and computer science, business strategy and military strategy, neuroscience and behavioral science, arms races and peace studies—and to unify them all under the aegis of a logical theory of rational interactions among purposeful agents.

Establishing the discipline on a coherent mathematical basis, von Neumann and Morgenstern took the study beyond zero-sum games, in which the winnings and losses of all parties add up to zero, to positive-sum games in which profits are generated and winnings exceed losses. This advance was critical. In zero-sum games, any winnings by an opponent come at the cost of other players. It is the law of the jungle and tends to degenerate to the war of all against all. The issue is how to convert such predatory games into positive-sum games of the golden rule, according to which the good fortune of others is also your own.

Von Neumann was always concerned with the dynamics of competitive processes and saw that economic systems could not achieve equilibrium outside an environment of growth. Capitalism by nature is a positive-sum game, in which every transaction theoretically can yield two or more winners. As long as the exchanges are voluntary, they will not occur unless both parties believe they will gain from them. This belief may sometimes be wrong. But since winnings accrue to those who arrange good deals for themselves and others, making them the dominant players in the game, the total of winnings—the economy—expands. Thus even less-skilled players also benefit, unless they opt out of the game by behaving in perverse and destructive ways. Shaul Olmert's theory of the global economy as a zero-sum game would have struck von Neumann as silly.

In politics, the occupation of Olmert senior, however, zero-sum elements do tend to prevail, with players contesting for a limited set of countries, government seats, and positions of authority in a finite planetary land mass. A longtime student of Morgenstern and admirer of von Neumann (who died too young for Aumann to have known him), Aumann built new and more robust bridges between the zero-sum predicament and the positive-sum world, taking the theory of games to a new level that casts unique light on the predicament of Israel.

Expounding his theory most relevantly and accessibly in "War and Peace," his Nobel lecture in Stockholm in December 2005, Aumann begins by making a clear distinction between one-time games and repetitive games. He shows that if you are not going to have any future relationships or transactions, the rational policy is predatory. The mugger or terrorist can be a rational man. The pursuer of a one-night stand has no reason not to lie and no incentive to gratify his prey. This grim fact is backed up by a large body of human experience and game-theory math.

It is repetition that makes cooperation achievable even when it cannot be summoned in one short game. Repetition of transactions over time and the extension of contracts through time is the heart of capitalism and of peaceful relationships among nations. Repetition is the bridge between the predatory present, the zero-sum moment, and the long-term sums of mutual learning and wealth.

In order to transform a zero-sum immediate game into a long-term economy, however, the long-term player must penalize bad behavior. If the predator gets away with his taking, he will continue to take. He will learn the law of the jungle. It is punishment that teaches him the greater gains of mutuality, investment, and trading.

The lesson for Israel is evident. "If you want peace now," Aumann says, "you may well never get peace. But if you have time—if you can wait—that changes the whole picture; *then* you may get peace now. This is one of the paradoxical, upside-down insights of game theory. . . . Wanting peace now may cause you never to get it—not now, and not in the future. But if you can wait, maybe you will get it now." And Israel can wait. Even the intifada did not interrupt the technology boom, while unilateralism in policy has worked very well.

Aumann's message is that civilization depends on long time horizons in repetitive games. In a single exchange, the rational policy is predatory. If predatory actions bring success, a player is never induced to extend the time horizon. By accommodating aggression, a nation invites it. Peace requires the imposition of penalties on aggression.

A critical element in all games is the discount rate, which determines the time value of the reward, the terms on which one can trade benefits now for benefits over the long run. In economics this factor is quantified as the rate of interest.

Capitalism works because of its long time horizons and low discount rates that optimize cooperative behavior. The time element is crucial to the deepening of capital and the generation of positive-sum games.

The more the players focus on politics rather than on economics, the more the game tends to deteriorate. Without capitalism, democracy is a zero-sum game and leads to conflict and war. Without the increasing economic rewards of an expanding pie of goods and assets, the democratic struggle for power hardly differs from a series of coups. In both cases, the losers are deprived not merely of political power but also of their livelihoods and their futures. The way to transcend the zero-sum trap into the golden-rule economy is to move from political and military relationships to the spirals of gain in capitalist economic interplay.

Missing a critical point, though, are utopian free marketeers, who imagine that a mere complex of free-trade agreements will bring about a world perfectly pacified by the lures of commerce. Essential to the transition is military power sufficient to defend against any feasible threat. Weakness enhances the rewards of adversaries' military strength. The kind of disarmament sought in the Peace Now spirit nearly always leads to war because it renders military strength relatively more rewarding than the saving and sacrifice needed for economic advance. Complete disarmament is the most dangerous situation of all since it offers the maximum reward for secret armament. Thus disarmament is likely to cause rapid and unpredictable acquisition of weapons and result in imbalances where aggression is rewarded. As the U.S. nuclear deterrent deteriorates, for example, the value of nuclear capabilities in Iran or other hostile countries rises inexorably.

Crucial to successful negotiation is commitment. Irrational behavior may be rational in a game if it conveys an absolute commitment to a goal. An example cited by Aumann is the "blackmailer's paradox."

Alice and Bob must divide a thousand dollars. It is not an ultimatum game; they can discuss it freely. Bob says to Alice, "Look, I want nine hundred of those thousand dollars. Take it or leave it. I will not walk out of this room with less than nine hundred dollars." Alice says, "Come on. That's crazy. We have a thousand dollars. We should divide it evenly."

"You may say it's crazy or not crazy, but I'm not walking out with less than nine hundred." Bob stands his ground, and since one hundred is better than nothing, Alice takes the hundred.

The paradox is that the irrational guy is Bob. He is crazy. But he gets nine hundred dollars. It would seem that in a rational game the irrational guy should get less rather than more. The answer to the paradox is that Alice can also declare that she's not walking out of here with less than nine hundred dollars. Then it becomes a test of wills and capabilities. The important thing is that the person who is making this demand has to convince the other one that he is absolutely serious.

Bob, when he says nine hundred dollars, has to convince

Alice that he is really serious. He's crazy, but he's serious. Alice, likewise—if she doesn't want to capitulate—has to convince Bob that she is serious. In order to convince the other person, you have to convince yourself. That is another part of the paradox. Conviction is a process of conversion in which identity itself is engaged. Such immovable convictions are often termed religious. In some sense, they transcend reason and partake of the domains of faith. The rational man at some point has to make a religious stand. He makes a commitment by declaring some entity as *holy*.

In this notion of sacred commitments are dissolved all the usual trite objections that game theory is valid only in a world inhabited by rational calculators engaged solely by materially calculable goals—by economic men. Focusing on behavior and response, the theory implicitly comprehends all motives, including sin and hate, love and worship. If the Palestinians, formed by more than a century of anti-Semitic propaganda, and current shame and envy, do in truth prefer killing Jews to life itself or to giving life to a Palestinian nation, then the game will accommodate that motive. Israel will build a fortress, backed by a nuclear deterrent and any further combination of needed deadly or defensive technologies. Precisely by taking the Palestinians at their word, the Israelis may cause them to think again. Perhaps life excluded from the wealthy fortress next door is not so attractive. Perhaps peace would at last seem preferable.

In early December 2008, I traveled to Toronto to see Aumann speak. It was a rare experience of the religion of rationality.

Aumann stood at the podium like a prophet, his giant, gnarly white beard splayed forth like a disheveled Santa's, his hoary voice tinged with hints of Hebrew, all lending a hallowed resonance to his words, which came slowly, one at a time, all at deliberate speed, as if extracted painfully and precariously from an aging brain, still lagging seven hours, or perhaps thirty-six centuries, behind the times of modern Toronto. For Aumann was trying to explain his ardent belief that his Canadian hosts for the evening, celebrating "Israel at Sixty"—and indeed most observers of Israel and its predicament—had gotten it wrong, way wrong, wrong by orders of magnitude.

As a preeminent living Israeli scientist and leading exponent of mathematical rationality, Aumann is one of the world's most modern thinkers. Although his prime field is game theory, he is one of the world's leading mathematicians and economists. But his audience tonight is a crowd of conservative Jews gathered in the comfort of the synagogue conference center of Aish Ha-Torah, meaning "Fire of the Torah." In the continuing conflict between the times and the Torah lies a revealing dimension of the Israel test. To the fire of the Torah, Aumann brings the ice of reason, but as the audience would learn, there is plenty of fire in his ice.

Nervous about Aumann's halting initial delivery and long, pregnant silences, some in his audience were shifting in their seats, half fearing that this crusty old prophet would break down. Others worried that he was coming down from his distant mountain in Jerusalem, enflamed with a vision of truth, to deliver an Israel test as a list of math problems. Or that he would unveil a series of stone tablets inscribed with a set of abstruse equations, together with the claim that his listeners must turn from the golden calves of commerce, the kosher feasts on the groaning boards of this gala event, and the numinous laws of the Torah upheld in this Orthodox synagogue, and bow to the revelation of mathematical logic. But Aumann had something else on his mind that evening. He would explain that his game-theory insights were all of a unity with his monotheistic Judaism. But his first observation was simple, factual, mathematical, and holy.

"Israel," he said, "is not sixty years old. It is *sixty times sixty* years old."

Gathered to celebrate and discuss "the state of our future" in black ties and evening ruffles, the audience was somber. Earlier in the evening Caroline Glick, the eloquent Cassandra of the *Jerusalem Post*, warned the group over dinner of the portentous meaning of the massacre of Jews a few days before at Mumbai's Chabad House in India, where jihadist terrorists took time off from an assault on the Taj Mahal Palace & Tower hotel and other monumental structures inherited from a long-gone empire to torture and kill a small assemblage of Jews at a non-descript school for orphans nearly a mile away.

"They did it," she said, "with long advanced planning and with an ecstatic relish of murderous hatred."

For twenty-four hours, the *New York Times*, CNN, and other notable media, as she reminded the audience, ignored the attack on the Chabad House. Then in subsequent days they appeared baffled by this digression in the path of terror, which struck the eminent editors of the *Times* as "senseless." They ruminated on the possible strategic significance of the Jewish center as a vantage point for an attack on Mumbai's more consequential targets, such as military bases or business centers. But Glick readily decoded the message from the bloody rubble and easily read the miasmic minds of the murderers.

"We recognize that wherever we are, the primary target is always us. The essential take-home lesson from Mumbai, the historic lesson from Mumbai, is that we are on our own. Our destiny is in no one's hands but our own. Our greatest achievements have come when we recognized that we must trust in ourselves. The greatest calamities come when we trust in others to save us. . . .

"That is what it means to be free. To look inside ourselves

and find what is valuable and good in ourselves and what must be defended. Depending on others is a form of slavery. It is self-awareness of worth and valor that separates a free person from a slave."

Glick's vision prepared the way for Aumann, who continued the lesson.

He began by reading the title of the conference from the program—"Israel at Sixty"—and then he told a story from scripture:

"Jacob and the man, the angel, struggled until the morning came and the man saw that he could not overcome Jacob, though he touched his rib and the rib moved. It was injured.

"The man said 'Send me away, the morning has come, make a truce with me, give me a cease-fire.' And Jacob responded: 'I will not send you away. I will not send you away, until you make peace with me . . . *until you have blessed me.*'

"And the angel asked him, 'What is your name?' and he said, 'Jacob.'"

"And the angel said, 'No longer will you be called Jacob, but *Israel.*'

"That was three thousand six hundred years ago. *Israel.* Why? Because you have struggled with angels and with peoples and you have been victorious. You made it. And he blessed him.

"Ladies and gentlemen," Aumann responded, "This is what is going on today. These verses reach down through the millennia. Jacob was left alone surrounded by enemies and then a man came and struggled with him. Who was that man? The spirit of Esau. The spirit of the nations, the spirit of the ages. That was the angel who struggled with Jacob. Jacob struggled not with a physical human being but with a conception: anti-Semitism. Beating down the Jews. He struggled with it. He does not give up. He is wounded. But he does not stop. Finally the angel said, 'I have to go.' Cease-fire. Let's make a truce. Let's go.

"'No,' responded Jacob, 'I will not stop until you accept me. You have to make peace with me. *You have to bless me.*'

"Then the angel said, 'OK, I bless you. Why do I bless you? Why do I make peace with you? Because you have held out in the struggle. You have shown to me you will not collapse. You are holding on to your principles. I have become finally convinced that you are not going to let go. You have convinced me of that. You will not let go. You have struggled with the concept, the idea of Esau, and with physical human beings, and you have overcome both on the spiritual plane and on the physical plane.'

"That is when Israel was created. It was three thousand six hundred years ago. Sixty times sixty years ago. Not sixty years ago.

"So it was up to Jacob. It was up to him and he did it. Just as in Caroline Glick's beautiful remarks at dinner, it's now up to us and we must do it. We have to keep on. If we want the blessing of our cousins, not only of our cousins, but if we want the blessing of the world, we have to keep up the struggle. Although we are wounded. In spite of our wounds. Which we have suffered again and again throughout this struggle, throughout this long night. This is what we have to do. If we want their blessing we have to keep up the struggle from our side."

Then, in the question and answer period, apparently in order to shake up his audience for a learning moment, he insisted, "The terrorists are rational. They are giving their lives. They are heroes of their people. They are heroes. . . ."

The moderator, Adrienne Gold, a Canadian TV personality, had had enough of this. She interrupted: "You mean there is no objective rationality? It's all relative?"

"Yes," he burst forth, "Of course there is no objective rationality. Congratulations. You have got it right. Rationality is the effective pursuit of your goals. The suicide bombers are rational, and they are getting their way. We have to understand they are rational in order to fight them."

"All right. But there *is* an objective morality. You don't deny that."

"Oh, now you are talking morality." Aumann said. "Morality is something else."

Morality perhaps is the rationality of the law. Or the rationality of the universe.

"For example, morality," Aumann said, "dictates not evicting people from their homes. Ever.

"Over history," he observed, "many peoples have been expelled from their homes. But never before have they expelled themselves. Only the Jews have been expelling themselves, their own people, from their own homes and synagogues, towns and farms. From Sinai, from Gaza, from the West Bank, from Jerusalem. Only the Jews. . . .

"Ladies and gentlemen," he concluded, "if we want to survive as a nation in Israel, we have to go back to Jewish values. There is no other way. We have to reclaim our belief in the holiness of our cause.

"The state of Israel was founded by the Jewish people sixty years ago. It was founded by and large by people who were not observant, [Chaim] Weizmann, Ben-Gurion, Moshe Dayan, Abba Eban, Golda Meir, people like this, and people who came before them. What these people did not realize is that Jewish values do not pass on automatically from generation to generation. They still had the vision. Their children didn't. Or if some of their children had it, their grandchildren did not.

"In Israel, in general, we do not have it any more, not just the political leadership, the intellectuals, the media, the universities, the courts, these people have lost the *raison d'être* of this state.

They have forgotten that it is not sixty years old; it is sixty times sixty years old. They have forgotten the struggle of Jacob with the angel. And so the whole thing comes apart in their hands."

Here Aumann entered into the realms of game theory: "What has happened is that nothing to us is *holy* any more."

Unifying his two visions of rationality and religion, Aumann believes that a vision of holiness is critical to a game's theoretic grasp of Israel's predicament.

He tells a story.

"About eighteen years ago, the last time there were serious discussions between Syria and Israel about some kind of understanding between the two countries, a high officer in Israel, a major general, came by my office in the Center for the Study of Rationality. Why do we call it the Center for Rationality? It's the only place in Israel where there is any rationality at all. It's on the second floor of the Feldman Building on the Givat-Ram campus of Hebrew University in Jerusalem. That's where it is.

"The general came to me and identified himself by his first name. He discussed the situation with Syria. Said if we are going to reach any accommodation with the Syrians, we are going to have to give up all the Golan Heights. We will have to expel all the Jews who have been living in the Golan Heights for forty years. They're going to have to leave the synagogues, leave [northern Galilee], which was one of the last bastions of the Jewish people in Israel at the time of the revolt against the Romans. We are going to have to leave all that, all the homes, all the farms, all the culture. Have to expel all the Jews.

"'Why?' I asked. 'Why can't you compromise with them? Why?'"

He said to me: "Because to the Syrians the land is *holy*."

I answered: "That's the trouble with us. Not only is the land *holy* to the Syrians, but they have managed to convince you that it is *not holy* to us. Nothing is holy to us. Not the Golan Heights, not Jerusalem. Not Tel Aviv. Nothing is holy to us. We do not have any red lines. Nothing at all. And because nothing is holy to us, we are going to be left nothing if we continue this way."

These echoes from the Torah and the primal religious predicament of the Jews might seem anomalous from a man who was awarded the Nobel for advances in a science invented by the very secular and eminently pragmatic titan von Neumann, a science that attempts to reduce to mathematical logic all the strategic interactions of human beings, from poker and chess to love and religion to naval maneuvers and nuclear war. It is a way, in the words of the late polymathic strategic-thinker Herman Kahn, to "think about the unthinkable," to extract the emotion and blood from scenes like Masada and Mumbai, Nagasaki and 9/11, and to arrive at purely rational rules and predictions that render these eruptions more manageable and amenable to mitigation, remedy, or deterrence.

Two years earlier, Aumann concluded his Nobel lecture with a comment on Isaiah: "When Isaiah speaks of lions lying down with lambs and nations beating their swords into plowshares and their spears into pruning hooks and nations learning war no more, he is describing what can happen when a central government prevails—in the presence of a Lord recognized by all. . . . "In the absence of such a dominant hierarchical power, one can perhaps have peace—no nation lifting up its sword against another. But the swords must continue to be there—they cannot be beaten into plowshares—and the nations must continue to learn war, in order not to fight."

This recognition is indispensable to the survival of Israel—and the United States.

CHAPTER FIFTEEN

The Meaning of Netanyahu

Both in the United States and in Israel, the twenty-first century's first decade ended with political change that brought the Israel test to the fore as the crucial conflict in international affairs.

In the United States was elected Barack Obama, a charismatic exponent of Peace Now, eloquent tribune of nuclear disarmament, fervent protagonist of the economics of envy, a compelling spokesman for third world causes and Muslim grievances, and a prominent believer in the idea that among the greatest threats to the world is the impending increase of a couple hundred parts per million (0.02 percent) in the accumulation of carbon dioxide in the atmosphere. The most talented speaker in high American office since Ronald Reagan and a masterly writer and teacher in the spirit of his community-activist mentor Saul Alinsky, Obama brings unusual intellect and ideological passion to the American scene.

One of Obama's early acts as president was to remove from the Oval Office a bust of Winston Churchill, sculpted by Sir

Jacob Epstein and loaned to President George W. Bush by the British after 9/11. To the new American president, it is safe to assume, Churchill represents a retrograde imperial figure sullied by his support for the British occupation of Obama's ancestral domains in Kenya.

Supported by 78 percent of American Jews, Obama's election was inopportune for Israel. He is a lawyer who sees the world in the guise not of a Churchillian struggle against evil but in the forensics of legal rights and torts, territorial claims and counterclaims, all suitable for arbitration and compromise. All his Middle East foreign policy advisors—Hillary Clinton, George Mitchell, Richard Holbrooke, Dennis Ross, Brent Scowcroft, et al.—believe in Palestinian statehood based on an Israeli amputation of "land for peace." In this regard these advisors are utterly conventional, differing little from the rest of the American intelligentsia in the media and the academy, including the eminent Condoleezza Rice, who ended her stint as secretary of state under Bush as an avid pursuer of appeasement. The chief public defenders of Israeli resistance to gouges in Golan and Gaza and jettisons of Judea and Samaria are unfashionable but inconveniently pithy and popular gentile figures such as Sarah Palin, who displays an Israeli flag in her office in Juneau; Thomas Sowell, in his pungent and visionary columns; Ann Coulter, in her defiant realism; Rush Limbaugh, day after day; and best seller of all except Coulter, the evangelical preacher John Hagee.

Obama's election victory with nearly 53 percent of the vote and a Democratic sweep of Congress has unleashed a resolute drive to create a Palestinian state in exchange for a robust barrier of legal paper between Israel and its enemies.

While the United States moves toward the Left and Peace Now legalism, Israel veers toward the Right and militant Reaganism. Its prime minister, Benjamin Netanyahu, is the obverse of Obama in nearly every way. Although his party won a smaller number of Knesset seats than his opponents combined, an additional fifteen slots were taken by Bibi's former chief of staff and intimate associate Avigdor ("Yvette") Lieberman, who is now foreign minister. These seats give the right-wing parties nearly the same percent—54 percent, in Israel's case—won by Obama. Running to the right of the newly statesmanlike and circumspect Netanyahu, Lieberman exploited widespread Israeli indignation at visible Arab–Israeli support for Hamas during the 2008 war in Gaza. He received, and perhaps even deserved, bad press for his demagoguery, but he is a rational man with whom Bibi has frequently worked in the past. In any case, under Netanyahu, Israel's leadership offers a striking contrast with America's.

While the youthful Obama was a community-action organizer and lawyer, Netanyahu was an anti-terrorist warrior. While Obama imagines that taxes in general are too low and inadequately progressive, Netanyahu is a sophisticated supply-side economist who believes that lower rates bring higher revenues and who opened his administration by advocating tax cuts. While in the past the United States has long offered a haven for frustrated Israeli entrepreneurs and other Jewish capitalists, Israel under Netanyahu will beckon as a land of hope and hospitality to frustrated American venture capitalists and entrepreneurs. While Obama believes that foreign aid is the answer to Palestinian poverty, Netanyahu knows that new opportunities opened up by Israeli enterprise are the only solution to the regional crisis.

While Obama believes that the United States has overreacted to the threat of terrorism, Netanyahu for nearly thirty years has championed and explained the war on terror in both the United States and Israel, in books, international meetings, and through the Jonathan Institute (named for his late older brother who died in the stunning Entebbe hostage rescue in Uganda). Netanyahu sees jihad as the single greatest threat to the West, and no other politician is so learned or so determined in combating it. While Obama thinks Churchill is a man whose time has passed, Netanyahu has read and pondered all of Churchill's works and admires the British titan "above all other gentiles." The time for Churchillian leadership, according to Netanyahu, is now.

Netanyahu offers far more than an ideological counterpoint to American liberalism. His life story and family legacy make his election a potential historic turning point in the relationship between the United States and Israel. Netanyahu is at once the most profoundly Zionist and the most deeply American of all Israeli leaders. In the increasingly global economy, facing an ascendant jihad, Netanyahu consummates the new capitalist Israel and incarnates an Israel–American partnership as deep and interdependent, and possibly as procreative, as any marriage. Out of it can emerge a new twenty-first-century Judeo–Christian alliance in economics, culture, military capabilities, and even religion.

Netanyahu comes from the most Zionist of families. On both sides, Bibi's grandparents moved to Palestine long before the establishment of Israel. Then called Mileikowsky, his father's forebears came in 1920, while his mother's Marcus ancestors arrived in 1896. On both sides, an oral and epistolary tradition depicts the almost empty land they settled. Netanyahu describes his mother's grandfather planting almond trees during the day and poring through the Talmud at night. As Bibi wrote, "By the time my mother was born in nearby Petah Tikva ('Gate of Hope') in 1912, the family was living, amid orchards they had planted, in a fine house with a promenade of palm trees leading up to it." The desert bloomed for Bibi's maternal forebears.

A more intellectual inspiration for Bibi was his paternal grandfather Nathan Mileikowsky, who though no tiller of sands became one of the most eloquent and compelling figures in the history of Zionism. Born in Lithuania in 1880, he was ordained a rabbi at age eighteen and emerged as a highly sought-after global lecturer by the age of twenty, a charismatic orator and "a fiery tribune of the [Jewish] people," who already at the time was proclaiming in speeches from Warsaw, Poland, to Harbin, China, the concept of settlement that Bibi mostly upholds today.

Described by a Jewish journalist as a "genius," who "with the breadth of his imagination . . . has the ability to raise his listeners to the highest ecstasy," Mileikowsky found himself trapped in Poland when it fell under German control early in World War I. The Germans proposed to send him to America to enlist U.S. Jews in a drive to keep America out of the war. Though proffered a "vast" payment by the German governor, he refused to comply unless the Kaiser would endorse a Jewish state in Palestine and press the Ottoman Turks to relinquish the territory. When no such deal could be set, Mileikowsky stayed in Poland until 1920, when he took his wife Sarah and their eight young children to Palestine, where he changed the family name to Netanyahu (meaning "given by God"). Eschewing any return to the soil, he accepted a missionary role as a manager of the Jewish National Fund, first in Europe and then in the United States. Here he encountered the eminent Zionist leader, Ze'ev Jabotinsky, who envisaged Israel "on both sides of the Jordan." As a young man, Bibi's father Benzion became Jabotinsky's assistant in the United States until the famed Zionist's death at sixty in 1940.

Although historians and journalists generally describe Jabotinsky and the elder Netanyahus, Nathan and Benzion, as extremists and reactionaries, the subsequent history of Israel vindicates their "Greater Israel" vision over the more adaptive posture of David Ben-Gurion, Golda Meir, and their followers. The prevailing notion of a diminutive Israel, with its constant offers to give up yet more land for peace, and with regular unilateral relinquishments of territory, has won the Israelis no gratitude or support whatsoever in the international community and has achieved precious little peace.

Netanyahu's Zionist roots and fiery passion for his country implies no parochial patriotism. More than any other foreign leader and even many American politicians, Bibi is immersed in American political culture and has deeply influenced the American political debate. After attending high school in Wyncote, Pennsylvania, a suburb of Philadelphia, where his father taught at a nearby small college, he earned both his undergraduate degree in architecture and his graduate degree in business management at MIT before going to work at the Boston Consulting Group (BCG) at the height of its influence and success in the late 1970s. Under the leadership of Bruce Henderson, carried on in a spin-off company by William Bain, BCG developed the learning curve and explained the resulting competitive dynamics of price cuts. BCG taught that aggressive price cuts and the attending increase in unit volume of sales are the most effective strategy in business, leading to a cascade of benefits, including greater market share, lower costs, higher margins, and competitive breakthroughs on the learning curve as larger production volumes yield experience. Fully aware of the close analogy with the dynamic global impact of tax-rate reductions, the BCG analysts supplied the most sophisticated version of the microeconomics of supply-side philosophy.

Working at BCG for two years, Netanyahu grasped the underlying assumptions of supply-side tax cuts as early as any American politician, including Jack Kemp and Ronald Reagan. During the early 1980s, in the heyday of the Reagan administration, Netanyahu served as a flamboyant political attaché for Israel in Washington, where he became a media favorite and befriended key members of the Reagan circle such as Kemp and Reagan's secretary of state George Schultz and UN ambassador Jeane Kirkpatrick. A cynosure for leading American Jewish businessmen, notably Ronald Lauder and Sheldon Adelson, he was willing to debate any of Israel's critics, such as noted Palestinian scholar Edward Said, and was able to crush most and hold his own with all. From his Washington splash, he went on to become Israeli ambassador to the United Nations, extending his charismatic presence to New York. Among his fans were talk-show star Larry King and *ABC News'* John Stossel.

All in all, the Netanyahu family has been more successful in the United States than in Israel. Not only did his father Benzion attain his greatest eminence as a historian of the Spanish Inquisition teaching at Cornell, but no fewer than six of Benzion's brothers became steel tycoons in the United States under the name Milo, adopted upon immigrating to America.

Bibi always kept in touch with his American uncles, and after hearing him speak on terrorism before a joint session of Congress after 9/11, his Uncle Zachary proudly observed that if Bibi had not been born in Tel Aviv, he might have become the first Jewish American president.

As prime minister in the 1990s and finance minister under Ariel Sharon from 2003 to 2005, Netanyahu led the drive to liberate and recast the Israeli economy as the leading force for prosperity in the Arab world—if only the Arabs would see it. Even if his dream of a transformation of the regional economy succeeds, however, no legacy of tax cuts, hedge fund performance fees, and single taxation of venture investors would prompt anyone to talk of Netanyahu in the same breath as Winston Churchill. Netanyahu's Churchillian role and reveille has come on the issue of Islamist terrorism: the global jihad against the United States and Israel. Just as Churchill gained a prophetic vantage merely by closely attending to the rhetoric of Adolf Hitler and his disciples, Netanyahu understands that the best way to grasp the intentions of organizations such as al–Qaida, Hezbollah, Hamas, and the Iranian mullahs is to listen to what they have to say.

Even more than Churchill, Netanyahu has been a warrior since his early years. Before entering college, he joined the elite General Staff Reconnaissance Unit—the secret Sayeret Matkal—or 269, that served as a spearhead for the Israel Defense Forces in their combat against terrorism. It was this unit that later led a re-taliatory attack against the perpetrators of the 1972 Munich Olympic Village attack on Israeli athletes by killing three of their leaders. Among the targets of Bibi's first operation with the unit, in 1968, in response to a mine attack on a bus full of young Is-raelis, was Yasser Arafat. The Palestinian was to be captured by a paratroop recon team, while Bibi's unit rescued injured members of an ambushed tank team. Arafat managed to escape disguised as a woman.

Toward the end of 1968, Bibi participated in a successful counter-terror operation against Middle East Airlines and Libyan Arab Airlines, destroying fourteen unoccupied planes at the Beirut International Airport in retaliation for an attack by Pales-tinian terrorists. Members of the Popular Front for the Libera-tion of Palestine had arrived in Athens, Greece, from Beirut airport and fired on an EL AL jet, killing an Israeli citizen, wounding a stewardess, and damaging the aircraft. Bibi also played a key role in securing the release of forty hostages from a hijacked Sabena Airlines plane at the Ben-Gurion Airport. (He was wounded in the arm by accidental friendly fire.)

In May 1969, he nearly lost his life in an action against Egyptian forces that had been laying traps for the Israelis near the Suez Canal. The team succeeded in destroying an Egyptian truck loaded with weapons, but two days later Egyptian troops opened fire on Netanyahu's inflated rubber boat operating in the canal. Laden with ammunition for his machine gun, Bibi discovered that he could neither swim nor disengage himself from his sling full of ammo. He had virtually drowned by the time he was rescued by a naval commando named Israel Assaf, who happened to notice bubbles of foam on the surface, felt for a head under the water, and extracted Bibi by his hair under intense Egyptian fire.

Focusing Bibi on the terrorist threat was the death of his brother Jonathan who had led the key rescue team at Entebbe in Uganda in 1976. A group of seven terrorists had seized an Air France Airbus on a flight to Paris from Tel Aviv. Bearing guns and grenades, they directed the pilot to fly to Libya to refuel, and then land at Entebbe, Uganda, 2,500 miles from Tel Aviv. Declaring the principle of no compromise with terror, Prime Minister Yitzhak Rabin ordered the elite unit to fly to Entebbe, kill the terrorists, free the 103 hostages who remained after gentile passengers were released, and bring them home. The operation was a stunning success. Only three hostages were killed in the fighting. An additional hostage—an elderly woman who had become ill in Uganda—could not be rescued because she had been taken to a hospital in Kampala; she was later murdered in her hospital bed under the orders of Idi Amin. But Jonathan, guiding the troops from outside the terminal, was shot dead by a Ugandan soldier from the top of the airport control tower.

This experience transformed Bibi's life, in much the way that the death of Joseph P. Kennedy in World War II changed the life of his brother John F. Kennedy Jr. In the United States at the time, Bibi resolved to enter politics, with a focus on combating terrorism.

After founding the Jonathan Institute, Netanyahu called a conference on terrorism in July of 1979 in Jerusalem. To it, he attracted such notables as George H. W. Bush, then a former head of the CIA, future Reagan cabinet leaders George Schultz and Ed Meese, then FBI Director William Webster, and soon-to-be UN ambassador Jeane Kirkpatrick. To this group Netanyahu offered shocking details of a Soviet network of training camps for Muslim terrorists.

Out of this conference came Netanyahu's first book, an edited compilation of the speeches from the event together with two analytical chapters by Bibi. It was called *International Terrorism: Challenge and Response*; *Proceedings of the Jerusalem Conference on International Terrorism.* The second conference was held at the Four Seasons Hotel in Washington, DC, in 1984, and attracted another assemblage of luminaries and produced another notable book, *Terrorism: How the West Can Win,* also edited and introduced by Bibi. George Schultz gave the book to Ronald Reagan, and he is said to have read it later on a plane to Asia. Then in 1995, Netanyahu wrote his own book, *Fighting Terrorism: How Democracies Can Defeat the International Terrorist Network*, which was republished after 9/11 with a foreword consisting of his September 20, 2001, speech to Congress.

Netanyahu shaped the response to terror of three American administrations. Like Churchill, he took his enemies at their own word and resolved to overcome them, whatever it may take. His own first administration ended in three years with an economic crisis caused by the bursting of the tech bubble, and he was defeated in a sweep by his former special forces commander Ehud Barak. But both Netanyahu's economic policies and his view of terrorism were vindicated by subsequent events.

Bibi is a flawed politician, but he is flawed like Churchill—stogies and drink (though Bibi is a piker compared to Churchill's boozing) and a succession of three wives. Like Churchill, Bibi was a decade ahead in grasping that the enemy is serious and that stated goals must be weighed seriously. Now he must confront the Iranians at a time when it appears that the only plausible path is the overthrow of their government. Perhaps, though, there is an implausible alternative.

"The first and most crucial thing to understand [about terrorism]," as Netanyahu told the U.S. Congress after 9/11, is that "there is no international terrorism without the support of sovereign states. . . . Terrorists are not suspended in midair. They train, arm, and indoctrinate their killers from within safe havens in the territories provided by terrorist states." The reality is that Hezbollah and Hamas are creatures of Iran, that al-Qaida is harbored by Pakistan, that the PLO depends on Egypt, Saudi Arabia, and the United Nations, and that the Kurdish PKK, the Islamic jihad, and Hamas all subsist on Syrian support. North Korea aids Iran and Pakistan in their nuclear ambitions, which portend the most extreme threat that terrorism poses.

Even suicide bombings, as Netanyahu observes, "are seldom carried out by solitary individuals. A whole array of people inculcate the suicide, provide him with explosives, guide him in their use, select the chosen target, arrange for his undetected arrival there, and promise to take care of his family after the deed is done. In short, suicide attacks require a significant infrastructure, and the people who provide it are anything but suicidal." These people are all ensconced in nation-states and sustained by them. In addition, he explains, the "terrorist states and terror organizations together form a terror network, whose constituent parts support each other operationally as well as politically."

Spurned by Netanyahu is the romantic image of the lone caveman terrorist who poses a mere police problem. As Boston University strategist Angelo Codevilla explains the issue, this concept "substitute[s] in our collective mind the soft myth that terrorism is the work of romantic rogues for the hard reality that it can happen only because certain states want it to happen or let it happen."

The influence on U.S. policy of Netanyahu's great insight has been both profound and lamentably limited. When George W. Bush responded to 9/11 by finally dropping the cops-and-robbers model of fighting terrorism, focusing instead on punishing the Taliban, the state sponsors of 9/11, he was following Netanyahu's prescription. Far more so than the pursuit of Osama bin Laden, the exemplary termination of the Taliban regime was the crucial response to 9/11, defining the risk to any state sponsors contemplating attacks on the United States.

Missing Netanyahu's message and perpetuating the myth of stateless terrorism is the U.S. practice of declaring war on something called "terror" while continuing to offer foreign aid and prestige to governments that enable and sponsor actual terrorist acts. Apart from drug dealing, none of the terrorist organizations have any substantial means of internal support. None of them are capable of running a country that partakes of the productive activities of humankind. Most of them run front organizations as shells for the collection of money from the West in a kind of global shakedown racket. As Michael Yon shows in his devastating portrait of al-Qaida in his book, *Moment of Truth in Iraq*, the terrorists' grip on the local population is driven more by fear and dependency than by any affair of the heart.

Sustaining this terrorist network of states is largely foreign aid to governments, together with environmental bars to energy production in the West that endow despots with economic power. Terrorism will continue as long as these suicidal Western policies continue. Without the support of the United Nations and U.S. foreign aid, many of the mendicant oppressor states of the third world would wither away, liberating their people to join the adventure of productive capitalism.

Netanyahu's message is that terrorist nations are not strong. They are pathetically weak. His counsel is to "oppose the bad things when they are small." Libya during the Qaddafi era was perhaps the leading perpetrator of terrorism, financing assassinations and bombings around the globe and killing Libyan exiles in the West. An effective program of sanctions against Libya coupled with the exclamation point of a bombing led to a rapid change in Libyan policy.

Terrorists gain all their power and momentum from the compulsive "negotiations," the multipronged founts of foreign aid, the "peace-keeping" forces, and the legal contortions of the cowering West. As Netanyahu points out, "Terrorism has the unfortunate quality of expanding to fill the vacuum left to it by passivity or weakness." But this murderous momentum, feeding on the pacifist flailing and self-abuse and outflung alms and oblations of the West, will rapidly reverse when faced with resolute resistance. He writes: "Once the terrorists know that virtually the entire population will stand behind the government's decision never to negotiate with them, the possibility of actually extracting political concessions [from the West] will begin to look exceedingly remote." The terrorist afflatus will dissipate and the momentum can be reversed.

The fight against terror must combine the United States and Israel. Netanyahu epitomizes the unity of the United States and Israel. His role dramatizes Israel as in effect an independent salient of America, an extension of Silicon Valley, a fount of our Judeo–Christian roots, a source of American genius. Over the years, from the time of Harry Truman, who boldly recognized the Israeli state against his pusillanimous State Department, through the era of Nixon and Kissinger during the Yom Kippur War in 1973, to the eras of Ronald Reagan and George W. Bush, the United States has often come to the defense of Israel. Today, in the continuing war on terror, the United States needs the leadership and guidance of Netanyahu as much as Israel needs the United States.

CHAPTER SIXTEEN

Land for War

The crucial assumption of the Peace Now movement is that it is within Israel's power to choose peace, that there is something that Israel can give, a price it can pay that would finally and fully purchase the peace.

This price is widely believed to be denominated in land. The utterly conventional and obviously fantastic consensus view of nearly all authorities on the subject, reflected in the policies of most of the world's governments led by the United States, is that the key problem in the Mideast is that *Israel has too much land.* Their remedy is for Israel *to give up land,* mostly to the Palestinian state as envisioned by the same experts. Awarded to the current Palestinian regime or to some similar successor, the result would be another fanatical anti-Jewish Muslim nation-state with no identity to sustain it beyond the Palestinian sense of grievance and its hatred of Israelis.

The dream of land for peace enchants Westerners precisely because it appears as a commercial proposition, suggesting that some price, this many square miles or that, would close the deal and reveal jihad as a negotiating tactic to be terminated at will when the Israelis pay up. Whether appeasement or extortion, the rationale hardly matters. After all, according to the stereotypes, Jews for millennia have bridled at extortion and then paid up as the price of doing business.

The evidence of tens of billions of dollars in tribute collected from the Israelis and the West since Oslo testifies that the Palestinian Authority is indeed an extortion racket. But the object of the racket has nothing to do with a few square miles of disputed land in the territories. The Palestinian regime has as little interest in land as it has in peace.

The "Peace" Process negotiations themselves affirm it. The sense that, by rational "commercial" standards, the parties are so close to agreement that, as Tzipi Livni would have it, "the dove is on the windowsill," powerfully sustains the land-for-peace illusion. With so little left to give, according to the negotiating maps, Israel could win peace with just minor concessions. The implication is that the Palestinians and their backers in the Arab world have waged jihad for decades, brought death and poverty and terror on their own land and people, and unceasingly pledged death to Israel and every Jew in its domains, as a negotiating *tactic* in pursuit of a fractionally better real estate deal.

Such a belief borders on insanity. As David Meir-Levi explains, "From 1949 to 1967 there were no settlements in the West Bank or the Gaza Strip. Nor was there peace. The settlements to which the Arabs objected at that time were Tel Aviv, Haifa, Hadera, Afula, etc.—in other words the settlement of Israel itself." That is still the stance of the Arabs and Iranians who count.

Why then do many Israelis, including most governments since 1967, seem to take this land-for-peace canard seriously?

The answer is to be found in another tenacious illusion: the always treacherous chimera of racialist self-determination, the most bewitching of all ersatz democratic ideologies and democracy's paramount enemy for more than one hundred and fifty years.

Israel is not racist and has imposed no racial standards in its own democracy. Arabs and Christians sit in the Knesset. Instead, the Israelis are the people in the world most universally and passionately accused of racism by—racists. Clinging together for safety, the Jews are reviled as clannish and chauvinistic conspirators. Jews often battle the libel by internalizing it, overcompensating for the accusation of tribalism by lowering the defenses of the tribe in the face of its enemies—the mostly Arab regimes that are the leading protagonists of the racialist cause in our time.

Goading Israel into this cul-de-sac of racial democracy is the "demographic threat," as neatly summed up in a May 2008 *Atlantic* magazine cover story by Jeffrey Goldberg entitled "Is Israel Finished?" What terrifies Goldberg is the prospect that "within the next several years, the number of Arabs under Israeli control—there are now more than 1.3 million Arab citizens of Israel (there are 5.4 million Jews), and an additional 3.4 million or more Arabs who live in the West Bank and Gaza—will be greater than the number of Jews." He cites a much-contested Israeli estimate that "by 2020, Jews will make up just 47 percent of the people who live between the Jordan River and the Mediterranean Sea." By extending Israel's domains beyond the regions where Jews outnumber Arabs, Goldberg and his ilk believe, the settlements jeopardize both the Jewish majority and Israeli legitimacy.

Goldberg's solution is essentially to uproot the some 400 thousand Jewish settlers in the West Bank and Eastern Jerusalem. That is right. The expert's solution is to remove 400 thousand people from their homes.

Goldberg's article justifies this brutal and ignominious surrender by suggesting that, together with the demographic trend, the West Bank settlements are "a catastrophe." Echoing Jimmy Carter's libelous sentiment in his book, *Palestine: Peace Not*

Apartheid, Goldberg even raises fears that "Israel will become a state like pre-Mandela South Africa, in which the minority ruled the majority."

Clinching the argument, Goldberg writes: "If the Arabs of the West Bank and Gaza were given the vote, then Israel, a country whose fundamental purpose has been to serve as a refuge for persecuted Jews, and allow those Jews to have the novel experience of being part of a majority, would disappear, to be replaced by an Arab-dominated 'bi-national' state."

Goldberg should be reassured. Judging from the behavior of virtually all other Arab states, any such bi-national state would be short-lived. An Arab-run Israel would quickly expel all its Jews and cripple its capitalist economy. Goldberg and company's notion of the rules of democracy amounts to an Israeli suicide pact.

In ceding territory to its enemies and conceding the claims of the racial parodists of democracy, Israel would betray not only herself, her children, and her Zionist fathers but also democracy and the West itself. It is precisely by resisting the era's most popular racialist perversion of the democratic idea that Israel defines, defends, vindicates, and illuminates democracy's true meaning. To the extent that Israel instead concedes the claims of mere racial majoritarianism, Israel betrays the democratic idea.

Elections—counting heads rather than breaking them—are a prime tool of democracy, but hardly its essence. Far from the arbitrary dictate of the latest election, democracy denotes the enduring self-rule of a people assumed to be equal under the Lord and the law. Elections every day would not make a democracy of a society in which the decisive political forces are teenage gangs with guns and terrorist courtiers doling out foreign aid to an intimidated populace.

No tenable theory of democracy allows the majority to destroy or expropriate the minority. Without a functioning and legally protected capitalist system, democracies swiftly sink into ochlocracies. Without the independent private sources of power imparted by free businesses, unbiased courts, and other institutions of economic order, any democracy becomes a despotism ruled by any tribe of thug politicians that manages to gain control. If it has oil or foreign aid, the regime may stay in power for decades. The failure of Israeli intellectuals and politicians (and their U.S. counterparts) to comprehend this reality is far more portentous than any supposed demographic trend.

Americans above all should understand this matter since it echoes the central trial of American history. As Lewis Lehrman wrote in *Lincoln at Peoria*, his book on the 1854 speech that launched Lincoln's career as the nemesis of slavery, the decisive issue between the future president and his rival Stephen Douglas was the limits of popular sovereignty. Do majority rights extend to the enslavement of minorities?

This is the same issue that currently convulses the Middle East and animates the Israel test. By claiming the right to banish or kill 5.5 million Jews, Arab leaders assert the supremacy of majorities to the point of enabling them to dispossess and displace and even to annihilate minorities. By supporting the expulsion of Jews from the West Bank and Gaza, American critics of Israel such as Jeffrey Goldberg and Thomas Friedman in principle accept this "democratic" imperative. Such a "democracy" of "one man, one vote, one time" can establish communism, Nazism, or any kind of slavery.

Even including the West Bank and Gaza, Israel is a tiny country. This "empire," this domineering colonialist, constitutes one-sixth of 1 percent of the Middle Eastern land area. The Jewish one-tenth of the West Bank population lives on about 2 percent of that area with perhaps another 4 percent reserved for roads and security. Minus the settled territories, Israel is nine miles wide at its narrowest point between the West Bank and the Mediterranean Sea. That's fourteen and a half kilometers, a distance that can be crossed by a runner, or a modern tank, in less than an hour.

An expulsion of Israelis from the West Bank would merely repeat the suicidal harvest of the previous Israeli flight from southern Lebanon and Gaza. Both capitulations led to the triumph of bristling deadly tyrannies, Hezbollah and Hamas, financed by Iran and institutional foreign aid. The surrender of the West Bank would be even more deadly, since its mountainous spine would provide Israel's enemies with an elevated staging area for a sudden invasion that could destroy the country.

Making a fetish of Israel's pre-1967 borders, Jimmy Carter pompously proclaims them unimpeachably "legal," embodied in UN resolution 242 in 1967 and UN resolution 338 in 1973, and accepted at Camp David in 1978 and in Oslo in 1993 by both Arabs and Israelis. His entire work is one perplexed and disgruntled screed against the Israelis for failing to observe their legal confinement. But Israel's agreement to accept most of the pre-1967 borders has always been contingent and must always be contingent on verifiable guarantees of its defense. Legal or not, those borders—so constricted that they have been termed "Auschwitz borders"—left Israel as an indefensible shard.

The pre-1967 borders have been fully tested. Whether an attractive nuisance or an irresistible temptation, their vulnerability resulted in attacks from three neighboring Arab states in 1967. Regardless of agreements or legalities, all the documents affirming the pre-1967 borders have been perforated and rescinded by the Arabs and their bullets, mortars, grenades, and bombs in four wars and innumerable raids and missile attacks.

A country surrounded by friendly neighbors could tolerate a nine-mile-wide waist guaranteed by the sort of "solemn pledges" that impress people like Jimmy Carter. But less than worthless are solemn pledges from Arab regimes that have trained their people for most of a century, from *madrasahs* to military drills to maniacal media screeds, that Israel is a diabolical expression of a verminous bacterial subhuman population.

Under these conditions, with a relentlessly indoctrinated electorate, jihadist democracy is the enemy. The intrinsically anti-democratic die was cast long ago by rabid anti-Semitic venom injected daily in Arabic for decades. Israel must command a defensible territory. That means expanded settlements and police constabulary on the mountainous spine of the West Bank and the Golan Heights that afford strategic access to Israel. It means police actions in the Gaza Strip, a frequent source of attacks on Israel.

Thomas Friedman, Shlomo Ben-Ami, and others believe the strategic situation changed radically with the emergence of missile technology, heralded by the Scuds that fell on Israel to wild Palestinian applause during the first Iraq war in 1991. With Israel, like the United States and all other modern nations, reachable from afar, these writers contend that the country no longer needs to hold a buffer of settlements to protect itself from nearby enemies. With Palestinians living among Israelis, the threat is no longer from outside but from within.

Benjamin Netanyahu rebuts this view in his book *A Durable Peace*: "The lesson for a small country like Israel is this: *In the age of missiles territory counts more, not less*. Long-range missiles increase the need for mobilization time, and short-range missiles can destroy strategic targets within their reach. For both reasons, the control of a contiguous buffer area becomes more, not less, important." He quotes the Left-oriented Jaffee Center for Strategic

Studies: "Territory is especially vital when it permits our forces to 'buy' time: in case of a surprise attack, this enables us to mobilize our reserves and bring them to the front lines before the aggressor succeeds in taking any part of our vital area."

Even if Netanyahu's argument were undermined by some new technology or strategy, the moral and democratic case is clear. Both the history of invasion and the present commitment of the Arabs to the death of Israel vindicate Israel's absolute and unilateral right to decide what land it must keep and what it may cede to the Palestinians, under what pre-conditions. Israel has no prior obligation to cede a single square inch of land except to advance its own security. If the right answer for Israel is to rule for a thousand years the territories on which reside enemies committed to its destruction, then no true principle of democracy compels them to do otherwise.

This confusion about the true nature and requirements of democracy enervates most of Israel's would-be advocates even as it emboldens its enemies. Perhaps the most influential writer on these issues is Thomas Friedman, who has combined all his illusions into a grand mythology. From his *New York Times* columns to his earlier book *From Beirut to Jerusalem*, which provided perhaps the most compulsively readable and courageously researched guidebook to this conflict, he insists that the obstacle to peace is not Arab violence but Israeli bellicosity.

In his book, he tells the story of his arrival in Beirut in 1982 as a committed Zionist since childhood and the tale of his eventual disillusionment. Beirut before his eyes became a snake pit of contending factions. When Yasser Arafat led the Palestinians into southern Lebanon as a vantage to attack Israel, it upset the balance between Maronite Christians and Muslims who had shared power. Muslims became a decisive majority. Because the Muslims as a majority had no tradition or intention of granting rights to minorities, the new situation was intolerable to the Maronites. Attacks came from all sides. While he was away, Friedman's apartment building was blown up with his driver's wife and children sheltering inside. Suicide bombs from the Iranian-financed terrorists of Hezbollah destroyed both the U.S. embassy and U.S. Marine headquarters.

The climax came in 1983 after the assassination by the PLO of the mildly pro-Israel Lebanese prime minister, Bashir Gemayel. Friedman reported a retaliatory massacre of some four hundred or more Palestinians at refugee camps Sabra and Shatila, near Beirut, committed by Maronite Christian Phalangists. Israeli soldiers still surrounding the area failed to stop the killings. Challenging the Israelis' claims that they had no foreknowledge of these crimes, his articles seethed with implications of unforgivable complicity. Friedman's series of investigations in the *New York Times* won him the Pulitzer Prize and durably sullied the reputation of the Israel Defense Forces. In a fabulous feat of moral equivalence, many writers compared Israel's behavior in Lebanon with the behavior of the Nazis in Europe.

Probing this scar tissue anew was the Academy Award-nominated Israeli film *Waltz with Bashir,* directed by Ari Folman, which occasioned many such suggestions by Israeli intellectuals that the most revealing and portentous event of the 1982 Lebanon War was this massacre, supposedly condoned by Israel.

Friedman, the *New York Times,* and the Pulitzer committee were following the venerable tradition in wartime journalism, tested in Vietnam, which holds that the vicissitudes and excesses inevitable in conflict become a saga of one-way scandals and salacious legal investigations. War is terrible, and soldiers of all nations often misstep in the fog. But Israel's offenses in Lebanon, producing perhaps a few thousand civilian casualties, occurred in the middle of a civil war that produced perhaps a half-million deaths. It is invidious and ultimately suicidal for journalists from free nations to focus on a few sensational disputed incidents in the middle of a fifteen-year bloodbath.

Israel occupied southern Lebanon only when it became a terrorist training center for jihadists around the Mideast and a source of repeated attacks on Israel. Regardless of Pulitzer craft and laurels, no reasonable journalistic standard permits the reporter to contemplate a self-defense against extermination and equate it with attacks by genocidal forces.

By stigmatizing the Israeli army and its defense minister Ariel Sharon, Friedman helped make any success in Lebanon impossible. A classic "useful idiot" in Leninist terms, Friedman helped trigger a movement that for a time deprived Israel of one of its greatest leaders and lent new momentum to the Palestinian cause.

Land for peace, however, does have a positive meaning. Beyond the delusional Peace Process, there is the vision of the land itself yielding peace as it endows those who live upon it with the raw materials of an orderly and productive life. It is only this goal that makes the proposed exchange of land for peace a credible idea. It is only the notion that the Palestinians might want land on which to make such a peace that suggests Israel might buy peace by giving it to them.

But if the Palestinians seek land for this purpose, why must it come from tiny Israel? The Palestinian Arabs are surrounded on all sides by spacious and compatible Arab countries of whom they theoretically could become citizens. Why not the East Bank? That's Jordan, where 300 thousand Palestinian Arabs fled during the 1967 war.

A Muslim–Arab state from time to time sustained by Israel and created as a home for the Palestinians, Jordan held the West

Bank until King Hussein's treacherous 1967 invasion and shelling of Jerusalem. Jordan retains a far more compelling obligation to these people than Israel does.

Should the Palestinians shun Jordan, perhaps they would prefer the Soviet jihadist state of Syria, which in its guise as "Greater Syria" stretches its reptilian claws throughout the region, including into nearby Lebanon. Egypt is contiguous with Gaza and could easily absorb the Gazan Palestinians who have put their democratic fate into the hands of the terrorists of Hamas.

Negotiators with illusions about their adversaries end up negotiating with themselves. Experts on business negotiation ordain that "whenever you start negotiating with yourself, you might as well give away the company." This is what the Israelis have been doing for decades, among all their gaggle of solipsistic political parties, each with its fluff of afflatus and acid of animus and symbolic banner of nationhood, each often willing to give away what some other Knesset party cherishes. For the Arabs, these are what-is-ours-is-ours negotiations; what is Israel's is negotiable and consumable.

Whatever the Arabs of the jihad and the intifada mean by the word "land" cannot be satisfied by giving up any particular patch of ground. Land to them is less transactional than transcendental and apocalyptic. As with all the ideologies of race and fatherland, all the cults of blood and soil, with all their ruinous and romantic rejections of modernity, inevitably making the Jews their first chosen enemies, they are haunted and driven by demons no Peace Process can exorcise.

Which is not to declare the Arabs beyond hope or help. Outside observers can easily assume a people are in the grip of a demonic ideology when they are actually only in the grasp of a despotic regime. Obscured in the terror applied by the regime against its own people is the reality that prior to the terrorists' seizure of power, there were other parties in the contest and real majorities for peace and productivity.

In conferring democracy on Germany, or even Japan, for two much-cited examples, the United States did not miraculously graft alien values onto an unwilling nation. The crucial process was not one of conversion at all. It was the total military defeat and destruction of the despotic faction and the transfer of power over time to already strong but obscured constituencies for capitalist democracy.

Peace can come to the Palestinians tomorrow and nationhood the day after if only they will take what is already in their grasp and go to work. They are prevented from doing this primarily by the rule of a terror regime—it hardly matters whether it calls itself Fatah or Hamas or by a dozen other names—that thrives on violence and chaos and hatred and is kept alive by money from jihadist states and intimidated Western powers.

The path to peace is not through negotiations but through invincible rejection of terror, joined to real opportunity for Palestinians who choose life over death. Over the next two decades, Israel will grow into the dominant economy in the Middle East and one of the most productive economies in the world. Palestinians must be made to see that displacing Israel is futile, but buying and selling its products and supplying labor for its factories and offices can make Palestinians once again the most successful of all Arabs, as they were between 1967 and 1987. Saved from the Nazi obsessions of their ruling clique, the Palestinians can become major beneficiaries of the emerging new global economy.

CHAPTER SEVENTEEN

Time for the Test

"Now, every human being on earth who cares about facts and can tell a lie from a truth knows that there was no such thing as 'Palestinian nationalism' until modern Zionism created it out of whole cloth, by placing enormous value on a piece of land that used to seem as precious to its landlords as a rat-ridden empty lot in a burnt-out neighborhood in the middle of nowhere, in the suburbs of nothing.

"The Jews gradually got possession of an arid stony wasteland . . . complete with the odd picturesque, crumbling, dirty town; and they loved it. They turned it into a gleaming, thriving, modern nation, not only a military but an intellectual powerhouse.

"And so it is only natural that the former owners' descendants want it back, and remember how much their ancestors loved it, and how the new owners only got possession by wickedness and deceit. Such memories have the strange property of growing clearer instead of cloudier every day. . . .

"There is no irreconcilable difference in the fight between Israel and the Palestinians, no bone-deep dispute that will haunt humanity forever. There is only greed and envy. They never disappear, but can easily move from one target to the next. The problem will be solved as soon as the world stops trying to solve it."

—David Gelernter,
The Weekly Standard, January 19, 2009

All right, now is the time for the test.

In the early 1940s in Europe, as Hitler ranted about the depravity of the Jews, the Nazis were already proceeding with the "final solution" that he had promised in *Mein Kampf*. They were preparing concentration camps near railroad lines at Treblinka, Bergen-Belsen, Dachau, Auschwitz, and dozens of other cities. They were lining up railroad cars and gas trucks. They were mobilizing scientists and engineers to develop efficient techniques for extermination. They were transforming a generation of young men into Brown Shirt brigades frothing with hate and lusting for violence against Jews. They were enlisting foreign allies such as the Grand Mufti Haj Amin al-Husseini to extend the killing to Palestine.

The world, then engulfed by a world war, mostly failed to focus on this particular threat, which seemed too bizarre and evil to be believed. The West lost 6 million of its most creative and productive citizens: kin of the same people who shaped twentieth-century science, enabled twentieth-century technology, and opened the horizons for the twenty-first-century economy—the people who largely enabled the West to prevail against the Axis powers and to win the cold war against the Soviet Union. We have to acknowledge today that in his most ardent cause and most fervent war aim, Hitler largely triumphed. Some sixty-five years later, the number of Jews is still over an estimated 5 million below the number in 1939. Poland, once home to almost 3.5 million Jews, has an estimated Jewish population of only 25,000 as of 2008. As expressed in the compulsive acts of condemnation of Israel by the United Nations, the Nazi obsession has attained a new respectability around the world.

Today, Hitler's rants have morphed into a global program of religious education and military ideology sustained by Arab and

Iranian oil money. The hundreds of thousands of Brown Shirts in Germany have become millions of frothing jihadi youths similarly inculcated with anti-Semitic hatred and a lust for violence. Leading politicians in Iran, Egypt, Syria, Malaysia, Venezuela, and other nations, and jihadi imams and mullahs around the globe have declared their resolve to destroy Israel.

Unlike the Germans, who faced a formidable technical challenge in carrying out their plan, the incumbent anti-Semites benefit from the increasing availability of nuclear weapons, which could render a new Holocaust both simpler and more effective than the first. Anti-Semites have the moral support of much of the UN bureaucracy, including its "human rights" apparatus, which is chiefly devoted to anti-Semitic agitprop. The UN General Assembly in 2008 directed 68 percent of its condemnatory resolutions and other strictures against Israel. The UN secretary-general has called for a global boycott of Israel for its efforts to defend itself against new campaigns of extermination. Aiding a new Holocaust is the vulnerability of the state where 5.5 million Jews are congregated.

Today, the most dangerous form of Holocaust denial is not rejection of the voluminous evidence of long-ago Nazi crimes but incredulity toward the voluminous evidence of the new Holocaust being planned by Israel's current enemies. Two Iranian presidents have resolved to acquire nuclear weapons for the specific purpose of "wiping Israel off the map." Scores of nations, representing 1.8 billion Muslims, have endorsed the jihad. After the genocidal crimes of World War II and the Communist empire and recent genocidal violence in Rwanda, the Sudan, Somalia, and Zaire, deniers of a new Holocaust agenda manifest blindness to human nature and human history. Showing no understanding of the central and indispensable contribution of capitalism to human welfare, the world political order is heavily focused on punishing capitalists, as epitomized by Israel and the United States.

The problem is not nuclear weapons themselves. They represent another major and irretrievable step in the history of weapons development. To condemn them is like condemning meteors or earthquakes or even the sun. They are an inexorable part of the world. Moreover, nuclear weapons have a positive aspect. They reflect a generally favorable move of the world from *quantitative* arms races to *qualitative* ones, from rivalries of mass mobilization of existing manpower and resources to intellectual competition in the development of new weapons and defenses.

Quantitative arms races focus on diverting wealth from private consumption to public mobilization. Quantitative arms races favor dictatorial regimes with large populations of young men. They reward the ability to extract resources from consumption and direct them to the job of reproducing the best existing military tools. Quantitative arms races make a billion youths inculcated with Wahhabi frenzies into a vast and possibly decisive weapon. Quantitative arms races lead either to economic exhaustion or to war.

Qualitative arms races can trump quantitative capabilities. During World War II, the perfection of radar, the emergence of computer decryption, and the mastery of nuclear weapons counteracted the apparently decisive advantages of the Axis countries in existing industrial power and military mobilization. During the cold war, the advance of U.S. guidance and communications technologies and steps toward effective missile defense countered the huge advantages in manpower of the Soviet Union and Communist China. In any qualitative rivalry, millions of Jewish individuals and other researchers and inventors operating in free societies can counteract billions of jihadists in mass movements and totalitarian confinement. As Peter Huber put it in an eloquent speech after 9/11, "Our silicon can beat their sons."

Today the superiority of America and its Israeli allies is growing ever greater. The campaigns of the qualitative arms race become increasingly more effective compared to the indoctrination of new Nazis. Hundreds of Talpions can trump millions of Brown Shirts or jihadi youth. However, there remains an acute danger. Countering the ever-growing American and Israeli lead in new technologies are widespread abolitionist attitudes toward nuclear weapons. Together with hostility toward anti-ballistic missiles, opposition to weapons in space, resistance to civil defense, and blindness to the urgent need for technological answers to nuclear terror, a suicidal pacifism in the United States endangers not only Israel's survival but ultimately America's as well.

Echoing the equally corrosive influence of levelers in economics, these attitudes in the West could so inhibit the development of new counter-weapons that a mere quantitative buildup of old weapons systems cobbled together from Western schematics could prevail. A window of opportunity may be opening for rogue powers that can acquire even primitive nuclear weapons. The archaic tools of quantitative competition could trump the superior capabilities of Israel and the West.

Under these conditions, no other issue is so important as the nuclear threat to Israel. The case of Israel gives the lie to every notion of unilateral disarmament, every illusion that the adversaries of the West are open to negotiation, every figment of belief that our enemies desire peace rather than destruction. Israel is not only a major source of Western technological supremacy and economic leadership—it is also the most vulnerable source of Western power and intelligence. It is not only the canary in the coal mine—it is also a crucial part of the mine.

Over the course of decades, Israel and the United States have made every possible overture toward Israel's enemies, lavishing them with funds, relinquishing land, endorsing statehood. If the

Arabs or Iranians desired peace, they would already have it. There would be a Palestinian state thriving next to Israel. But instead, Israel faces a global mobilization against its very existence. In a world of nuclear weapons, the continued determination to destroy Israel represents a direct threat to New York and Washington as well.

In the conflict with the jihadists, inapt are the lessons of the cold war, in which we carefully learned to live with a nuclear USSR until communism cracked under the pressure of U.S. military advances. During the cold war, the United States and the Soviet Union learned to live with nuclear weapons by developing a careful etiquette, both in their rhetoric and in their military movements. In relation to Israel, Iran and other jihadist movements are brutally breaching that etiquette. When high officials in major countries announce their intention to use nuclear weapons to "destroy" a nation, they must be addressed in a way unnecessary when they merely spoke of driving the nation into the sea. All the qualitative resources of the West—all its current military powers and sources of new technology creation—must be brought to bear on the threat.

The defense of Israel cannot be reactive. It probably cannot be public. It must mobilize all our resources of intelligence, technology, and surprise. It must succeed.

Like the Germans and Japanese in World War II, our adversaries will not wait for the West to prepare. They will attempt to achieve surprise. With no qualitative capabilities to cultivate, they know that time is their enemy. Whether against the United States or Israel, they must launch their blows as soon as they are ready.

By eliciting the early declarations and announcements of Iran and other jihadist states, Israel has performed a huge service to the West. When they can, these countries will obviously assault the Great Satan as well as Satan Minor. The Israel test makes the challenge clear. It signals the real predicament of the West.

The predicament of the West is the plight of the world and all its people. The defense of Israel is vital to the defense of the world economy. People are all we have. They are the ultimate resource and the most precious one. Only in peace can they thrive and reproduce.

An inescapable fact of life is that people—and peoples—vary tremendously in their talents and capabilities, and moral integrity, and thus in their capacity to sustain life on earth against nihilist movements such as the jihad. People differ hugely in their ability to conceive the algorithms of economic advance and military defense. Shaped by baffling mixtures of genes and culture, history and faith, civics and law, nations show a broad spectrum, from an animus for land and blood to an afflatus for creativity and peace.

Just as free economies are necessary for the survival of the human population of the planet, the survival of the Jews is vital to the triumph of free economies. If Israel is quelled or destroyed, we will be succumbing to forces targeting capitalism and freedom everywhere. We will allow a fatal triumph of the barbarian masses that may well end up demoralizing and destroying the United States as well. Any global regime of UN redistribution of resources and suppression of wealth creators will doom the globe to a slow retreat to a radically smaller population of primitive peoples.

If we have a free, competitive, and collaborative world economy, however, some people and countries will far outperform others. Their outperformance is what makes it remotely possible to feed 6 billion people. As Matt Ridley observes in his upcoming book *The Bright Side*, without technological innovations, "we'd have needed about 85 earths to feed 6 billion people . . . if we'd gone on as 1950 organic farmers without a lot of fertilizer, we'd have needed 82 percent of the world's land area for cultivation, as opposed to the 38 percent that we farm at the moment." Many of the enabling technologies, from desalinization to distributed solar power to targeted irrigation, originated in Israel or were crucially advanced there. The United States contributed the world's most potent agricultural machinery and fertilization tools. The universe is hierarchical, and economic freedom is what makes it possible for some humans to climb the hierarchies of knowledge and build systems to sustain life.

Economists and politicians talk of natural endowments, energy supplies, landmasses and sea-lanes, choke points and channels, money supplies and trade balances and capital investment. Environmentalists prattle about global warming and other alleged planetary disorders. Law professors talk of constitutional penumbra and class action suits and the "freedom to choose."

None of these concerns can hold a candle in importance to the talents of a country's human beings and their commitment to the disciplines and devotions that drive the global economy. What permits the human race to thrive and prosper is the willingness to unleash and affirm the genius of an incredibly small number of people: to embrace excellence and collaborate with it rather than succumb to envy and suppress achievement. The twentieth century was shaped and animated and endowed largely by a tiny cohort of the earth's population usually called the Jews. In much of the world, they were suppressed and constricted by various dictatorial regimes, some of which they supported. But the achievements of the twentieth century are heavily attributable to the prevalence of capitalism in the West and its ability to accommodate the genius of the Jews. Without them, the world would be radically poorer and its prospects for the future would be decisively dimmed.

All around the globe today, however, the leaders of nations and international organizations, prestigious academics, and passionate writers denounce the very countries in which Jews are allowed to create and succeed. These leaders claim to be anti-Zionist, anti-Israel, anti-American, or anti-capitalist, but the distinctions dissolve in the crucial animus of anti-Semitism.

People who obsessively denounce Jews have a name; they are Nazis. The Palestinian Arab leaders have shown themselves to be mostly Nazis. Anyone who believes these men should command a nation-state ensconced next to Israel is delusional. There is only one answer to the claims and demands and threats of such people and that is "no."

The leaders of Iran are proud Nazis. Anyone who believes that the West can stand aside and conduct negotiations while they acquire access to nuclear weapons is a gull who has failed to learn anything from the history of the twentieth century. The president of Syria is equally obsessed with Jews and Israel. The Wahhabis of Saudi Arabia in their *madrasahs* around the globe are cultivating new armies of young Brown Shirts. The civilized world must show enough courage of its convictions to answer all the neo-Nazis with a resounding "no."

In the United States, however, most elite opinion believes that this is a moment in human history when disarmament is a tenable option, a moment for intensified concessionary diplomacy in the Middle East, a moment when the supreme priority should be "climate change." Such beliefs place the very survival of the United States into question.

The Holocaust threat only begins with Israel. The entire West is vulnerable to the jihad. It can be stopped only through a combination of resolve and technology. On the front lines, Israel must face the menace earlier than the United States. Israel has already demonstrated the effectiveness of civil defense programs against missile attacks. By fleeing to underground shelters, Israelis have incurred only a handful of deaths from thousands of hits on Israeli towns. The Israelis have maintained military forces that long succeeded in holding the jihad at bay.

The Israel test forces the capitalist world to recognize the necessity of armament and civil defense. Today the nuclear threat seems chiefly addressed to Israel. But increasing steadily is the possibility of infiltrating nuclear weapons into American cities, exploding them offshore near American ports, or detonating bombs above America's critical electronic infrastructure. A nuclear explosion over the central part of the United States might precipitate a cascading electromagnetic pulse that could paralyze the power grid and destroy much of the microchip technology that runs our economy. The United States must mobilize all its capabilities of intelligence and defense against these threats.

The Israel test impels us to forgo the illusion of opting out of the arms race. All too many Americans still subscribe to the "strangest dream" school of international relations, as I called it after singing along with Joan Baez at Club 47 on Mount Auburn Street in Cambridge as a college student in the 1960s: *Last night I had the strangest dream / I ever dreamed before / I dreamed the world had all agreed / To put an end to war / I dreamed I saw a mighty room / The room was filled with men / And the paper they were signing said / They'd never fight again.*

The song and the sentiment are as infectious and deadly as the Oxford peace movement that anesthetized Britain before World War II, as the Peace Now mantra that inebriates Israel, as the campaigns for nuclear disarmament that seduce American liberals. The single greatest domestic threat to the United States is not the jihad but the peace movement. Countries that fail to meet the challenge of qualitative armament, of military technology, end up at war.

Ronald Reagan's best moment was his commitment to build anti-ballistic missiles. His worst, most self-indulgent, and foolish moment was his speech advocating the destruction of nuclear weapons. Regardless of any caveats he included, the speech was a horrible blunder that played into the hands of America's enemies and is still a major weapon in their portfolios. It was his strangest dream moment, and if it were to come true, it would doom the country that he loved.

Now President Barack Obama also is entertaining this fatuous dream. At moments of weakness, he speaks of nuclear disarmament. Within a week of assuming office he spoke of destroying 80 percent of America's nuclear stockpiles. He contemplates abandoning missile defense. His chief asset in making such proposals is his ability to cite Reagan as a precursor on the road to disarmament. To the extent he pursues it, Obama can jeopardize the very existence of this country. With nuclear weapons in the hands of others and without anti-missiles and other advanced technologies, the United States cannot survive as a free country. Arms races are the inexorable burden of all free peoples.

No major nation in history has succeeded in preserving its integrity and sovereignty without meeting the challenge of ever-advancing armaments. For Israel, the issue is obvious. Without maintaining leadership in military technology, the country has no chance at all of survival. But many American intellectuals still imagine that the United States is different, that it is possible or desirable for us to negotiate an "end to the arms race."

Our enemies will always want to end the arms race because they know only free nations can win it. The crucial test of American leadership is to see through the constant stream of proposals for technological disarmament. All our enemies want to confront us without our qualitative superiority.

An end to the arms race would deprive the capitalist countries of their greatest asset in combating barbarism. The result would bring no relief from military competition but rather its transformation. Arms rivalry would shift from qualitative goals that favor free countries such as the United States and Israel toward quantitative rivalry that will favor our barbarian enemies.

The predicament of Israel is ultimately the predicament of world capitalism. If the United States, with its world-leading armaments, is incapable of defending Israel, it will prove unable to defend anything else. The Israel test is finally our own test of survival as a free nation.

My Own Israel Test

I n the current arenas of controversy, where Israel is a foreign policy issue and a legal argument and a historic debate, I am presenting it chiefly as a test. It begins for everyone as a personal test. It is a test that climaxes the long experience of American gentiles with Jewish immigration and rivalry. It is a test for Jews who wish to proceed with their lives without concern for Middle Eastern conflicts and moral claims. For Jews and gentiles, it is a test now embroiled in confusions, evasions, and misunderstandings on all sides. But I believe that the test is clear and definitive.

In the modern capitalist world, in which the historical extremes of poverty have been widely overcome, the most acute moral issues relate to recognition of accomplishment and superiority—treatment not of the poor but of the excellent and gifted people whose work is indispensable to providing opportunities for the poor and everyone else. In capitalism, as I wrote in *Wealth & Poverty* some thirty years ago, the great conflict is not between rich and poor but between incumbent elites and existing forms of capital and the new elites and superior forms of capital that must necessarily displace them if economic progress is to occur.

Thus the paramount conflict in capitalism is between the established system—entrepreneurs, businesses, political movements, and bureaucracies—and the superior minds and methods, vessels of excellence and innovation, that threaten to usurp them. On one side stand the alliances of governments and elites, in democracies and tyrannies alike, that distort economies around the globe by protecting the past in the name of social fashions and special interests. On the other side are the inventors, entrepreneurs, industrial innovators, and visionary artists who challenge every establishment.

The Israel test revolves around a fact that is recognized by most people in some form, surreptitious or partial, but is rarely acknowledged openly or explored for its consequences: in any rivalry with intellectual dimensions, disproportionate numbers both of the challengers and of the winners will be Jewish.

Today in America and around the world many of the incumbent rich and powerful are Jewish as well. But few people seem to worry much about existing wealth. We are relatively comfortable with incumbent wealth and privilege and enjoy the scandals and follies of the rich and famous. What is threatening is creative destruction from brilliant and ambitious outsiders. The French have been so preoccupied with this phenomenon that they have supplied us with no fewer than three pejoratives to capture it: *nouveau riche, arriviste,* and *parvenu.* All three terms apply readily to Jewish immigrants and business successes as well as to Israel, an allegedly upstart nation-state in the Middle East.

In most advanced countries, according to the available data, a hugely disproportionate number of brilliant and ambitious outsiders engaged in intellectual and entrepreneurial activities are Jews. Around the globe, wherever freedom opens up, however briefly in historical terms, Jews quickly tend to rise up and prevail. Jews, historically, have shown vigilance toward the main chance and valiance in taking it. Together with superior knowledge and talent, this visionary audacity is the essence of entrepreneurial prowess. Understanding and combating the rise of anti-Semitism and anti-Zionism requires fathoming the anxious sense of vulnerability of incumbent establishments—intellectual, commercial, military, political, and cultural—as they face the Israel test.

As a youth I learned first hand the temptations of anti-Semitism. Attending Phillips Exeter Academy in New Hampshire, I devoted nearly all my efforts as a junior at the school to writing for the *Exonian*, the school's daily newspaper, and managed barely to scrape by in my classes. I expected to be named an editor of the school paper for my senior year. For generations, my forebears had been editors. I was entitled. Since virtually no other undergraduate had written as many stories, features, reviews, and editorials, I thought my ascension was assured.

When the next editorial board was announced, I was shocked to discover that the editor-in-chief was to be a student named Peter Sobol, whom I had scarcely met and who had contributed nothing notable to the paper. I found that most of the other prospective new editors were also only occasional contributors. Three of them were "New York Jews," as I invidiously observed, who unlike me had achieved high grades, almost effortlessly as it seemed, while I struggled to eke out Cs. If truth be known, at the time, they were also more accomplished writers than I.

That summer, in a parental campaign to help me catch up on my studies, I was assigned a Radcliffe student as a tutor in the classical languages. In an effort to avoid famously demanding Exeter courses such as American history and calculus, I was aiming for a Classics diploma. The Radcliffe girl (in those times of atavistic "sexism," we still called college students "girls") was named Valerie Ann Leval. The name still can suffuse my brain with remembered effervescence and longing.

Hired to teach me the Greek language so I could qualify for second-year Greek in my senior year at Exeter, she was a tall, willowy creature, both intelligent and beautiful. On long walks through the fields and over the hills of Tyringham Valley, Massachusetts, I accompanied her in besotted bliss as we recited Greek phrases and conjugated polymorphous Greek verbs from a textbook coauthored by my Exeter teacher.

One day toward the end of the summer, as we strode up a sylvan dirt road by the Gilder Farm in the late afternoon, en route to a hilltop field spread out with mosses and tufted with blueberry bushes and reaching out toward rolling horizons and wide sunset vistas, she asked me how I liked Exeter.

How I ached to impress her! I knew that she would not be taken with callow effusions about the virtues of this famous preparatory school, its oval tables, its fabled teachers, its austere standards. I hesitated to tout Exeter's athletic exploits, my true enthusiasm, to this refined intellectual girl. What to say? We beat Andover 36 to 0? I chose what seemed to me at the time a path of seductive candor and salty sophistication. Echoing sentiments I had heard both at home and at school, I responded, "Exeter's fine, except that there are too many New York Jews."

At first, Valerie did not reply. We continued crunching up the dirt road. I sensed there was something wrong. My hopes for the evening seemed to be slipping fast away while Valerie contemplated how to respond. Then she commented dryly: "You know, of course, that I am a New York Jew myself."

My stomach turned over like a cement mixer. I gasped and blathered. I cannot remember exactly what it was I said. I suppose I prattled something about all my Jewish friends and my well-known offbeat sense of humor.

To this day I recall the moment as a supreme mortification and as a turning point. Rather than recognizing my shortcomings and inferiority and resolving to overcome them in the future, I had blamed the people who had outperformed me. I had let envy rush in and usurp understanding and admiration. I had succumbed to the lamest of all the world's excuses for failure—blame the victor. I would pay by losing the respect of this woman I then cared about more than any other. I had flunked my own Israel test. But I had learned my lesson.

I was brought up in a highly literary and artistic Anglo-Saxon Protestant family in New York City and western Massachusetts. I had learned the family legends. We were classic WASPs all, scions of stained-glass artist Louis Comfort Tiffany, the *Century Magazine* editor Richard Watson Gilder, Episcopal pastor Reese Fell Alsop of the Church of St. Ann's in Brooklyn Heights, and Chester W. Chapin of the Boston and Albany Railroad. Gilder forebears and their children had been painted exhaustively by Cecilia Beaux and engraved in bronze by Augustus Saint-Gaudens. My great-aunt Mary O'Hara had written the equine sagas of the *Flicka* series.

One of the favorite family stories recounted an exploit of my great-grandmother, Helena de Kay Gilder, who was an obsession of the artist Winslow Homer. At her wedding to my great-grandfather, Homer presented to her a special painting. It depicted Helena in a chair, dressed in black. At her feet was a red rose, symbolizing, according to art historians, Homer's heart.

Homer was just one of many artists and writers in my family's circle. My great-grandfather was a close friend to both Mark Twain and Walt Whitman, among many others who visited at our farm in the Berkshires. When Twain's wife died, he retreated to Tyringham and rented from my great-grandfather a house next to ours. But among all the literary figures in the family circle, Helena and my great-grandfather were particularly close friends and backers of Emma Lazarus, the now-celebrated Jewish American poet who wrote the inscription on the Statue of Liberty in New York:

The New Colossus
"Keep ancient lands, your storied pomp!" cries she
With silent lips. "Give me your tired, your poor,
Your huddled masses yearning to breathe free,
The wretched refuse of your teeming shore.
Send these, the homeless, tempest-tost to me,
I lift my lamp beside the golden door!"

In the *Century Magazine*, Richard Watson Gilder published both her poems and her prophetic but sometimes disdained Zionist essays. One of her poems calling for a new homeland was entitled "The New Ezekiel" and "celebrates," in Esther Schor's words, "the coming together of all the dry bones of Israel":

Say to the wind, Come forth and breathe afresh
Even that they may live upon these slain,
And bone to bone shall leap, and flesh to flesh . . .
. . . I ope your graves, my people, saith the Lord,
And I shall place you living in your land.

Prompting the Lazarus poems and essays were the ongoing pogroms in Russia that also inspired "The New Colossus" and brought millions of Jews to the United States. Here they began their relentless rise through all the nation's hierarchies and ladders of accomplishment. Here they challenged all the established powers and principalities.

At the time, WASPs were impregnably on top, running the businesses and media of the day. With notable friendships with two U.S. presidents and such leading lights of literature as Twain, my family was perched near the top of the American establishment. Like most exalted WASP families, my forebears and their descendants were about to face their Israel test.

Lazarus's biography by Esther Schor is heavily based on hundreds of letters of correspondence between Lazarus and Helena Gilder and reports a suspected romance between Lazarus and Helena's brother, the poet Charles de Kay. By usual standards, my family was actively philo-Semitic. A leading Zionist professor at Columbia told Richard Gilder: "My people owe thanks to you at the *Century* more than to any other publication."

A Tiffany sister of my grandmother was Dorothy Burlingham, a lifetime best friend and collaborator of Anna Freud, daughter of Sigmund, one of the prime forces of modernist Jewish intellect in the twentieth century. The tempestuous story of Anna and Dorothy is well told by her grandson Michael in his book *The Last Tiffany*. On all sides I had relatives with intimate links to Jews.

In our family, however, we were not immune to the general miasma of ambivalent disdain, admiration, and anxiety toward Jews. We took for granted that a person's religion and ethnicity were significant elements of "background." This background stuff was important, and lots of people failed the background test. In describing someone, we regarded their roots to be as worthy of note as their fruits. Jokes about rabbis, priests, and preachers, inflected in rich accents, evoked uproarious laughter around our dinner table. It was another era, I might nervously opine, when one did not consider it offensive to exalt one's own heritage over others or to laugh at ethnic foibles. We were led to believe that our cultural heritage was supreme, and, with some ambivalence, we knew that it had roots entangled in the heritage of the Jews. I suppose we knew also that Jewish intellectuals and entrepreneurs were challenging the preeminence of WASPs in American cultural and commercial life.

Jews were beginning to move into Harvard University in significant numbers. As a student at Harvard in the class of 1936, my father roomed with a Jewish classmate named Walter Rosen, who became my own godfather before he, like my father, too, died as a pilot in World War II. Several of my father's other good friends were Jewish. Aunts and cousins married Jews. After graduation, my father visited Germany with another roommate, David Rockefeller, and returned with a passionate revulsion against Hitler's frothing anti-Semitic speeches. My father was convinced that Nazism was a dire threat to civilization and must be stopped by military force.

In 1938, one of the youngest members of the Council on Foreign Relations (to this day the library is named after him), my father famously and impertinently confronted John Foster Dulles, later to become secretary of state, for believing that some rapprochement between Germany and the United States was still possible. In sophisticated circles there persisted a fashionable belief, fostered in part by Bloomsbury economist-philosopher John Maynard Keynes, that Germany was somehow a victim of World War I and of the postwar settlement and reparations. There was a notion abroad that Germany had earned by this grievance a moral edge against the winners of that horrendous conflict.

My father was having none of it. In a conviction that air power would be decisive in the coming war, he took up civilian flight training to be ready while working as an executive trainee at his grandfather's firm, Tiffany and Company. My father died in 1943 commanding a squad of B-17 bombers, called Flying Fortresses, on the way to the war in Europe. The entire squad was lost to what was suspected to have been sabotage at the Gander, Newfoundland, fueling station.

A piano teacher and performer, my mother, Anne, after the war became a close friend of the famed virtuoso William Kapell and taught him how to drive a car in the Berkshires, where he practiced his incandescent musical art in a converted red barn next to our house. Only six or seven at the time, I remember chiefly how loudly he played compared to my mother. We were all shocked and dismayed by his death in a plane crash in San Francisco while returning from a triumphant concert tour in Australia. When tapes of Kapell's performances in Australia were rediscovered early in this new century, the event was front-page news in the *New York Times*.

Several years younger than my mother, Kapell consulted her about his romantic pursuit of a mutual friend and gave her piano lessons. At the time, he was her favorite pianist, but other Jews soon joined the lists of virtuosi, including Serkin, Horowitz, Rubinstein, Cliburn, Fleisher, Gilels, Gould, and Ax, as Jewish genius dominated the global culture of the piano.

On my father's side, Tiffany and Company is no longer independent, having been absorbed by Avon Products, as the "family" jewelry business surrendered to Jewish entrepreneurs, who outperformed the stodgy WASPs in control at Tiffany.

In many walks of life, from finance to films, American WASPs have undergone such a displacement. Some are ambivalent about it, but very few in my experience are anti-Semitic, and even those admire many Jews. Nearly all cherish their Jewish friends, associates, and connections. They are proud to know Henry Kissinger, who became my tutor at Harvard, just as they boast of their youthful encounter with Bob Dylan or appreciation of the supremacy of Leonard Cohen or Irving Berlin as a songwriter. The American economy and culture is not a zero-sum game, and the creative ferment fostered by Jewish inventors and entrepreneurs has enriched the entire nation and made the current generation of WASPs the most prosperous and successful in history. Jews have not only succeeded in America but have saved America as well. They are now so deeply entwined in American culture and enterprise—and in the lives of most Americans—that it is difficult to imagine life in the United States without its Jewish leadership and leaven.

Virtually all Americans who have achieved anything important in the twentieth century have had crucial Jewish colleagues and collaborators. Virtually none of the significant scientific and technological feats of the twentieth century would have been possible without critical contributions by Jews. Even some of the best Christian preachers and theologians turn out to be Jewish.

As with all nations and cultures faced through history by the plain facts of Jewish excellence and success, we have a choice. We can resent it or embrace it as a divine gift to the world. But although our choice is free, the result of our choice is intractably set by the moral law that governs the outcome of human endeavor as strictly as the laws of physics govern the planets. The envy of excellence leads to perdition, the love of it leads to the light.

Today this choice, with all its relentless implications, is focused not on the Jews in the neighborhood but on the Jews as a nation.

America is a profoundly Judeo–Christian nation, and without the Jewish role, it might well not have prevailed or even survived in its present form. Israel is a national expression of the Jewish genius and achievement that has long been manifest in American life and commerce. We need Israel today as much as Israel needs us, as much as we needed Jewish physicists and chemists, such as Leó Szilárd, John von Neumann, and J. Robert Oppenheimer, to bring to fruition the Manhattan Project that won World War II, as much as we needed Jewish entrepreneurs and inventors to consummate the technologies of Silicon Valley, and as much as we needed Jewish engineers to maintain our national defenses throughout the cold war and after.

The lesson of the ascendancy of Jews in America is the same as the lesson of Israel today. It is not primarily a tale of sentimental tolerance in which WASP Americans sheltered the needy Jews, but a tale in which America, including American WASPs, incomparably benefited by passing an often brutal and exacting moral test, and accepted, if sometimes grudgingly, the superior performance of another, in some ways, alien people. The point of Lazarus's great poem is not to celebrate America as a vast homeless shelter but as a nation whose genius has been to know that the huddled masses—in their very yearning to breathe free—would surpass all the storied posh and pomp of Europe.

As with America, so with Israel. Israel is not a dispensable Jewish "best friend," a noble but doomed democracy, or even a charitable dependency we can no longer afford. It is an indispensable ally, and in the past twenty years it has evolved into perhaps our most valuable partner.

Yet, for most Americans, ultimately our loyalty to Israel arises not from a cold calculus of survival, but from a sense of the holy. What Americans must fathom with both heart and mind is that this instinct is true—and vital to our survival—that if we would live, we must defend this Holy Land.

ENDNOTES

PART ONE: ZERIZUS

1 I found the word *zerizus* in the introductory matter at the estimable *Jewish World Review* Web page, where it was defined as the "blessed willpower and aspiration that leads to exceptional achievement." I am informed that the word is more commonly spelled "*zerizut*" and means "alacrity." I am adopting the *JWR* concept as the spirit of Jewish enterprise.

CHAPTER ONE
The Central Issue

4 *Caroline Glick, the dauntless* . . . Personal communication with author, December 1, 2008, Aish Ha Torah conference center, Toronto, Canada.

4 *Today tiny Israel, with* . . . Deloitte and Touche, LLP, *Global Trends in Venture Capital 2008 Survey*, Venture Capital Services: Technology, Media, and Telecommunications (NY: Deloitte, 2008), pp. 23–24 and passim; *Israel High Tech & Investment Report*, June 2005; Sara Aharoni and Meir Aharoni, eds., *Industry and Economy in Israel*, (Kfar-Sava, Israel: Miksam, 2006), pp. 6–25, 29–30, and passim; Helen Davis and Douglas Davis, *Israel in the World: Changing Lives Through Innovation* (London, UK: Weidenfeld & Nicolson, 2005), pp. 12–21 and passim; Jonathan Medved, "Israel Beyond the Conflict," presentation and interview, December 2008.

4 *The 2008 World Factbook:* Israel; West Bank; Gaza, Central Intelligence Agency Web page, www.cia.gov, last updated May 26, 2009.

6 *In an elaborately mounted* . . . Rafael Reuveny, "The Last Colonialist: Israel in the Occupied Territories since 1967," *The Independent Review* 12, no. 3 (Winter 2008), pp. 325–374.

8 *With a gross domestic . . . The 2008 World Factbook:* Israel, Central Intelligence Agency Web page, www.cia.gov, last updated May 26, 2009.

8 *Jews lead all other . . .* Thomas Sowell, *Ethnic America: A History* (NY: Basic Books, 1981), p. 5. Table shows Jews a decisive first among all ethnic groups in incomes in 1980. Sowell has since documented this Jewish lead in incomes in a variety of later publications and cites census data and the 2000–2001 National Jewish Population Survey (NJPS), which compare data on education, employment, occupation, and income for the total U.S. population with the combined, weighted sample of respondents to NJPS and the National Survey of Religion and Ethnicity (NSRE). In 2001, more than one-third of Jewish households (34%) reported income over $75,000, compared to 17% of all U.S. households. Proportionally fewer Jewish households (22%) than total U.S. households (28%) reported household income under $25,000. The median income of Jewish households is $54,000, 29% higher than the median U.S. household income of $42,000 in the 2000 census. In 1990, the median income of Jewish households was $39,000, 34% higher than the median income of $29,000 for all U.S. households.

9 *Like former president Jimmy . . .* Jimmy Carter, *Palestine: Peace Not Apartheid* (NY: Simon & Schuster, 2006); Shlomo Ben-Ami, "A War to Start All Wars: Will Israel Ever Seal the Victory of 1948?" *Foreign Affairs* (September/October 2008). Ben-Ami writes: "Israel should pull back settlements and give up its '67 gains in order to secure its '48 victory." Bernard-Henri Lévy in "Pondering, Discussing, Traveling Amid and Defending the Inevitable War," *New York Times Magazine*, August 6, 2006, states: "I have always agitated for the Israeli state to leave the occupied territories and, in exchange, win security and peace." Also urging creation of a Palestinian state in the West Bank: Lévy, *Left in Dark Times: A Stand Against the New Barbarism* (NY: Random House, 2008); and Thomas Friedman, *From Beirut to Jerusalem*, Rev. Kindle ed. (NY: Farrar, Straus & Giroux, 2007).

In early 2009, boldly and felicitously abandoning a three-decade stance and refuting proposals for a feral Palestinian state in the West Bank was the eminent revisionist historian Benny Morris: *One State, Two States: Resolving the Israel/Palestine Conflict* (New Haven: Yale University Press, 2009), pp. 161–201. He champions a Jordanian solution.

10 *But creating no such . . .* David Meir-Levi, *History Upside Down: The Roots*

of Palestinian Fascism and the Myth of Israeli Aggression (NY: Encounter Books, 2007), p. 64.

11 *José Ortega y Gasset* . . . José Ortega y Gasset, *The Revolt of the Masses* (NY: W. W. Norton, 1936), pp. 94–95.

14 *Capitalist wealth, as Pierre* . . . Pierre-Joseph Proudhon, *What is Property?* (NY: Cosimo Classics, 2007), p. 14.

14 *In an 1883 diary* . . . Paul Lawrence Rose, *Wagner: Race and Revolution* (New Haven: Yale University Press, 1996), p. 64.

15 *Inescapably, it poses the* . . . Thomas Sowell, "Are Jews Generic?" in *Black Rednecks and White Liberals* (San Francisco: Encounter Books, 2006), pp. 65–110. See also: Thomas Sowell, *Conquests and Cultures: An International History* (NY: Basic Books, 1998).

15 *"Everywhere," as I wrote* . . . George Gilder, *Wealth & Poverty, A New Edition of the Classic,* 2nd ed. (San Francisco: ICS Press, 1993), p. 109.

CHAPTER TWO

The Blindness of the Experts

19 *G. K. Chesterton got it* . . . G. K. Chesterton, "The Twelve Men," in *Tremendous Trifles* (Beaconsfield, UK: Darwen Finlayson, 1968), p. 55.

19 *From the virtuoso tracts* . . . Alan Dershowitz, *The Case for Israel* (Hoboken, NJ: Wiley, 2004); Dershowitz, *The Case Against Israel's Enemies* (Hoboken, NJ: Wiley, 2008).

20 *Dershowitz cogently contests the* . . . Dershowitz, *The Case for Israel*, pp. 181–188.

21 *Dershowitz devastates the likes* . . . Statement of UN General Assembly President Miguel d'Escoto Brockmann on the Question of Palestine, UN General Assembly, November 29, 2008.

21 *As Larry Summers put* . . . Karen W. Arenson, "Harvard President Sees Rise in Anti-Semitism on Campus," *NY Times*, September 21, 2002.

22 *Long preceding the formation* . . . Benny Morris, *One State, Two States: Resolving the Israel/Palestine Conflict*, pp. 110–111 and passim, in which he details the expulsionist tenets of the PLO, Hamas, and Hezbollah charters; Dershowitz, *The Case for Israel*, p. 94; Bill Bennett, Jack Kemp, and Jeane Kirkpatrick, "Twenty Facts about Israel and the Middle East" (Washington, DC: Empower America, 2002), reproduced on the *Jewish World Review* Web site, May 21, 2002.

22 *From the PLO's 1964* . . . Bill Bennett, Jack Kemp, and Jeane Kirkpatrick, "Twenty Facts."

23 *By this measure, the* . . . Meir-Levi, *History Upside Down: The Roots of*

Palestinian Fascism and the Myth of Israeli Aggression (NY: Encounter Books, 2008), pp. 7–12. See also: Chuck Morse, *The Nazi Connection to Islamic Terrorism: Adolph Hitler and Haj Amin al-Husseini* (Lincoln, NE: iUniverse, 2003), pp. 15–36, complete with illustrations; Bernard-Henri Lévy, *Left in Dark Times: A Stand Against the New Barbarism* (NY: Random House, 2008), which offers a footnote on p. 220 describing the memoirs of Haj Amin al-Husseini as published in Damascus in 1999 by *Al-Ahali* documenting his relationship to Himmler, Eichmann, et al. "He was one of Eichmann's best friends and had constantly incited him to accelerate the extermination measures."

23 *Fresh from aiding the* . . . David Pryce-Jones, c. 8, "The Rescue of the Mufti of Jerusalem," in *Betrayal: France, the Arabs, and the Jews* (NY: Encounter Books, 2008).

24 *Still unsated in his* . . . Morse, *The Nazi Connection to Islamic Terrorism*, p. 84.

24 *Arafat characteristically bought Hitler's* . . . Morton A. Klein, national chairman of the Zionist Organization of America, press release, September 10, 1999.

25 *Devoted to the destruction* . . . Ruth R. Wisse, *Jews and Power* (NY: Schocken, 2007), p. 158. Wisse writes: "Palestinian terrorist leaders were coached by Soviet intelligence agencies and educated at Soviet universities. Mahmoud Abbas . . . received his PhD from the People's Friendship University in Moscow for a dissertation on 'secret relations between Nazism and the leadership of the Zionist movement.'"

25 *Perhaps the most menacing* . . . Lévy, *Left in Dark Times: A Stand Against the New Barbarism*, pp. 171–172.

26 *Under Israeli management, economic* . . . Oussama Kanaan, "Recent Experience and Prospects," in Steven Barnett et al., *The Economy of the West Bank and Gaza Strip: Recent Experience, Prospects, and Challenges to Private Sector Development* (Washington, DC: Middle Eastern Department, International Monetary Fund, 1998), pp. 14–28.

26 *Evicted were more than* . . . Meir-Levi, *History Upside Down: The Roots of Palestinian Fascism and the Myth of Israeli Aggression*, p. 64.

27 *Winston Churchill proclaimed the* . . . Martin Gilbert, *Churchill and the Jews* (Toronto: McClelland & Stewart, 2007), pp. 160–161.

28 *That says it all,* . . . Hillel Halkin, "Why the Settlements Should Stay," *Commentary*, June 2002, pp. 21–27. He sums up: "There is indeed something unacceptable about telling Jews that although they may live anywhere they wish, in New York and London, in Moscow and

Buenos Aires, there is one part of the world they may not live in—namely, Judea and Samaria, those regions of the land of Israel most intimately connected with the Bible, with the Second Temple period, and with Jewish historical memory, and most longed-for by the Jewish people over the ages."

CHAPTER THREE
Tale of the Bell Curve

29 *The most compelling book* . . . Dennis Prager and Joseph Telushkin, *Why the Jews? The Reason for Antisemitism*, Rev. ed. (NY: Touchstone, a division of Simon & Schuster, 2003), pp. 7–8.

31 *Opening the book is* . . . Ibid., *frontispiece.*

31 *Benzion Netanyahu, the historian* . . . Benzion Netanyahu, *The Origins of the Inquisition in Fifteenth-Century Spain*, 2nd ed. (NY. New York Review Books, 2001), p. 90.

32 *As eminent Russian pro-Semite* . . . quoted in Yuri Slezkine, *The Jewish Century* (Princeton, NJ: Princeton University Press, 2004), pp. 164–165. Choice quotes from the Berkeley professor Slezkine: "The most notable thing about Jewish students in the Soviet Union and Jewish students in the United States was the fact that, whereas Soviet colleges produced Communists, the American colleges also produced Communists." (p. 361). "While young Soviet Jews turned toward Zionism and capitalism, U.S. Jewish students turned toward socialism and anti-Zionism." (p. 338). "It is true that Jews suffered immeasurably from the pogroms, but was not the revolution a universal pogrom? . . . Or is condemning a whole social class to extermination . . . a 'revolution' . . . and killing and robbing Jews a pogrom? Why such honor for Marx and his followers?" (p. 183).

32 *In* The Bell Curve . . . Richard J. Herrnstein and Charles Murray, *The Bell Curve: Intelligence and Class Structure in American Life* (NY: Free Press, 1994).

32 *As Murray later distilled* . . . Charles Murray, "Jewish Genius," *Commentary*, vol. 123, no. 4, April 2007, pp. 29–35.

33 *As recently as 1999,* . . . David Rosenberg, *Cloning Silicon Valley: The Next Generation High-Tech Hotspots* (Upper Saddle River, NJ: Financial Times/Prentice Hall, 2001), p. 26. More recent data published in *Seed* magazine, December 2008, p. 75, showed that although Israel was tied with the United States in the share of GDP devoted to education, Israeli fifteen-year-olds ranked behind Americans on the

OECD's PISA science test, though the United States ranked only 37 out of the 57 listed.

34 *Murray's later work,* Human . . . Charles Murray, *Human Accomplishment: The Pursuit of Excellence in the Arts and Sciences; 800 B.C. to 1950* (NY: HarperCollins, 2003).

35 *Social psychologist David McClelland* . . . David C. McClelland, *The Achieving Society* (Princeton, NJ: D. Van Nostrand, 1961), pp. 43, 365.

36 *Edward B. Roberts of* . . . Edward B. Roberts, *Entrepreneurs in High Technology: Lessons from MIT and Beyond* (NY: Oxford University Press, 1991), pp. 58–59.

37 *Thomas Sowell of the* . . . Thomas Sowell, "Are Jews Generic?" in *Black Rednecks and White Liberals* (San Francisco: Encounter Books, 2006), pp. 65–110. See also: Slezkine, *The Jewish Century,* pp. 33–39 on anti-Sinitic violence against overseas Chinese.

39 *It is unseemly, as* . . . Sowell, *Ethnic America,* p. 5.

40 *As Walter Lippmann eloquently* . . . Walter Lippmann, *The Good Society* (NY: Grosset & Dunlap, 1943); quoted from paperback (Piscataway, NJ: Transaction Books, 2004), pp. 193–194.

40 *Yes, "Jew-hatred is unique"* . . . Dennis Prager and Joseph Telushkin, *Why the Jews? The Reason for Antisemitism,* p. 3.

CHAPTER FOUR
The Palestinian Economy

45 *There are similar numbers* . . . *The 2008 World Factbook*: Israel; West Bank; Gaza, Central Intelligence Agency Web page, www.cia.gov, last updated May 26, 2009.

46 *With the Arab population* . . . Ami Isseroff et al., *The Population of Palestine Prior to 1948,* MidEastWeb, www.mideastweb.org/palpop.htm, p. 2; Fadle Naqib, *The Palestinian Economy and Prospects for Regional Cooperation,* Geneva, Switzerland, United Nations Conference on Trade and Development (UNCTAD), Special Economic Unit, June 30, 1998, pp. 14–15; Jonathan Adelman, *The Rise of Israel: A History of a Revolutionary State* (NY: Routledge, 2008), pp. 23–24 and passim.

46 *Only invasion by five* . . . Malcolm B. Russell, *The Middle East and South East Asia* (Ann Arbor: Stryker-Post, 1982), p. 122.

47 *Increasing flows of unearned* . . . Steven Stotsky, "Does Foreign Aid Fuel Palestinian Violence?" *Middle East Quarterly* (Summer 2008), pp. 23–30. For a two-year period, the Republic of Congo eclipsed the PLO as a per-capita foreign-aid recipient, but over the last two decades, Palestine

is number one. A more vivid account of the foreign-aid funding of Palestinian terrorism occurs in Aaron Klein, *Schmoozing with Terrorists: From Hollywood to the Holy Land; Jihadists Reveal Their Global Plans—to a Jew!* (Los Angeles: WND Books, 2007), pp. 109–132.

47 *The late Lord Peter* . . . P. T. Bauer, "Foreign Aid and Its Hydra-Headed Rationalization" in *Equality, The Third World, and Economic Delusion* (Cambridge, MA: Harvard, 1981), pp. 86–137; P. T. Bauer, "Foreign Aid: Issues and Implications," *Reality and Rhetoric: Studies in the Economics of Development* (Cambridge, MA: Harvard University Press, 1981), pp. 38–62. See also: P. T. Bauer, *Dissent on Development: Studies, and Debates in Development Economics* (Cambridge, MA: Harvard, 1972), pp. 96–146.

47 *The first era of* . . . Ami Isseroff et al., *The Population of Palestine Prior to 1948*, MidEastWeb, www.mideastweb.org/palpop.htm, Tables 7, 10, and passim; *Israel and Palestine: A Brief History*, MidEastWeb, http://www.mideastweb.org/briefhistory.htm.

48 *The most significant of* . . . Arthur Goldschmidt Jr. and Lawrence Davidson, *A Concise History of the Middle East*, 8th ed. (Boulder, CO: Westview Press, 1994), p. 297; *The 2008 World Factbook*: Israel; West Bank.

48 *Gaza, the other territory* . . . *Times* (UK) online, "The Gaza Strip; Facts and Figures," June 18, 2007.

48 *As Hillel Halkin observed* . . . Hillel Halkin, "Why the Settlements Should Stay," *Commentary*, June 2002, p. 24.

48 *In this first phase* . . . Don Peretz, *The West Bank: History, Politics, Society, and Economy*, Illustrated ed. (Boulder, CO: Westview Press, 1986), p. 89 and passim; Joseph Nevo and Illan Pappé, *Jordan in the Middle East: The Making of a Pivotal State*, Illustrated ed. (NY: Routledge, 1994), p. 236 and passim.

48 *Many leading Palestinian entrepreneurs* . . . A. J. Meyer, *Middle Eastern Capitalism: Nine Essays* (Cambridge, MA: Harvard University Press, 1959), p. 38. "The Palestine Arab refugee is typical. During the past decade [1948–1958] these stateless and second-class citizens have established models of enterprise in the Levant far more sophisticated than earlier establishments. The best garage and machine shop (by Western standards) in Beirut is run by Palestinians. Locally financed and managed casualty and life insurance has been largely a creation of a Palestinian group. Perhaps the most aggressive banking and industrial combine yet to operate in the Arab East is completely owned and managed by Christian and Moslem Palestinians."

49 *During these twenty years . . .* Oussama Kanaan, "Recent Experience and Prospects," in Steven Barnett et al., *The Economy of the West Bank and Gaza Strip: Recent Experience, Prospects, and Challenges to Private Sector Development* (Washington, DC: Middle Eastern Department, International Monetary Fund, 1998), pp. 15, 18 (quote: "The Way It Turned Out"), and passim. Between 1969 and 1991, investment and GDP rose more than tenfold.

49 *Efraim Karsh tells the . . .* Efraim Karsh, "What Occupation?" *Commentary*, July/August 2002.

50 *In 1993, impelled by . . .* Israel Ministry of Foreign Affairs, Israel–PLO Recognition: Exchange of Letters between PM Rabin and Chairman Arafat, Israel Ministry of Foreign Affairs Web site, September 9, 1993.

50 *As Oussama Kanaan wrote . . .* Oussama Kanaan, "Uncertainty Deters Private Investment in the West Bank and Gaza Strip," International Monetary Fund Report, *Finance & Development*, vol. 35, issue 2, June 1, 1998.

51 *With massive aid flowing . . .* Steven Stotsky, "Does Foreign Aid Fuel Palestinian Violence?" *Middle East Quarterly* (Summer 2008), pp. 23–30.

51 *Previously, under the Israeli . . .* A. J. Meyer, *Middle Eastern Capitalism: Nine Essays* (Cambridge, MA: Harvard University Press, 1959), p. 38.

52 *The increase in foreign . . .* Ziv Hellman, "Terminal Situation," *Jerusalem Post*, Issue 18, December 24, 2007.

53 *In 1948, when Arabs . . .* Efraim Karsh, *Israel: The First Hundred Years*, Illustrated ed. (NY: Routledge, 2000), p. 104; Kanaan, pp. 14–28.

53 *By 1992, the economy . . .* Oussama Kanaan, "Recent Experience and Prospects," in Steven Barnett et al., *The Economy of the West Bank and Gaza Strip: Recent Experience, Prospects, and Challenges to Private Sector Development* (Washington, DC: Middle Eastern Department, International Monetary Fund, 1998), pp. 14–28.

54 *A recent thicket of . . .* Raja Khalidi, "Sixty Years After the UN Partition Resolution: What Future for the Arab Economy in Israel?" Edited by Rashid Khalidi, *Journal of Palestine Studies: A Quarterly on Palestinian Affairs and the Arab–Israeli Conflict* 146, vol. xxxvii, no. 2, Berkeley: University of California Press published for the Institute for Palestine Studies (Winter 2008), pp. 6–22.

54 *Alas, 1992 would turn . . .* Ziv Hellman, "Terminal Situation," *Jerusalem Post*, December 10, 2007.

57 *Contrary to the claims . . .* "The Economic Status of Arab Citizens of Israel: An Overview," Mossawa Center, The Advocacy Center for Arab

Citizens of Israel, 2008, p. 6; *The 2008 World Factbook*: Jordan, Central Intelligence Agency Web page, www.cia.gov, last updated May 26, 2009.

57 *The life expectancy of* . . . Yaakov Kop and Robert E. Litan, *Sticking Together: The Israeli Experiment in Pluralism* (Washington, DC: Brookings Institution Press, 2002), p. 54. Chart based on data from Central Bureau of Statistics, Statistical Abstract of Israel, vol. 51 (Jerusalem: Central Bureau of Statistics, 2000), pp. 3–30. It shows that Arab women in Israel live 77.4 years and Arab men live 74.2 years, while Jewish men and women live roughly two years longer. Arab longevity in Israel is significantly greater than Arab longevity in the rest of the Middle East, with the possible exception of Syria, where life expectancy is 74 years.

58 *Arabs constitute roughly 50* . . . *The 2008 World Factbook*, Central Intelligence Agency Web page, www.cia.gov, last updated May 26, 2009.

58 *Amid all the dismal* . . . Raja Khalidi, "Sixty Years after the UN Partition Resolution: What Future for the Arab Economy in Israel?" Edited by Rashid Khalidi, *Journal of Palestine, Journal of Palestine Studies: A Quarterly on Palestinian Affairs and the Arab–Israeli Conflict* 146, vol. xxxvii, no. 2, pp. 6–22.

59 *When Ben-Gurion told* . . . Walter Laqueur, *Dying for Jerusalem: The Past, Present, and Future of the Holiest City* (Naperville, IL: Sourcebooks, 2005), p. 161.

59 *After the Gaza war* . . . Claudia Rosett, "Can We Give to Gaza without Giving to Hamas?" *Forbes*.com, March 5, 2009.

CHAPTER FIVE

The Economics of Hate

61 *In a great prophetic* . . . Ludwig von Mises, "A Draft of Guidelines for the Reconstruction of Austria," *Selected Writings of Ludwig von Mises: The Political Economy of International Reform and Reconstruction,* edited and with an intro. by Richard M. Ebeling [Hillsdale College, Hillsdale, Michigan] (Indianapolis: Liberty Fund, 2000), pp. 133–168. A similar moment of truth struck Michael Bloomberg, mayor of New York, in early 2009, when he realized the tiny group of entrepreneurs who provide the bulk of the revenues for the city. "Charging that it's 'easy to rile against the rich,' Mayor Bloomberg warned yesterday that the income-tax increases being considered for the wealthiest New Yorkers would drive them from the city. 'One percent of the households that file in this city pay something like 50 percent of the taxes.

In the city, that's something like 40,000 people. If a handful left, any raise would make it revenue neutral,' the billionaire mayor said on his weekly radio show. 'The question is what's fair. If 1 percent are paying 50 percent of the taxes, you want to make it even more? Anybody below that 1 percent, no taxes?'" (David Seifman, *New York Post*, February 14, 2009).

62 *Explaining this Austrian catastrophe* . . . Adolf Hitler, *Mein Kampf*, trans. James Murphy (NY: Random House, 1988). See c. 10, "Why the Second Reich Collapsed," and, particularly, c. 11, "Race and People."

63 *Mein Kampf, however, is* . . . David Pryce-Jones, "Their Kampf: Hitler's Book in Arab Hands," *National Review*, July 29, 2002. Pryce-Jones cites Lukasz Hirszowicz, author of *The Third Reich and the Arab East* (London: Routledge & Kegan Paul, 1966), a Polish-born scholar who, as Pryce-Jones reports, examines in careful detail how Hitler's Germany sought to woo Arabs through anti-British and anti-Jewish policies. Nazi personalities like Josef Goebbels and Baldur von Schirach of the Hitlerjugend (Hitler Youth movement) carried out goodwill tours. Various German agents financed and armed clandestine Arab Fascist groups. The first Arabic translation of *Mein Kampf* appeared in 1938, and Hitler himself tactfully proposed to omit from it his "racial ladder" theory, which assigned to Arabs a rung just above Jews.

65 *Adumbrating Mearsheimer and Walt* . . . John L. Mearsheimer and Stephen M. Walt, *The Israel Lobby and U.S. Foreign Policy*, Illustrated ed. (NY: Macmillan, 2007).

66 *Michael Milken, for example* . . . George Gilder, *Telecosm: The World After Bandwidth Abundance*, Rev. ed. (NY: Touchstone, a division of Simon & Schuster, 2002), p. 168.

CHAPTER SIX
The Archetype and the Algorithm

72 *Pushing this contrary tide* . . . Reuven Brenner, *The Financial Century: From Turmoils to Triumphs* (Toronto: Stoddart, 2001), p. 2. Brenner explains the phenomenon: "[I]n many countries, sudden economic success has less to do with the entrepreneurialism of the local population than it does with the political blunders of other nations . . . [that] lead to the rapid outflow of both capital and talented people [who] take their knowledge, skills, networks, and resources to new places, which thrive as a result. Hong Kong, Israel, and the United States are all countries

where such a sequence of events brought about rapid prosperity. The countries the migrants left, meanwhile, fell behind."

74 *But as Eugene Wigner* . . . Eugene Wigner and Andrew Szanton, *The Recollections of Eugene P. Wigner: as told to Andrew Szanton* (NY: Plenum Press, 1992), p. 174.

76 *As Macrae describes it* . . . Norman Macrae, *John von Neumann: The Scientific Genius Who Pioneered the Modern Computer, Game Theory, Nuclear Deterrence, and Much More* (NY: American Mathematical Society, 1999), pp. 31–84; quote, p. 33.

77 *Steve J. Heims's fascinating* . . . Steve J. Heims, *John von Neumann and Norbert Wiener: From Mathematics to the Technologies of Life and Death* (Cambridge, MA: MIT Press, 1982), pp. 30–32.

78 *In 1919, a brutal* . . . Macrae, *John von Neumann*, p. 81.

79 *As he told his* . . . Wigner and Szanton, *The Recollections*, p. 174.

80 *As Heims explained: "It* . . . Heims, *John von Neumann*, p. 109.

82 *As Kati Marton wrote* . . . Kati Marton, *The Great Escape: Nine Jews Who Fled Hitler And Changed The World* (NY: Simon & Schuster, 2006), p. 37.

83 *As Kati Marton explained* . . . Ibid., p. 38.

83 *Always von Neumann's vantage* . . . David Berlinski, *The Advent of the Algorithm: The Idea that Rules the World* (NY: Harcourt, 2000), pp. 215–216.

84 *Heims explains von Neumann's* . . . Heims, *John von Neumann*, p. 129.

84 *Induction requires theories—every* . . . Joseph B. Soloveitchik, *The Halakhic Mind: An Essay on Jewish Tradition and Modern Thought* (Ardmore, PA: Seth Press, 1986). A brilliant exposition of the limitations of bottom-up inductive science and the opportunity it opens for the "Halakhic mind" of monotheistic religion and what Soloveitchik terms the "logos." Notable quotes: "We are confronted with an amusing situation. While the fathers of modern physics regard their own constructs with skeptical reservation, the enthusiastic positivists attribute final veracity to them. However, the opinion of the builders of modern physics is decisive, and *volens nolens,* philosophy will have to adjust . . ." (p. 27). "The White Light of divinity is always refracted through reality's 'dome of many-colored glass.'" (p. 46).

84 *As he told a* . . . Marton, *The Great Escape*, p. 38.

85 *The crucial step to* . . . Miklós Rédei, ed., *John von Neumann: Selected Letters* (Providence, RI: American Mathematical Society, 2005), pp. 32–38. See also: William Aspray, *John von Neumann and the Origins of Modern Computing* (Cambridge, MA: MIT Press, 1990), pp. 40–42, 53,

and passim. "I think it is soberly true to say that the existence of such a computer would open up to mathematicians, physicists, and other scholars areas of knowledge in the same remarkable way that the two-hundred-inch telescope promises to bring under observation universes which are at present entirely outside the range of any instrument now existing." (p. 55).

86 *Von Neumann was the* . . . Aspray, *John von Neumann and the Origins of Modern Computing,* pp. 61–62.

86 *The von Neumann machine* . . . Martin Davis, *The Universal Computer: The Road from Leibniz to Turing* (NY: W. W. Norton & Co., 2000), p. 182 and passim.

87 *Recalling this debate is* . . . Author's interview with Eyal Talmi at the Weizmann Institute in December 2008. See also: "The Weizac Days," *Interface* magazine, pp. 317–339; "Said Einstein: But There Is Hardly Even a Computer in Europe," *Chicago Jewish Star*, November 26, 2004.

88 *Even if no one* . . . Josef Moneta, *Information Technology: Proceedings of the 3rd Jerusalem Conference on Information Technology,* Illustrated ed., (Amsterdam: North-Holland, 1978), p. 323.

90 *Admiral Lewis Strauss, chairman* . . . quoted in Macrae, *John von Neumann: The Scientific Genius Who Pioneered the Modern Computer, Game Theory, Nuclear Deterrence, and Much More,* pp. 4–5.

90 *As Edward Teller sagely* . . . Author's interview with Teller at Century Association in New York City, around 1985.

92 *The Nazi education minister* . . . David Gries and Fred B. Schneider, *A Logical Approach to Discrete Math,* 3rd ed., Illustrated (NY: Springer, 1993), p. 111.

PART TWO: ISRAEL INSIDE

CHAPTER SEVEN
From Last to First

98 *The first company I* . . . George Gilder, c. 17, "The Terabeam Era," in *Telecosm: The World After Bandwidth Abundance* (NY: Touchstone, a division of Simon & Schuster, 2002), pp. 232–241.

98 *His latest surprise in* . . . David Medved, *Hidden Light: Science Secrets of the Bible* (Jerusalem: Toby Press, 2008).

99 *I was familiar with* . . . Daniel Roth, "Driven: Shai Agassi's Plan to Put Electric Cars on the Road," *Wired*, September 2008, p. 118 and passim.

101 *Before July of 1985* . . . Alan Reynolds, "National Miracles Are No Mystery," *Orbis*, vol. 40, no. 2, Spring 1996; "Economic Myths Explained: National Prosperity Is No Mystery"; "The Case of Israel," *Journal on U.S. Foreign Policy* (April 1, 1996) pp. 208–209. Also: "Projections had been that tax revenue would not change much [with the 20 percent drop in rates]. In the event, however, all categories of tax revenue increased, and especially income-tax revenue . . . and inflation was down to about 11 percent by 1993, belying once again the notion that lower inflation requires 'austerity,' or that rapid real growth raises inflation." See also: Gregory S. Mahler, ed., *Israel After Begin: Conference on Israel in the Post-Begin Era: Papers* (NY: SUNY Press, 1990), pp. 297–298.

102 *Writing in 1990, Michael* . . . Michael Porter, *The Competitive Advantage of Nations* (NY: Free Press, 1998), p. 149.

102 *As late as 1965* . . . Dan Breznitz, "The Development of the IT Industry in Israel: Maximization of R&D as an Industrial Policy," in *Innovation and the State: Political Choice and Strategies for Growth in Israel, Taiwan, and Ireland* (New Haven: Yale University Press, 2007).

103 *Ignorant of Albert Einstein's* . . . Carl Alpert, *Technion: The Story of Israel's Institute of Technology* (NY: American Technion Society, 1982), p. 19.

103 *"In the world of* . . . Ibid.

104 *This failure came despite* . . . I was informed of Rosen's role by my daughter Louisa Gilder, author of *The Age of Entanglement: How Quantum Physics Was Reborn* (NY: Knopf, 2008), which describes Rosen's contribution to the Einstein, Podolsky, Rosen paper, now the Einstein work most quoted in the professional literature because of its role in the history of entanglement and the development of quantum computing.

104 *A team of American* . . . A. J. Meyer, *Middle Eastern Capitalism: Nine Essays* (Cambridge, MA: Harvard University Press, 1959), pp. 44–45.

105 *These Jews, as the* . . . Midge Decter, "The Legacy of Henrietta Szold," in *The Commentary Reader*, edited by Norman Podhoretz (NY: Atheneum, 1966), p. 281.

105 *They assigned close to* . . . Lisa Kaess, "Can Israel Play in the Big Leagues?" *The International Economy*, vol. v, no. 5 (September/October 1991), pp. 45–49.

106 *This influx of Russian* . . . Ibid., p. 47. See also: Philip Spiegel, *Triumph Over Tyranny: The Heroic Campaigns That Saved 2,000,000 Soviet Jews*, with foreword by Natan Sharansky (NY: Devora, 2008); Noah Lewin-Epstein, Yaacov Ro'i, and Paul Ritterband, eds., *Russian Jews on Three Continents: Migration and Resettlement* (NY: Routledge 1997); and Yuri Slezkine, *The Jewish Century* (Princeton, NJ: Princeton University Press, 2004), pp. 350–359 and passim.

107 *At the same time* . . . Author's interview with Jonathan Medved, December 2008.

107 *Throw in natural leadership* . . . Author's interview with Natan Sharansky, December 2008.

108 *These throngs were not* . . . Author's interview with Tal Keinan, December 2008.

108 *Labor Party chief Shimon* . . . Kaess, "Can Israel Play in the Big Leagues?" p. 46.

109 *Today, on a per* . . . Avi Fiegenbaum, *The Take-off of Israeli High-Tech Entrepreneurship in the 1990's: A Strategic Management Research Perspective* (Oxford, UK: Elsevier, 2007), pp. 1–2. See also: Breznitz, c. 2 in *Innovation and the State: Political Choice and Strategies for Growth in Israel, Taiwan, and Ireland* (New Haven: Yale University Press, 2007).

110 *In 2006, Israel's nearly* . . . State of Israel Ministry of Trade and Labor, Venture Capital Industrial Cooperation Authority, State of Israel Web site, accessed June 1, 2009.

110 *A 2008 survey of* . . . Deloitte and Touche, LLP, *Global Trends in Venture Capital 2008 Survey*, Venture Capital Services: Technology, Media, and Telecommunications (NY: Deloitte, 2008), pp. 23–24 and passim. See also: Jonathan Medved, "Israel Beyond the Conflict," presentation and interview, December 2008.

CHAPTER EIGHT
Inside the Computer Revolution

114 *In the 1970s, commanding* . . . George Gilder, *Microcosm: The Quantum Revolution in Economics and Technology* (NY: Free Press, 1990), pp. 91–113.

115 *A Hungarian Jew who* . . . Andrew S. Grove, *Only the Paranoid Survive: How to Exploit the Crisis Points That Challenge Every Company* (NY: Broadway Business, 1999). See also: Grove, *Swimming Across: A Memoir* (NY: Warner Books, 2001), and Richard Tedlow, *Andy Grove: The Life and Times of an American Business Icon* (NY: Penguin, 2006).

115 *Frohman remains close* . . . Dov Frohman, with Robert Howard, *Leadership the Hard Way* (San Francisco: Jossey-Bass, a Wiley imprint, 2008), p. 5.

116 *The first Intel invention* . . . George Gilder, *The Silicon Eye* (NY: W.W. Norton, Atlas Books, 2005), pp. 69–86.

117 *During the early 1980s* . . . Author's interview with Boaz Eitan, December 2008.

119 *Frohman knew that "the* . . . Frohman, *Leadership*, p. 46.

120 *Conceiving the key network* . . . George Gilder, *Telecosm: The World After Bandwidth Abundance*, Rev. ed. (NY: Touchstone, a division of Simon & Schuster, 2002), pp. 69–81.

120 *Von Neumann's final contribution* . . . John von Neumann, *The Computer and the Brain* (New Haven: Yale University Press, 1958).

122 *Among humans, common sense* . . . Gilder, *The Silicon Eye*, p. 88.

122 *In any case, Hillis* . . . W. Daniel Hillis, *The Connection Machine* (Cambridge, MA: MIT Press, 1989), pp. 4–5.

122 *Hillis explained the problem* . . . George Gilder, *The Silicon Eye* (NY: W. W. Norton, Atlas Books, 2005), p. 88.

123 *"Dumber than an airport* . . . Gilder, *Telecosm*, p. 90.

123 *Computers might be "general* . . . Anya Hurlburt and Thomas Poggio quoted in Gilder, *Microcosm,* p. 294.

CHAPTER NINE
Inside the Internet

Most of this chapter is based on author's interviews with Eli Fruchter, Amir Eyal, Guy Koren, and others, between 2000 and 2008.

The technology of EZchip network processors is explored by Ran Giladi in *Network Processors: Architecture, Programming, and Implementation* (Burlington, MA: Morgan Kaufmann, 2008). Also, Giladi, "Maximizing Parallelism in NP," speech, August 23, 2006.

CHAPTER TEN
The Next Generation

Company accounts come from author's interviews in Israel and the United States. I was alerted to several of these companies by Joel Bainerman, "Reaping What Has Been Sown," *Electronics World*, August 2008, pp. 11–13.

137 *I found him first* . . . Helen Davis and Douglas Davis, *Israel in the World, Changing Lives through Innovation* (London: Weidenfeld & Nicolson,

2005), pp. 110–113. Although I never got to meet Zohar Zisapel, this interview brings out the charismatic character of this pioneer of Israeli technology.

CHAPTER ELEVEN
The Shoshana Algorithm

The details of Martin Gerstel's life and the launch of Compugen come from author's interviews with Gerstel in December 2008 and May 2009.

147 *An algorithm, explains David* . . . David Berlinski, *The Advent of the Algorithm: The Idea that Rules the World* (NY: Harcourt, 2000), after p. xviii.

157 *As Crick put it* . . . Matt Ridley, *Francis Crick: Discoverer of the Genetic Code* (NY: Atlas Books, Eminent Lives, 2006), pp. 106–107.

158 *As Yale biologists Michael* . . . Michael Seringhaus and Mark Gerstein, "Genomics Confounds Gene Classification," *The American Scientist*, November/December 2008, pp. 466–471.

162 *At the heart of* . . . Raymond Kurzweil, *The Singularity is Near: When Humans Transcend Biology* (NY: Viking, 2005), pp. 232–233 and passim.

162 *Ehud Shapiro of the* . . . Ehud Shapiro and Yaakov Benenson, "Bringing DNA Computers to Life," *Scientific American*, vol. 294, no. 5, May 2006, pp. 44–49.

163 *From Given Imaging's ingestible* . . . Avi Fiegenbaum, c. 11 and c. 12 in *The Take-off of Israeli High-Tech Entrepreneurship in the 1990's: A Strategic Management Research Perspective* (Oxford, UK: Elsevier, 2007), pp. 163–192. "Over the years, medical technology developed into one of Israel's principal export industries, rendering Israel a world leader in the field . . . [with] products sold on over 250 export markets [rising] from $622 million [in 1995] . . . surpassing the billion dollar mark [in 2000]."

CHAPTER TWELVE
Hong Kong in the Desert

Author's interview with Tal Keinan, Tel Aviv, December 2008.

166 *For decades Israelis doggedly.* . . Ronald I. McKinnon, *Money & Capital in Economic Development* (Washington, DC: Brookings Institution Press, 1973).

167 *Aiding these early efforts* . . . Alan Reynolds, "Economic Myths Explained: National Prosperity Is No Mystery," *Journal on U.S. Foreign Policy* (April 1, 1996).

168 *"We'd put up the* . . . Gary Winnick, personal conversation with author.

170 *Israel would have to* . . . Keinan, interview, December 2008.

170 *As Netanyahu put it* . . . Sara Aharoni and Meir Aharoni, eds., *Industry and Economy in Israel* (Kfar-Sava, Israel: Miksam, 2006), p. 60.

170 *First Histadrut had to* . . . Keinan, interview, December 2008.

PART THREE: THE PARADOX OF PEACE

CHAPTER THIRTEEN
Peace Now

177 *Our host for the* . . . This chapter is heavily based on author's interview with Shaul Olmert and his colleague Itzik Ben-Bassat in December 2008.

177 *Named after a novel* . . . Ruth R. Wisse, *Jews and Power* (NY: Schocken, 2007), p. 114.

178 *As the Irgun argued* . . . Ibid., p. 131.

179 *"In Israel," explains the* . . . For an account of the survival tactics of Is-raeli businesses, see Dan Carrison, *Business under Fire: How Israeli Com-panies Are Succeeding in the Face of Terror and What We Can Learn from Them* (NY: AMACOM, a division of the American Management Asso-ciation, 2004). Also: Dov Frohman, with Robert Howard, *Leadership the Hard Way: Why Leadership Can't Be Taught; And How You Can Learn It Anyway* (San Francisco: Jossey-Bass, a Wiley imprint, 2008).

180 *The entire state is* . . . Dan Senor and Saul Singer, *Start-Up Nation: The Story of Israel's Economic Miracle* (NY: McClelland & Stewart, 2009). (November).

182 *As Jonathan Adiri, a* . . . Author's interview with Jonathan Adiri, De-cember 2008.

184 *Olmert reminded me of* . . . Bernard Avishai, *The Hebrew Republic: How Secular Democracy and Global Enterprise Will Bring Israel Peace at Last* (NY: Harcourt, 2008), pp. 198–201. A pungent discussion of Avishai's views occurs in David Billet, "Undoing the Jewish State," *Commentary,* April 2008. He sums up: "In recent years, and in the face of a ferocious inter-national movement to delegitimize the Jewish state, a little industry has sprung up among some Jewish intellectuals to question the need for the state's existence in the first place and to dream up an alternative that will remove this evident thorn from their personal and ideological com-fort zones. To the names of Noam Chomsky, Tony Judt, and others can be added that of Bernard Avishai, still yearning, like that 60s' Mon-

treal adolescent, for the heaven of 'authenticity,' and cursing the Jews who have wickedly deprived him of it."

185 *"The vital signs seem* . . . Avishai, *The Hebrew Republic*, p. 198.

186 *Told that Bibi Netanyahu* . . . Ibid., p. 200.

186 *Frohman disparages the surge* . . . Ibid.

186 *He asks Avishai:* "What . . . Ibid.

187 *All these Israeli dissidents* . . . John Leonard, *When the Kissing Had to Stop* (NY: New Press, 1999), p. 321.

189 *A week later some* . . . "Billions Pledged to Rebuild Gaza," BBC News online, March 2, 2009.

190 *Similarly, after the 1967* . . . Ruth R. Wisse, *Jews and Power* (NY: Schocken, 2007), p. 156 and passim.

190 *As Ruth Wisse observed* . . . Ibid., pp. 154–155.

191 *In conversation with Sadat* . . . Daniel Gordis, *Saving Israel: How the Jewish People Can Win a War That Will Never End* (Hoboken, NJ: Wiley, 2009), p. 180.

191 *As Wisse writes,* "This . . . Ibid., p. 156.

CHAPTER FOURTEEN
Games of War and Holiness

Much of this chapter is based on interviews with Robert Aumann in Toronto and Jerusalem and with Caroline Glick in Toronto, as well as on Aumann's speech in Toronto, December 1, 2008.

194 *Their masterpiece, the* Theory . . . John von Neumann and Oskar Morgenstern, *Theory of Games and Economic Behavior*, 60 Anv. ed. (Princeton, NJ: Princeton University Press, 2004).

196 *Expounding his theory most* . . . Robert Aumann, "War and Peace," Nobel Prize Lecture, Stockholm, December 2005.

201 *It is a way* . . . Sharon Ghamari-Tabrizi, *The Worlds of Herman Kahn: The Intuitive Science of Thermonuclear War* (Cambridge, MA: Harvard University Press, 2005), p. 290.

206 *"When Isaiah speaks of* . . . Aumann, "War and Peace," December 2005.

CHAPTER FIFTEEN
The Meaning of Netanyahu

Most of the biographical details in this chapter come from Ben Caspit and Ilan Kfir in *Netanyahu, The Road to Power* (Secaucus, NJ: Birch Lane Press, 1998). On Netanyahu in Washington, DC, in the early 1980s: interview with Douglas Feith, March 2009.

207 *One of Obama's early* . . . Katie Connolly, "Busted: The Churchill Flap," *Newsweek*, March 2, 2009.

204 *Supported by 78 percent* . . . Hilary Leila Krieger, "Exit Polls: 78% of Jews Voted for Obama," *Jerusalem Post* Web page, November 5, 2008.

210 *While Obama thinks Churchill* . . . "An Israeli Churchill," *Investor's Business Daily*, editorial, January 30, 2009; Tim McGirk, "Israel's Netanyahu: Taking a Turn toward Pragmatism? *Time* online, May 18, 2009.

210 *As Bibi wrote, "By* . . . A Durable Peace: Israel and Its Place Among the Nations (New York: Grand Central, 2000) p. 38.

215 *Focusing Bibi on the* . . . Benjamin Netanyahu, ed., *Self-Portrait of a Hero: The Letters of Jonathan Netanyahu 1963–1976*, with Iddo Netanyahu (NY: Little, Brown & Co., 1998,) p. 22.

216 *Out of this conference* . . . Benjamin Netanyahu, ed., *International Terrorism: Challenge and Response; Proceedings of the Jerusalem Conference on International Terrorism* (New Brunswick, NJ: Transaction Publishers, 1982), p. 88.

216 *The second conference was* . . . Benjamin Netanyahu, ed., *Terrorism: How the West Can Win* (NY: Avon Books, 1987), p. 106.

216 *Then in 1995, Netanyahu* . . . Benjamin Netanyahu, *Fighting Terrorism: How Democracies Can Defeat Domestic and International Terrorists* (NY: Farrar, Straus & Giroux, 2001).

217 *"The first and most* . . . Netanyahu, *Fighting Terrorism*, p. xiii.

217 *Even suicide bombings, as* . . . Ibid., p. 108.

217 *In addition, he explains* . . . Ibid., p. xiv.

217 *As Boston University strategist* . . . Angelo Codevilla, "Osama bin Elvis," *The American Spectator*, March 2009.

218 *As Michael Yon shows* . . . Michael Yon, *Moment of Truth in Iraq* (Minneapolis: Richard Vigilante Books, 2008).

218 *His counsel is to* . . . Netanyahu, *Fighting Terrorism*, p. 130.

219 *As Netanyahu points out* . . . Ibid., p. 141.

219 *He writes: "Once the* . . . Ibid., p. 147.

CHAPTER SIXTEEN
Land for War

222 *The sense that, by* . . . Rory McCarthy, "Profile: Tzipi Livni," World News, www.guardian.co.uk, February 10, 2009.

222 *As David Meir-Levi explains,* . . . David Meir-Levi, *History Upside Down: The Roots of Palestinian Fascism and the Myth of Israeli Aggression* (NY: Encounter Books, 2008), p. 88.

223 *Goading Israel into this* . . . Jeffrey Goldberg, "Is Israel Finished?" *Atlantic*, May 2008, cover story; ("Unforgiven," inside title).

223 *Echoing Jimmy Carter's libelous* . . . Ibid.

224 *Clinching the argument, Goldberg* . . . Ibid.

224 *Goading Israel into this* . . . Ibid.

225 *As Lewis Lehrman wrote* . . . Lewis Lehrman, *Lincoln at Peoria* (Mechanicsburg, PA: Stackpole Books, 2008), pp. 127–130.

225 *Even including the West* . . . Jonathan Medved, "Israel beyond the Conflict," presentation and interview, December 2008.

226 *Making a fetish of Israel* . . . Jimmy Carter, *Palestine: Peace Not Apartheid* (NY: Simon & Schuster, 2006).

227 *Benjamin Netanyahu rebuts this* . . . Benjamin Netanyahu, *A Durable Peace* (NY: Grand Central, 2000), p. 303.

227 *He quotes the Left-oriented* . . . Ibid.

228 *In his book, he* . . . Thomas Friedman, *From Beirut to Jerusalem*, Rev. Kindle ed. (NY: Farrar, Straus & Giroux, 2007).

230 *That's Jordan, where 300* . . . "The Hashemite Kingdom of Jordan," History section, A Living Tribute to King Hussein I Web site.

CHAPTER SEVENTEEN
Time for the Test

234 *Some sixty-five years later* . . .Martin Gilbert, *The Holocaust: A History of the Jews of Europe During the Second World War*, (NY: Macmillan, 1987), p. 18; "Poland's Jews Alive and Kicking," CNN.com/EUROPE, October 6, 2008.

235 *Scores of nations, representing* . . . Muslim Population Worldwide, www.muslimpopulation.com, accessed January 10, 2009.

235 *The UN General Assembly* . . . Mona Charon, "Camera-Ready Victims: Hamas Practices Human Sacrifice: The World Shrugs," *National Review Online*, January 16, 2009.

236 *They reflect a generally* . . . I first encountered this distinction between qualitative and quantitative arms races fifty years ago in Samuel P. Huntington, "Arms Races: Prerequisites and Results," *Public Policy*, vol. 8, C. J. Friedrich and S. E. Harris, eds. (Cambridge, MA: Graduate School of Public Administration, Harvard University, 1958).

236 *As Peter Huber put* . . . Peter Huber, "Silicon Security, Killer Apps, and the Coming Boom," speech given at the Gilder–Forbes Telecosm V Conference, San Francisco, November 5, 2001.

239 *As Matt Ridley observes* . . . Ridley's book will be published in 2010, but

Ridley made these points in an interview, with Ronald Bailey of *Reason,* in "Chiefs, Thieves, and Priests," February 2009.

AFTERWORD
My Own Israel Test

246 *We are relatively comfortable* . . . Thomas Sowell, *Black Rednecks and White Liberals* (San Francisco: Encounter Books, 2006), p. 77. Sowell explains: "the rise of middleman minorities from poverty to prosperity has been like a slap across the face. . . . Someone who was born rich represents no such assault on the ego. . . . When people are presented with the alternatives of hating themselves for their failure or hating others for their success, they seldom choose to hate themselves."

249 *But among all the* . . . Esther Schor, *Emma Lazarus*, Illustrated ed. (NY: Schocken, 2006), a poignant and probing biography that tells the complex and fascinating story of the relationship between the Gilders and Lazarus.

BIBLIOGRAPHY

– A –

Adelman, Jonathan. *The Rise of Israel: A History of a Revolutionary State.* NY: Routledge, 2008.

Aharoni, Meir, and Sara Aharoni, eds. *Industry and Economy in Israel.* Kfar-Sava, Israel: Miksam, 2006.

Alpert, Carl. *Technion: The Story of Israel's Institute of Technology.* NY: American Technion Society, 1982.

Aspray, William. *John von Neumann and the Origins of Modern Computing.* Cambridge, MA: MIT Press, 1990.

Avishai, Bernard. *The Hebrew Republic: How Secular Democracy and Global Enterprise Will Bring Israel Peace at Last.* NY: Harcourt, 2008.

– B –

Bailey, Ronald. "Chiefs, Thieves, and Priests." *Reason,* February 2009.

Baker, Ronald J. *Mind Over Matter: Why Intellectual Capital is the Chief Source of Wealth.* Hoboken, NJ: Wiley, 2007.

Bauer, P. T. *Dissent on Development, Studies, and Debates in Development Economics.* Cambridge, MA: Harvard, 1972.

—. "Foreign Aid and Its Hydra-Headed Rationalization." *Equality, the Third World, and Economic Delusion.* Cambridge, MA: Harvard, 1981.

—. "Foreign Aid: Issues and Implications." *Reality and Rhetoric: Studies in the Economics of Development.* Cambridge, MA: Harvard University Press, 1981.

Ben-Ami, Shlomo. "A War to Start All Wars: Will Israel Ever Seal the Victory of 1948?" *Foreign Affairs* (September/October 2008).

Bennett, Bill, Jack Kemp, and Jeane Kirkpatrick. "Twenty Facts about Israel and the Middle East." Washington, DC: Empower America, 2002.

Berlinski, David. *The Advent of the Algorithm: The Idea That Rules the World.* NY: Harcourt, 2000.

Billet, David. "Undoing the Jewish State." *Commentary,* April 2008.

Brenner, Reuven. *The Financial Century: From Turmoils to Triumphs.* Toronto: Stoddart, 2001.

Breznitz, Dan. "The Development of the IT Industry in Israel: Maximization of R&D as an Industrial Policy." *Innovation and the State: Political Choice and Strategies for Growth in Israel, Taiwan, and Ireland.* New Haven: Yale University Press, 2007.

– C –

Carrison, Dan. *Business under Fire: How Israeli Companies Are Succeeding in the Face of Terror and What We Can Learn from Them.* NY: AMACOM, a division of American Management Association, 2004.

Carter, Jimmy. *Palestine: Peace Not Apartheid.* NY: Simon & Schuster, 2006.

Caspit, Ben, and Ilan Kfir. *Netanyahu: The Road to Power.* Translated by Ora Cummings. Secaucus, NJ: Birch Lane Press, 1998.

Chesterton, G. K. *Tremendous Trifles.* Beaconsfield, UK: Darwen Finlayson, 1968.

Codevilla, Angelo. "Osama bin Elvis." *The American Spectator,* March 2009.

– D –

Davis, Helen, and Douglas Davis. *Israel in the World: Changing Lives through Innovation.* London: Weidenfeld & Nicolson, 2005.

Davis, Martin. *The Universal Computer: The Road from Leibniz to Turing.* NY: W. W. Norton, 2000.

Decter, Midge. "The Legacy of Henrietta Szold." *The Commentary Reader.* Edited by Norman Podhoretz. NY: Atheneum, 1966.

Deloitte and Touche, LLP. *Global Trends in Venture Capital 2008 Survey.* Venture Capital Services: Technology, Media, and Telecommunications. NY: Deloitte, 2008.

Dershowitz, Alan. *The Case against Israel's Enemies.* Hoboken, NJ: Wiley, 2008.

—. *The Case for Israel*. Hoboken, NJ: Wiley, 2004.

Drucker, Peter F. *Adventures of a Bystander*. NY: HarperCollins, 1991.

– E –

Ebeling, Richard M., ed. "A Draft of Guidelines for the Reconstruction of Austria." *Selected Writings of Ludwig von Mises: The Political Economy of International Reform and Reconstruction*. [Hillsdale College, Hillsdale, Michigan] Indianapolis: Liberty Fund, 2000.

– F –

Fiegenbaum, Avi. *The Take-off of Israeli High-Tech Entrepreneurship During the 1990's: A Strategic Management Research Perspective*. Oxford, UK: Elsevier Science, 2007.

Friedman, Thomas. *From Beirut to Jerusalem*. Rev. Kindle ed. NY: Farrar, Straus & Giroux, 2007.

Frohman, Dov, with Robert Howard. *Leadership the Hard Way: Why Leadership Can't Be Taught—And How You Can Learn It Anyway*. San Francisco: Jossey-Bass, a Wiley imprint, 2008.

– G –

Giladi, Ran. *Network Processors: Architecture, Programming, and Implementation*. Burlington, MA: Morgan Kaufmann, 2008.

Gilbert, Martin. *Churchill and the Jews*. Toronto: McClelland & Stewart, 2007.

Gilder, George. *Microcosm: The Quantum Revolution in Economics and Technology*. NY: Free Press, 1990.

—. *The Silicon Eye*. W. W. Norton, Atlas Books, 2005.

—. *Telecosm: The World After Bandwidth Abundance*. Rev. ed. NY: Touchstone, a division of Simon & Schuster, 2002.

—. *Wealth & Poverty: A New Edition of the Classic*. 2nd ed. San Francisco: ICS Press, 1993.

Gilder, Louisa. *The Age of Entanglement: How Quantum Physics was Reborn*. NY: Knopf, 2008.

Goldberg, Jeffrey. "Is Israel Finished?" *Atlantic,* May 2008.

Goldberg, Jonah. *Liberal Fascism: The Secret History of the American Left: From Mussolini to the Politics of Meaning*. NY: Doubleday, 2008.

Goldberg, Steven. *Fads and Fallacies in the Social Sciences*. Amherst, NY: Humanity Books, 2003.

Gordis, Daniel. *Saving Israel: How the Jewish People Can Win a War That May Never End*. Hoboken, NJ: Wiley, 2009.

Grove, Andrew S. *Only the Paranoid Survive: How to Exploit the Crisis Points That Challenge Every Company*. NY: Broadway Business, 1999.

—. *Swimming Across: A Memoir*. NY: Warner Books, 2001.

– H –

Hagee, John. *Jerusalem Countdown: A Warning to the World*. Later print. ed. Lake Mary, FL: FrontLine, 2006.

Halkin, Hillel. "Why the Settlements Should Stay." *Commentary,* June 2002.

Heims, Steve J. *John von Neumann and Norbert Wiener: From Mathematics to the Technologies of Life and Death*. Cambridge, MA: MIT Press, 1982.

Herrnstein, Richard J., and Charles Murray. *The Bell Curve: Intelligence and Class Structure in American Life*. NY: Free Press, 1994.

Hillis, W. Daniel. *The Connection Machine*. Cambridge, MA: MIT Press, 1989.

Hitler, Adolf. *Mein Kampf*. Translated by James Murphy. NY: Random House, 1988.

Huntington, Samuel P., and C. J. Friedrich, and S. E. Harris, eds. "Arms Races: Prerequisites and Results." *Public Policy*, vol. 8. Cambridge, MA: Graduate School of Public Administration, Harvard University, 1958.

– I –

Isseroff, Ami et al. *The Population of Palestine Prior to 1948*. MidEastWeb. http://www.mideastweb.org/palpop.htm.

—. *Israel and Palestine: A Brief History*. MidEastWeb. http://www.mideast-web.org/briefhistory.htm.

– K –

Kaess, Lisa. "Can Israel Play in the Big Leagues?" *International Economy*, vol. v, no. 5, September/October 1991.

Kanaan, Oussama. "Recent Experience and Prospects." *The Economy of the West Bank and Gaza Strip: Recent Experience, Prospects, and Challenges to Private Sector Development*. Edited by Steven Barnett. Washington, DC: Middle Eastern Department, International Monetary Fund, 1998.

Karsh, Efraim. "What Occupation?" *Commentary,* July/August 2002.

—. "1948, Israel, and the Palestinians—The True Story." *Commentary,* May 2008.

Khalidi, Raja. "Sixty Years after the UN Partition Resolution: What Future for the Arab Economy in Israel?" Edited by Rashid Khalidi. *Journal of Palestine Studies: A Quarterly on Palestinian Affairs and the Arab–Israeli Conflict* 146, vol. xxxvii, no. 2. Berkeley, CA: University of CA Press for the Institute of Palestine Studies (Winter 2008).

Khalidi, Rashid. *The Iron Cage: The Story of the Palestinian Struggle for Statehood.* Boston: Beacon Press, 2006.

—. *Sowing Crisis: The Cold War and American Dominance in the Middle East.* Boston: Beacon Press, 2009.

Klein, Aaron. *Schmoozing with Terrorists: From Hollywood to the Holy Land; Jihadists Reveal Their Global Plans—to a Jew!* Los Angeles: WND Books, 2007.

Kop, Yaakov, and Robert E. Litan. *Sticking Together: The Israeli Experiment in Pluralism.* Washington, DC: Brookings Institution Press, 2002.

Kurzweil, Raymond. *The Singularity is Near: When Humans Transcend Biology.* NY: Viking, 2005.

– L –

Laqueur, Walter. *Dying for Jerusalem: The Past, Present, and Future of the Holiest City.* Naperville, IL: Sourcebooks, 2005.

Leonard, John. *When the Kissing Had to Stop.* NY: New Press, 1999.

Lévy, Bernard-Henri. *Left in Dark Times: A Stand against the New Barbarism.* NY: Random House, 2008.

—. "Pondering, Discussing, Traveling Amid, and Defending the Inevitable War." *New York Times Magazine,* August 6, 2006.

Lehrman, Lewis E. *Lincoln at Peoria.* Mechanicsburg, PA: Stackpole Books, 2008.

Lewin-Epstein, Noah, and Yaacov Ro'i, and Paul Ritterband, eds. *Russian Jews on Three Continents: Migration and Resettlement.* NY: Routledge, 1997.

Lippmann, Walter. *The Good Society.* NY: Grosset & Dunlap, 1943; Ppbk. ed. Piscataway, NJ: Transaction Books, 2004.

– M –

Macrae, Norman. *John von Neumann: The Scientific Genius Who Pioneered the Modern Computer, Game Theory, Nuclear Deterrence, and Much More.* NY: American Mathematical Society, 1999.

Mahler, Gregory S., ed. *Israel after Begin: Conference on Israel in the Post-Begin Era: Papers*. NY: SUNY Press, 1990.

Marton, Kati. *The Great Escape: Nine Jews Who Fled Hitler And Changed The World*. NY: Simon & Schuster, 2006.

McClelland, David C. *The Achieving Society*. Princeton, NJ: D. Van Nostrand, 1961.

McKinnon, Ronald I. *Money & Capital in Economic Development*. Washington, DC: Brookings Institution Press, 1973.

Medved, David. *Hidden Light: Science Secrets of the Bible*. Jerusalem: Toby Press, 2008.

Meir-Levi, David. *History Upside Down: The Roots of Palestinian Fascism and the Myth of Israeli Aggression*. NY: Encounter Books, 2008.

Meyer, A. J. *Middle Eastern Capitalism: Nine Essays*. Cambridge, MA: Harvard University Press, 1959.

Morris, Benny. *One State, Two States: Resolving the Israel/Palestine Conflict*. New Haven: Yale University Press, 2009.

Morse, Chuck. *The Nazi Connection to Islamic Terrorism: Adolf Hitler and Haj Amin al-Husseini*. Lincoln, NE: iUniverse, 2003.

Murray, Charles. *Human Accomplishment: The Pursuit of Excellence in the Arts and Sciences; 800 B.C. to 1950*. NY: HarperCollins, 2003.

—. "Jewish Genius." *Commentary*, vol. 123, no. 4, April 2007.

– N –

Netanyahu, Benjamin. *A Durable Peace: Israel and Its Place Among the Nations*. NY: Grand Central, 2000.

—. *Fighting Terrorism: How Democracies Can Defeat Domestic and International Terrorists*. 2nd ed. NY: Farrar, Straus & Giroux, 2001.

—, ed. *International Terrorism: Challenge and Response; Proceedings of the Jerusalem Conference on International Terrorism*. New Brunswick, NJ: Transaction Publishers, 1982.

—, ed. (with Iddo Netanyahu). *Self-Portrait of a Hero: The Letters of Jonathan Netanyahu 1963–1976*. NY: Little, Brown & Co., 1998.

—, ed. *Terrorism: How the West Can Win*. NY: Avon Books, 1987.

Netanyahu, Benzion. *The Origins of the Inquisition in Fifteenth-Century Spain*. 2nd ed. NY: New York Review of Books, 2001.

– P –

Podhoretz, Norman. *The Norman Podhoretz Reader: A Selection of His Writings from the 1950s through the 1990s.* Edited by Thomas L. Jeffers. NY: Free Press, 1992.

—. *World War IV: The Long Struggle against Islamofascism.* NY: Doubleday, 2007.

Porter, Michael E. *The Competitive Advantage of Nations.* NY: Free Press, 1998.

Prager, Dennis, and Joseph Telushkin. *Why the Jews? The Reason for Anti-semitism.* Rev. ed. NY: Touchstone, a division of Simon & Schuster, 2003.

Proudhon, Pierre-Joseph. *What is Property?* NY: Cosimo Classics, 2007.

Pryce-Jones, David. "Their Kampf: Hitler's Book in Arab Hands." *National Review,* July 29, 2002.

—. "The Rescue of the Mufti of Jerusalem." *Betrayal: France, the Arabs, and the Jews.* NY: Encounter Books, 2008.

– R –

Rédei, Miklós, ed. *John von Neumann: Selected Letters.* Providence, RI: American Mathematical Society, 2005.

Reuveny, Rafael. "The Last Colonialist: Israel in the Occupied Territories since 1967." *The Independent Review* 12, no. 3 (Winter 2008).

Reynolds, Alan. "Economic Myths Explained: National Prosperity is No Mystery." *Journal on U.S. Foreign Policy* (April 1, 1996).

—. "National Miracles Are No Mystery." *Orbis,* vol. 40, no. 2, Spring 1996.

Ridley, Matt. *Francis Crick: Discoverer of the Genetic Code.* NY: Atlas Books, Eminent Lives, 2006.

Roberts, Edward B. "Entrepreneurs in High Technology." *Lessons from MIT and Beyond.* NY: Oxford University Press, 1991.

Rose, Paul Lawrence. *Wagner: Race and Revolution.* New Haven: Yale University Press, 1996.

Rosenberg, David. *Cloning Silicon Valley: The Next Generation High-Tech Spots.* Upper Saddle River, NJ: Financial Times/Prentice Hall, 2001.

Roth, Daniel. "Driven: Shai Agassi's Plan to Put Electric Cars on the Road." *Wired,* September 2008.

– S –

Schor, Esther. *Emma Lazarus.* Illustrated ed. NY: Schocken, 2006.

Shlaim, Avi. *The Iron Wall: Israel and the Arab World.* NY: W. W. Norton, 2001.

Senor, Dan, and Saul Singer. *Start-Up Nation: The Story of Israel's Economic Miracle*. NY: McClelland & Stewart, 2009 (November).

Seringhaus, Michael, and Mark Gerstein. "Genomics Confounds Gene Classification." *The American Scientist*, November/December 2008.

Shapiro, Ehud, and Yaakov Benenson. "Bringing DNA Computers to Life." *Scientific American*, vol. 294, no. 5, May 2006.

Slezkine, Yuri. *The Jewish Century*. Princeton, NJ: Princeton University Press, 2004.

Soloveitchik, Joseph B. *The Halakhic Mind: An Essay on Jewish Tradition and Modern Thought*. Ardmore, PA: Seth Press, 1986.

Sowell, Thomas. *Black Rednecks and White Liberals*. San Francisco: Encounter Books, 2006.

—. *Conquests and Cultures. An International History*. NY: Basic Books, 1998.

—. *Ethnic America: A History*. NY: Basic Books, 1981.

Spiegel, Philip. Foreword by Natan Sharansky. *Triumph Over Tyranny: The Heroic Campaigns that Saved 2,000,000 Soviet Jews*. NY: Devora, 2008.

Stotsky, Steven. "Does Foreign Aid Fuel Palestinian Violence?" *Middle East Quarterly* (Summer 2008).

– T –

Tedlow, Richard. *Andy Grove: The Life and Times of an American Business Icon*. NY: Penguin, 2006.

Tiger, Lionel, and Joseph Shepher. *Women in the Kibbutz*. NY: Harcourt Brace Javonovich, 1974.

– U –

Ulam, S. et al. "John von Neumann: 1903–1957." Edited by J. C. Oxtoby et al. *Bulletin of the American Mathematical Society*, vol. 64, no. 3, pt. 2 (May 1958).

United Nations Conference on Trade and Development (UNCTAD). Special Economic Unit. *The Palestinian Economy and Prospects for Regional Cooperation*. Geneva, Switzerland, June 30, 1998.

– V –

von Neumann, John, and Oskar Morgenstern. *Theory of Games and Economic Behavior*. 60 Anv. ed. Princeton, NJ: Princeton University Press, 2004.

– W –

"The Weizac Years." *IEEE Annals*, vol. 13 (November 4, 1991).
Wigner, Eugene Paul, and Andrew Szanton. *The Recollections of Eugene P. Wigner: as told to Andrew Szanton.* NY: Plenum Press, 1992.
Wisse, Ruth R. *Jews and Power.* NY: Schocken, 2007.

– Y –

Yon, Michael. *Moment of Truth in Iraq.* Minneapolis: Richard Vigilante Books, 2008.

ACKNOWLEDGMENTS

In the interest of full disclosure I should begin by saying that, as a practicing venture capitalist, at this writing I am an investor in several of the companies mentioned in this book and may invest in others in the future. Crucial assistance in researching, writing, editing, and checking this book came from many people who may well not wish to be associated with its controversial theses. My college roommate, editor, and friend of fifty years, Bruce Chapman and my friend and colleague Thomas Lehrman accompanied and guided me on extended trips to Israel. Buoying and abetting my first visit were Howard and Roberta Ahmanson and Dr. Steven Ferguson of The Fieldstead Company. Mark Gerson gave me valuable introductions in Israel and an astringent critique of the book.

Pointing me to essential sources and ideas were Lewis Lehrman and Jeffrey Satinover in their own many profound writings and in personal consultations. Marie Lavinio provided expert supervision of copyediting and final processing of the manuscript. David Billet of *Commentary* and Daniel Halper provided acute and insightful readings. The look and layout of the physical book was deftly supplied by Charles Bork.

Among all the world's writers I was most fortunate to have the supreme editorial guidance of Richard Vigilante.

Alissa Grainger and Charles Burger of my own company lent me constant support and needed advice that sustained me through the throes of crash and creation. Mary Collins George and Tina Chase kept the Gilder–Forbes Telecosm Conference, Friday Letter, and the Telecosm Forum going strong.

Louisa, Mellie, Richard, and Nannina made it all worthwhile, and my wife Nini juggled me, my book, Louisa's book, and two books of her own with all the aplomb of an air traffic controller and landed us all safely at home again and again.

George Gilder
Tyringham, Massachusetts
May 25, 2009

INDEX